BORN OF SAND AND SUN

Petra Bašnákova

Dewi Lewis Publishing

to Nadia and Saqer

What is the true happiness that mankind is in such a hurry to find? Which we are all looking for? Does it exist at all? Can we grab it, squeeze it and never let go? Or do we just waste time in the fleetingness of the moment, letting ourselves be carried away by its ideal and at the end of the day feeling empty again?

I only discovered mine after meeting those who call it Inshallah. If Allah wills. Whose lifeblood is a kind of lightness of being, relieved of unimportant thoughts and with a belief in simplicity. Knowing that we are made of stardust trying to reach its cosmic origin. I only discovered my universe with them. With the desert Nomads, who helped me to be reborn with different values to those I had perceived so far.

One October morning at the turn of 2019, I set out across the wrinkled surface of the Judean Desert, covered with oil stones, radiating absorbed heat from the sun's rays. Their fervour attracted the heartbeat of every earthly being, including me. Mother Nature herself engulfed me in her pliable blanket, formed from a mixture of dust and sand. As I lay there so fragile, dreaming, alone, surrounded by wasteland, a miracle happened. I was awakened from my dream by a boy with a deep look, sitting on a white donkey, followed by two black goats. He gave me his hand and with a vigorous movement of it indicated that I was welcome to join his flock. Almost breathlessly, I obeyed the boy, and followed him blindly as if he was a messiah who knows the way to redemption. I had no idea where he was leading me and what he wanted from me, but even so, my heart decided to follow him. We embarked on a journey of trust between two strangers from different worlds, which led us to the most precious thing – family. In that moment, Usama's decision to show his own vulnerability formed a bond between me and the unique culture of the desert nation, who, after I had gained their trust, accepted me as one of their own. And this is the beginning of my story – a journey of knowledge across the fabulous Palestine, during which its inhabitants revealed the secret of inner peace to me in my new home, the desert, where the Sun shines more penetratingly and the silence is many times quieter.

Petra Bašnákova

Gradually, through mutual coexistence and through a greater understanding of the current factors in a territory besieged by the Israeli-Palestinian conflict, I knew why the path of my life had crossed with the Bedouins – survivors of the terrible consequences of the 1948 Palestinian war, when they faced a mass expulsion from their own homes, which sadly continues to this day. Military raids, the demolition of dwellings, bans on grazing goats and much more. Yet, despite this difficult fate, they could not break the strong bond with the heart of their culture hidden in the vast desert. They decided to persevere, to not give up, even though, for decades, they have endured injustice and humiliation from those on the other side of the segregation wall. Today, the number of Bedouins inhabiting their original territories is decreasing and many are gradually losing their identity – the identity of being a freely roaming Nomad across your country.

I was told many things; I witnessed the different destinies of families, we grieved and rejoiced over life events and tried to understand each other. And at that moment, when I felt that I was beginning to be one of them, I understood my mission. What consolidates the Bedouin tribes into a united force is not anger and resentment towards those who drove them to the border of freedom, but the hope that one day they will be able to cross that border again and take a full breath of freedom and sea breeze.

Their devotion to their homeland and their bravery and determination not to give up, make them modern-day heroes of a Holy War. Born of Sand and Sun is a visual metaphor for the threat of the gradual disappearance of the brave Palestinian Bedouin nation and the beauty hidden in the depths of their culture. Over time it can only turn to fragments covered in sand, which also turn into sand. Interwoven with pictorial symbols, which created a plot line for the story, I gradually uncovered intimate moments of their lives. For me it was an essential transformation, the discovery of grace in the grief that has fuelled the nation for the past decades. The beauty of a land that no human creature could have shaped and the home of anyone who touches its heated earth.

One evening nearing the full moon, whose light grew with the setting sun, Nadia led me to the edge of a desert cliff. Beneath it lay an unsuspecting herd of about forty camels grazing carelessly in the shadow of the night. We stood motionless watching the beauty and fragility of these majestic beings as she took my hand and said, "One day we will be like them. Inshallah. Thank you for showing me that even people from the other side of the wall are trying to understand and help us. That they can be good." At that moment I couldn't bring myself to say a word, but I knew that I owed a debt to Nadia and that, thanks to her, I could find my inner peace and become part of the remarkable life of those whose hope never fades.

From the Bedouin perspective
the desert is considered an open space.

شكراً لله !! أيتها الصحراء الحبيبة لأنك علمتنا الصبر وعلمتنا كيف
نتحمل الأعداء والإهانات، ما دفعنا فوق المسائل التافهة ونتغلب على الشر
بدون الخير، ونتحمل الجمال، حتى نحمي آذاننا من الكلام القذر، أنا أحبك
أيتها الحلقة العارية، بابتسامة واسعة وشوقة ملكوت، كما أنني لم أعد
أراك رغم ما يزال مسكني فيك، كيف لي أن لا أحبك وسعادتي منبعثة من كل
حبة رمل.

نحن معاً واحد سنظل، كذلك إلى الأبد يا حبيبتي كيف علمتني أن أفارقك إلى الأبد؟
أرى كثبان الرمال تغير شكلها بفعل الرياح.
ومع ذلك تظل الصحراء ثابتة. كيف علمتني أن أفارقك وأنت الفارس، لا تتركوا
أثراً، تسترشد بضوء الليل، حيث نجمات نور السماء واللطف تجاه الضيوف وعمل
الخير، هل تعلم لماذا ابتعدنا عن السواحل وركبنا الأرض الجافة؟ لا يمكنك
رؤية الشيء سواء رمالك الذهبية في البعد، كما لو كنت فضاءً مفتوحاً يملك
التنفس فيه بحرية دون أن تشعر بالملل يا سيد العالم الساحر والمثير.
لا تفتقر إلى وطني كأوهام من الحجارة والسيارات، وطني هو الصحراء التي تعلمت
منها تحررت أن أكره العزلة. نعم، أنا بدوي ومجتمعي لا يعرف معنى العزلة.
لا تدعو بيتي يشتعل وتحبو حرية حركة الحيوانات في الفضاء المفتوح إلى مساحات
ضيقة حيث لا يمكن للبشر التنفس، وفوق كل ذلك احترم ملكتي العارية،
لتكون هدفاً لحياتكم وأسلحتكم كما لو كانت ساحة اختبار، كما لو أنكم تجهلون من
تغيير الفرص التي خلقت من أجله البشرية.

أربعة وثلاثون سنة مضت، محاصر في ذلك الكهف، في هذه العزلة الصامتة - تعتبر العزلة، البداية لو لم يستطع أن يتملكها المرء لما استطاع الوصول للخطوة التالية. أركب موجه البحر، أصل الجزيرة، محصور في عزلة الصحراء، التي من خلالها عليك أن تبحث عن ذاتك.

نعم الصحراء، لا أعلم لماذا عندما نسمع كلمة "الصحراء" نفكر فيها على الفور كعدو للأشجار، أرض محروقة لا يوجد فيها أمل للحياة. إنها كوحش الليل الذي يختلف عن لياليكم المضيئة بالمصابيح والقناديل يا معشر أهل المدينة. من وجهة نظر البدو تعتبر الصحراء مساحة مفتوحة. الصحراء هي روح عارية، وبالنسبة للروح العارية هناك قوانين مختلفة مقارنة بالروح المخفية في الجسد أو في الطبيعة. لذا، يجب أن يكون هناك تقنية خاصة لتجربة هذا المبدأ "الروح العارية".

البدو هم الذين يعتمدون على تربية المواشي كمصدر لقوتهم ويعيشون نمط حياة البدو بحثاً عن الطعام والماء.

نمط حياتنا هو تقليد ثقافي عربي محدد وهناك خصائص كثيرة تحددنا؛ وواحدة من هذه الخصائص هي أننا لسنا ماديين، حتى لا نملك مالاً أو ممتلكات ونعيش في خيام سوداء مصنوعة من شعر الماعز المنسوج.

الحيوانات تعتبر مهمة وخاصة الجمال وهي وسيلة النقل المهمة والأساسية بالنسبة لنا. نعتمد على منتجات الألبان من الماعز كمصدر غذاء رئيسي لنا

From the Bedouin perspective
the desert is considered an open space.

أليس الإنسان خليفة للتأمل والتفكير! تصبح الصحراء ملجأً أولاً لكل من يسعى للتأمل والتفكير في غياب هذه الحياة. إنها تفتقد أي شخص لا يستطيع قبول القيود في حياته. تتسائل عن جسيمات رمالها في الصحراء، تتوسط الأحلام أمامها ورمالها التي لا تقيدها الصخور ولا تقطعها الحدود لذا يشعر الإنسان بالحرية والسلام من نفسه، وهي عناصر لا غنى عنها في الحياة الصحراوية والعربية كجو أشكال الصحراء تبدو أنها تحب أنها ليست مجرد لوحة لا تتغير الحال بل بالأحرى حب وعواطف وإحساس وتحرر وجمال ممزوج معاً في خليط لا يعلمه سوى الله أن يحبه في الصحراء، وآمل أن يجرب الجميع يوماً ما إلى الصحراء ويشهد ما عشته.

Saqer Alkawazba

34 years ago, in that cave, in that silent solitude my journey started. Clawing the way, the beginning that one must build on in order to reach the next step. Sailing the sea, reaching the island, dwelling, submerged in the solitude of the desert, through which you may seek your own truth. Yes, the desert. I don't blame you when you hear the word "desert" and immediately think of it as the enemy of trees, a burned land where there is no hope for life. It's as if it's a night beast that differs from your illuminated nights with lanterns or lamps, O beloved people of the city.

From the Bedouin perspective, the desert is considered an open space. The desert is a naked soul and for the naked soul, there are different laws compared to the hidden soul in the body or in nature. Therefore, there must be a special technique to experience this principle of the naked soul.

The Bedouins are those who rely on livestock herding for their livelihood and live a nomadic lifestyle in a search for food and water. Our lifestyle is a specific Arab cultural tradition and there are distinct characteristics that define us. One of these characteristics is that we are not materialistic. We do not possess money or belongings. We live in black tents made of woven goat hair. Animals are considered important, especially camels, which are an essential and primary means of transportation for us. We also rely on dairy products as our main source of food. Thank you! O beloved desert, for granting us patience and teaching us to endure adversaries and insults, to rise above trivial matters, to overcome evil, to not suffer fools gladly as well as to guard our ears from dirty talk. You! O naked queen, I address you with a broad smile and supressed longing, as if I no longer see you even though I still dwell within you. How can I not praise you, my happiness is scattered across every grain of sand? Together, we are one and the same forever more, my beauty. How can I depart from you forever. I see the sand dunes changing their form with the wind. Yet the desert remains unchanged. How can I depart from you when you are the horseman ship, leaving no trace and navigating through the guidance of your shining stars, when you have implanted in me generosity and kindness towards guests and practices of good deeds? Do you know why we moved away from the coast and ride the dry land? The distance of the eye sees nothing but your golden sands, as if you were an open space where you can breathe deeply without getting bored. O master of the captivating and thrilling science, do not perceive my homeland as piles of stones and cars. My homeland is the desert, teaching us by instinct to hate defeat.

Yes. I'm a Bedouin and my community does not know the meaning of defeat. Don't let my house be burnt down or restrict my animals from the movement from the open space to narrow ranges, where humans can breathe. On top of that, you have chosen my naked queen to be the target for your lies and weapons as if she were a testing ground. It is as if they want to change what humanity was created for. Isn't mankind created for meditation and reflection? The desert becomes the first refuge for all those who seek meditation and reflection in the absence of this life. It embraces anyone who can not accept boundaries in their life, as they wander its sand particles. In the desert, dreams mediate its skies and sands that are not bounded by rocks or hindered by limits. So, one feels the freedom and peace in their breath, which are considered inseparable elements of desert and wilderness, life in all its forms.

The desert, on its own is a miracle. It is not merely a word, as money may imagine, but rather it is love, emotions, sensations, worries and beauty blended together in a mix that only God can gather. I hope that one day everyone will escape to the desert and experience what we Bedouins have experienced.

Between sun and sand

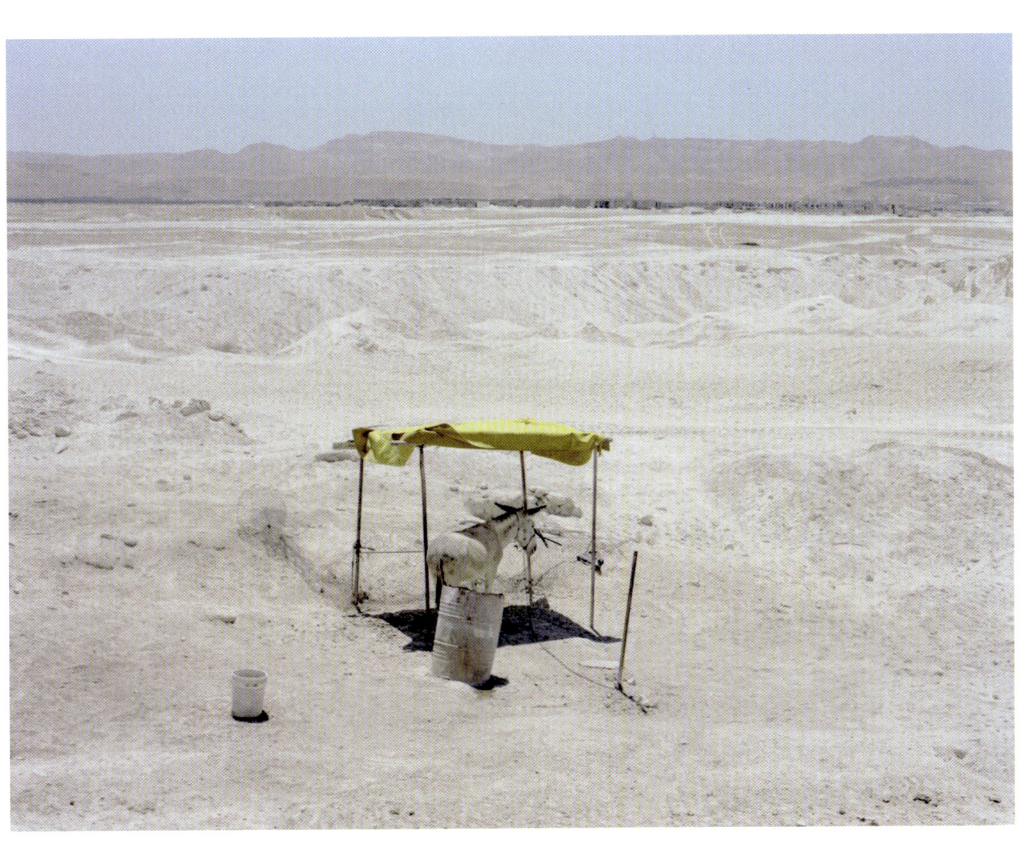

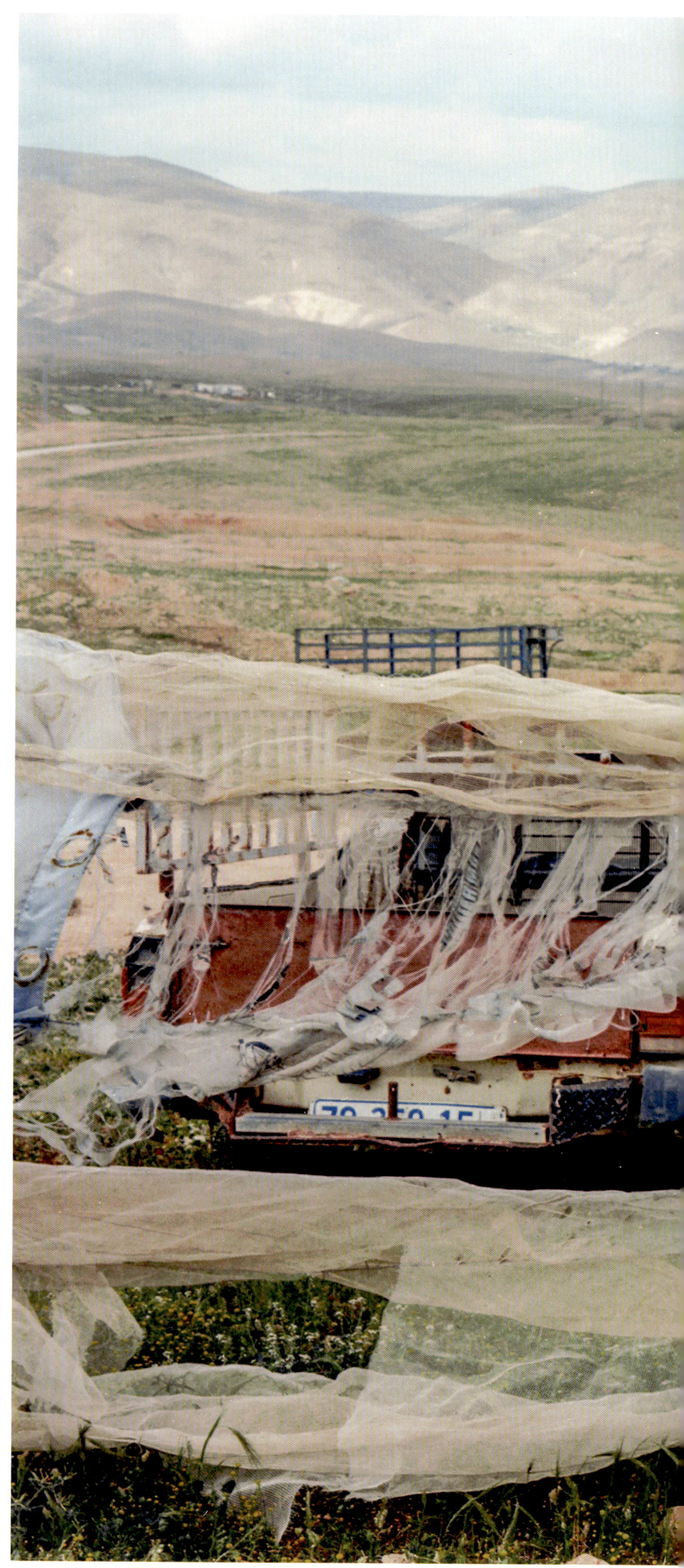

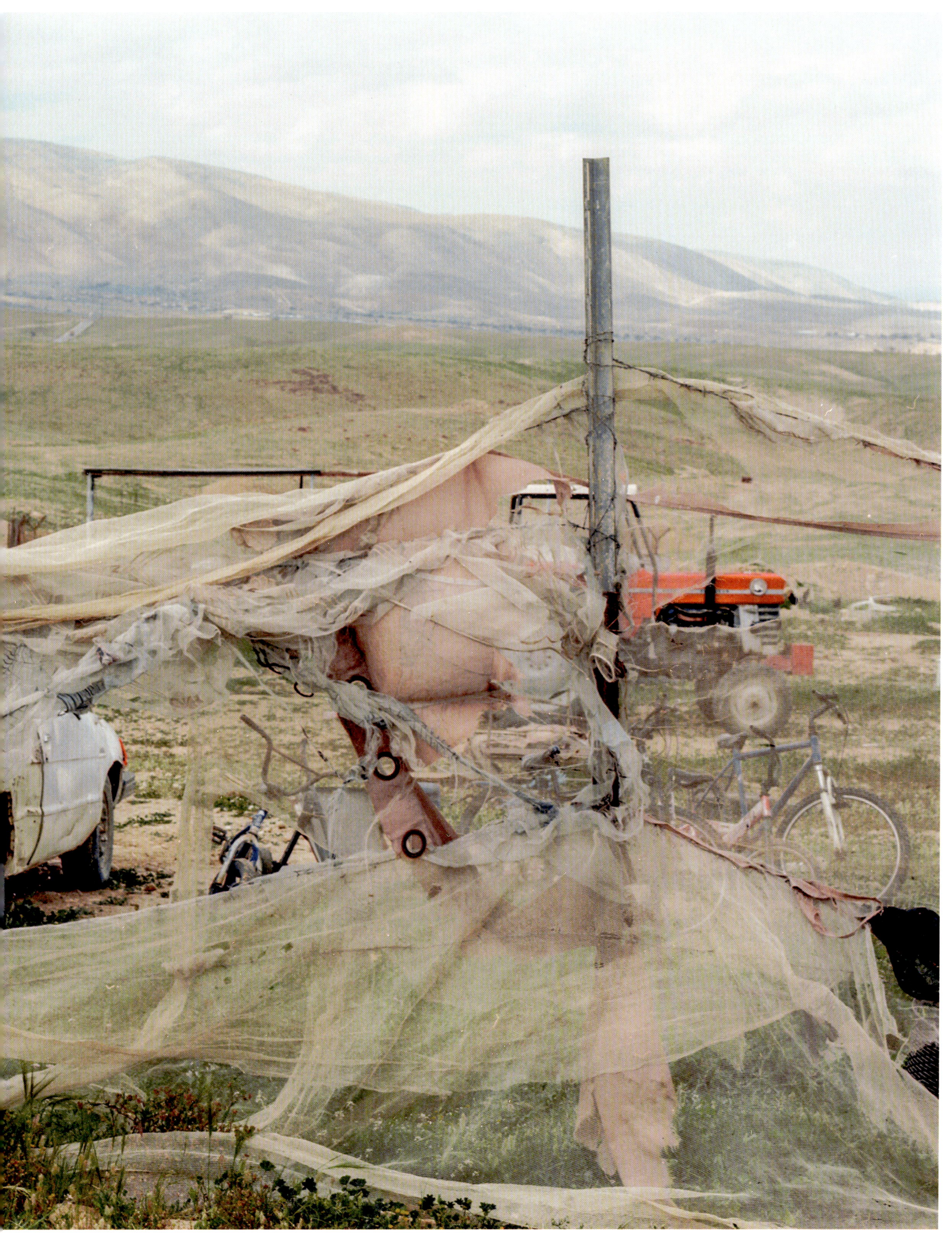

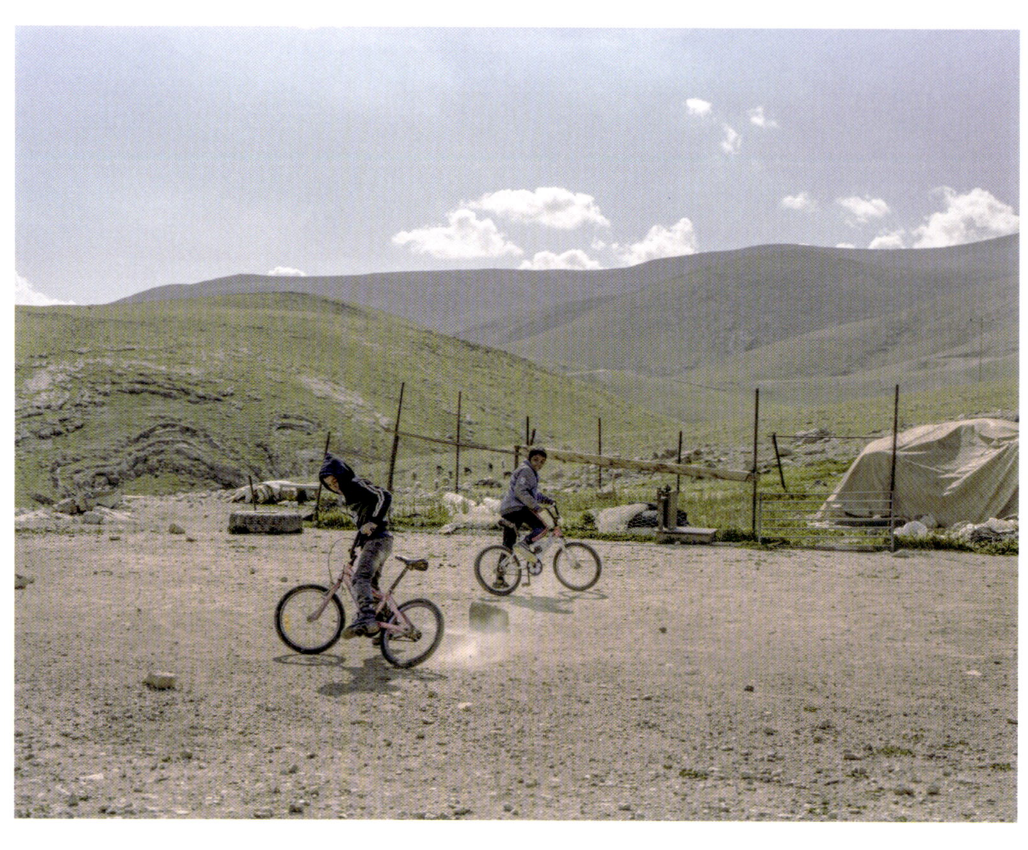

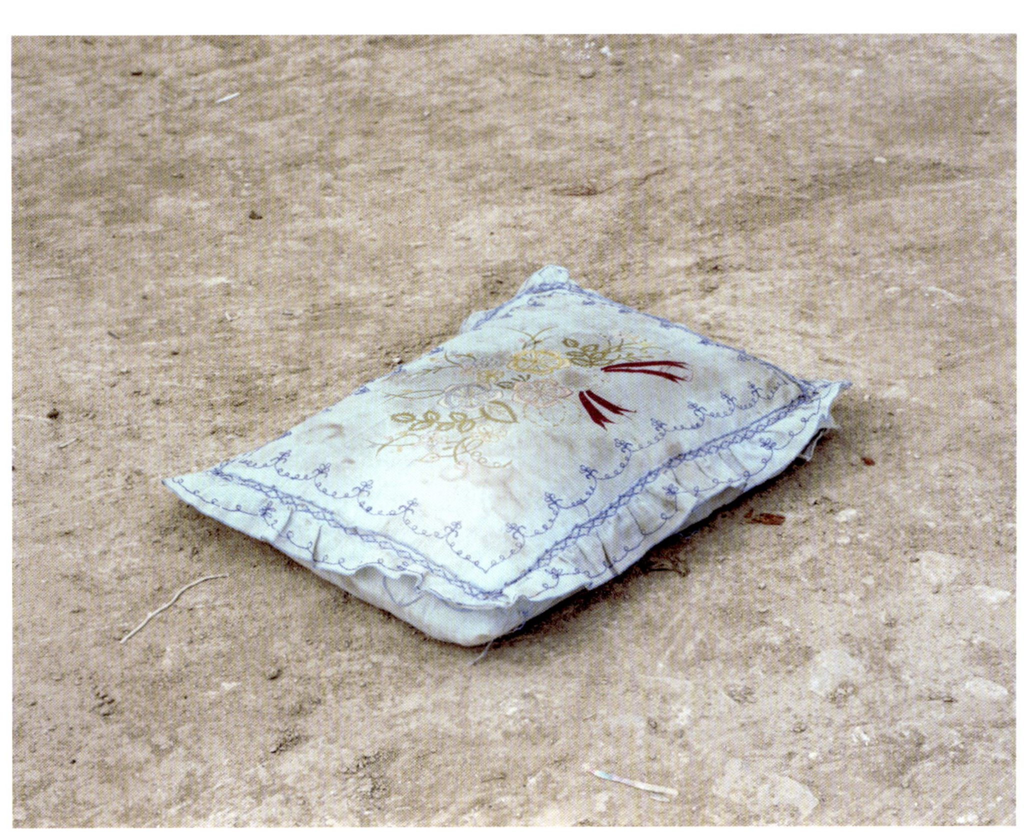

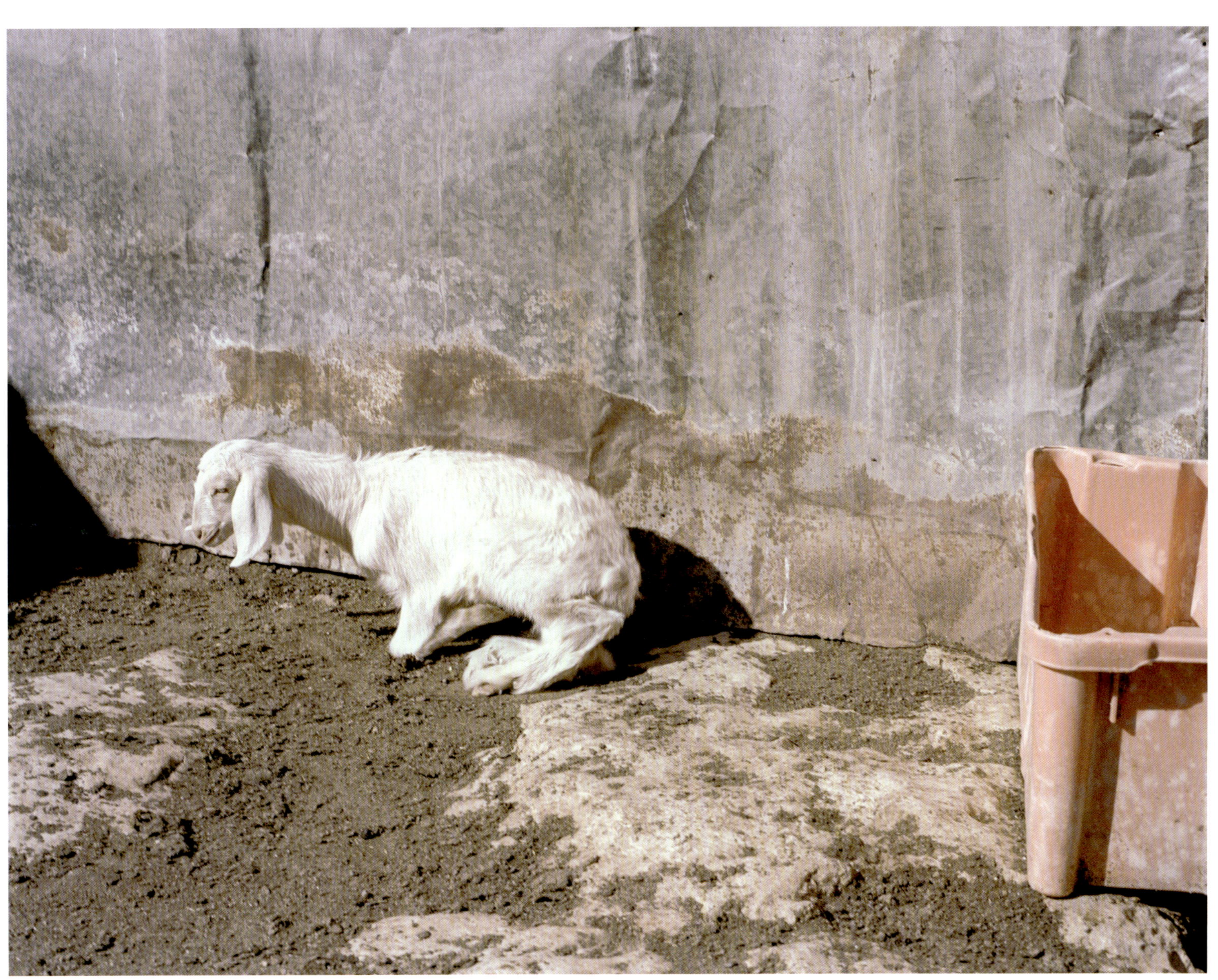

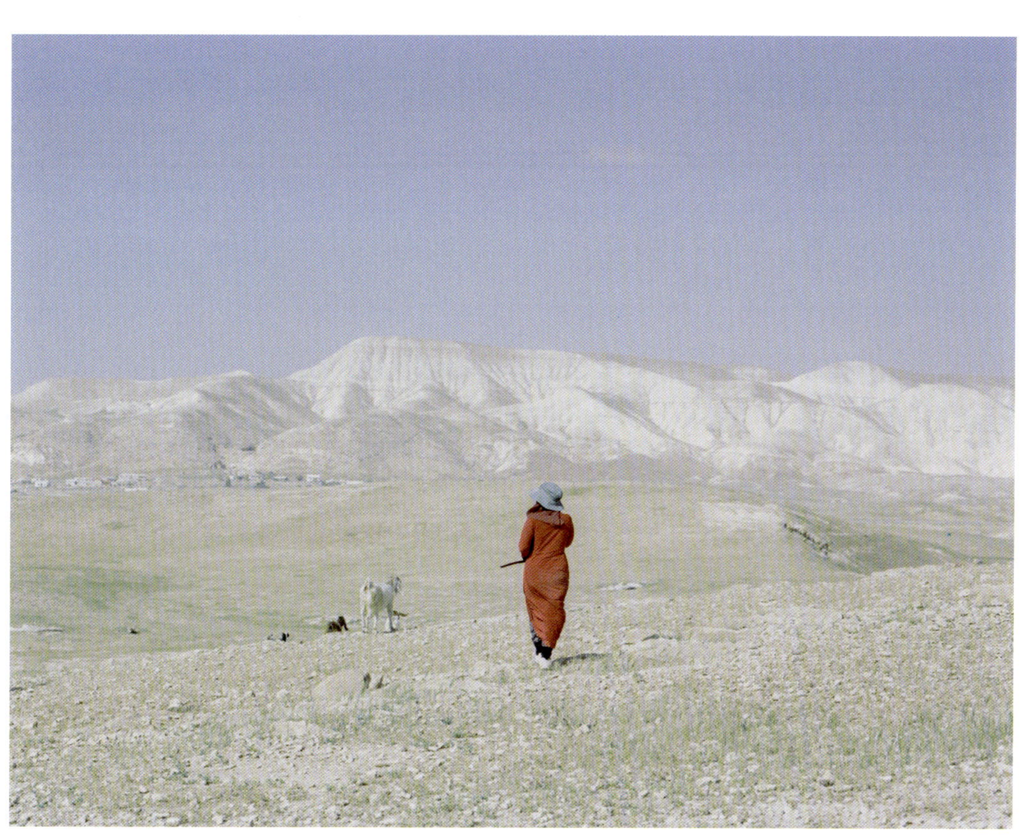

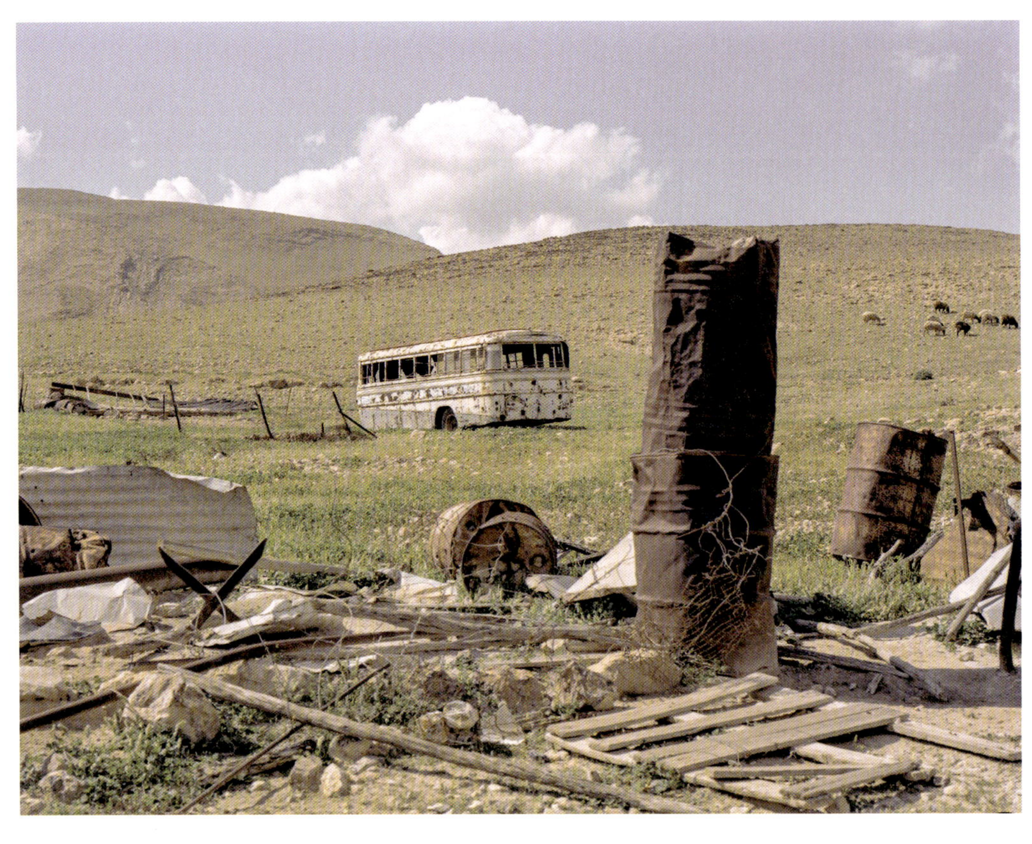

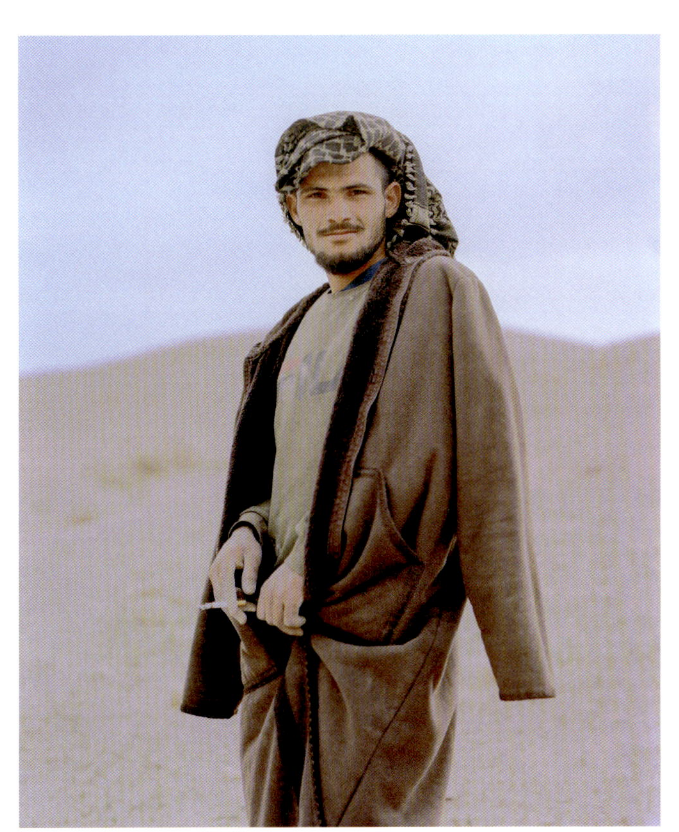

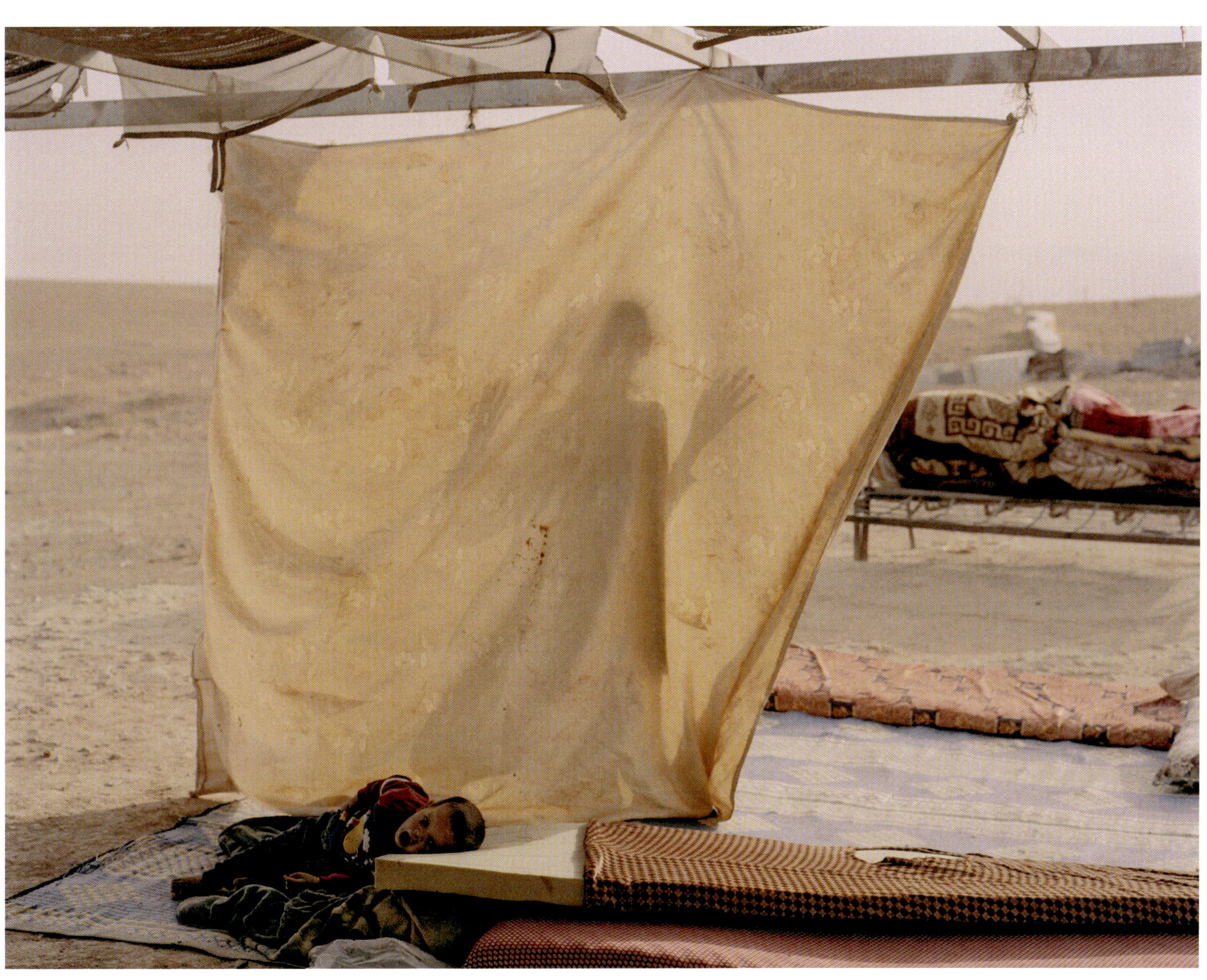

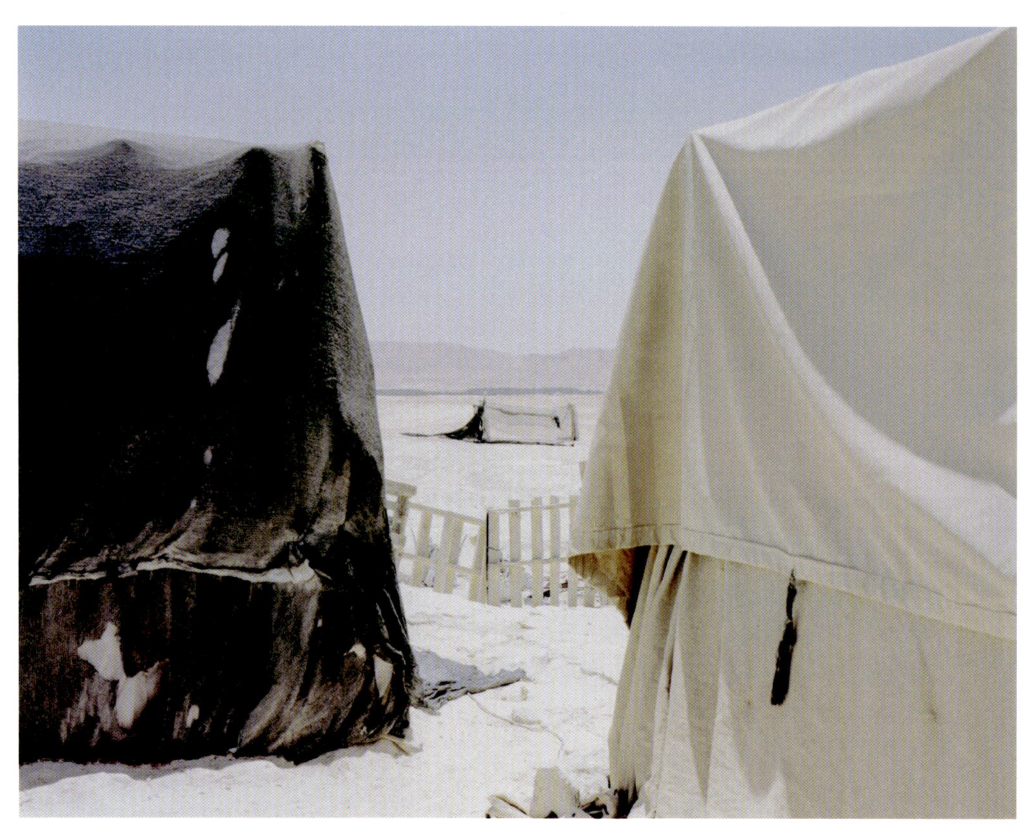

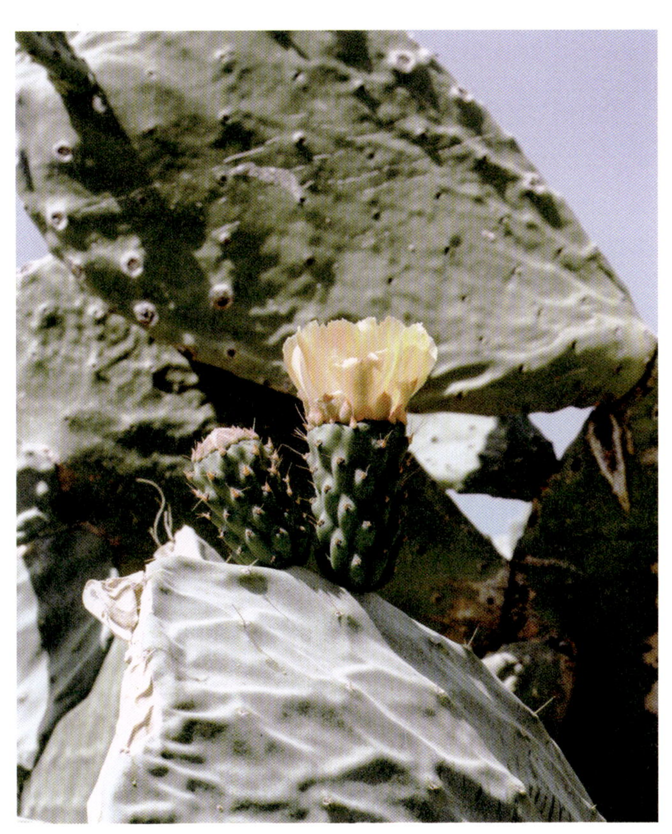

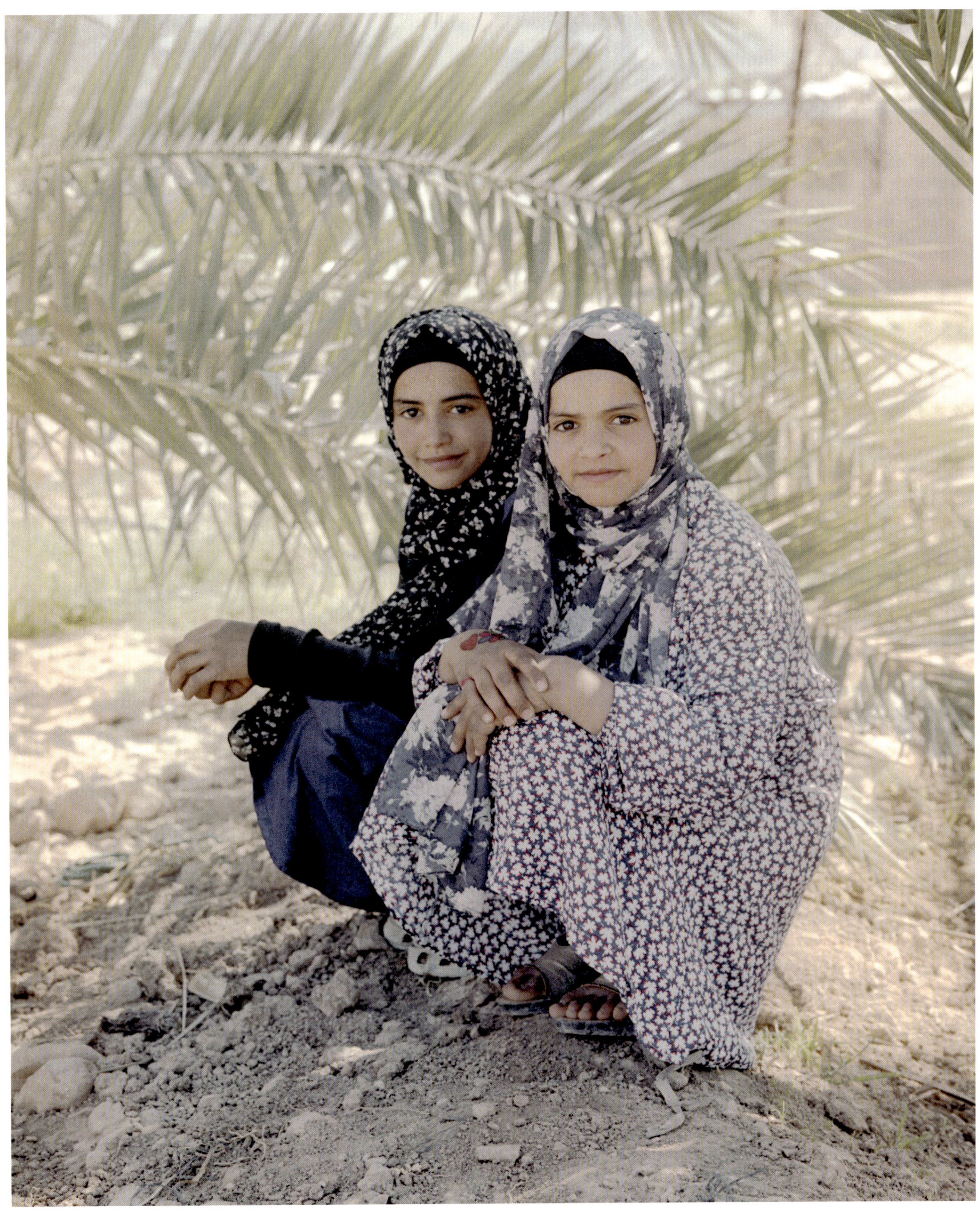

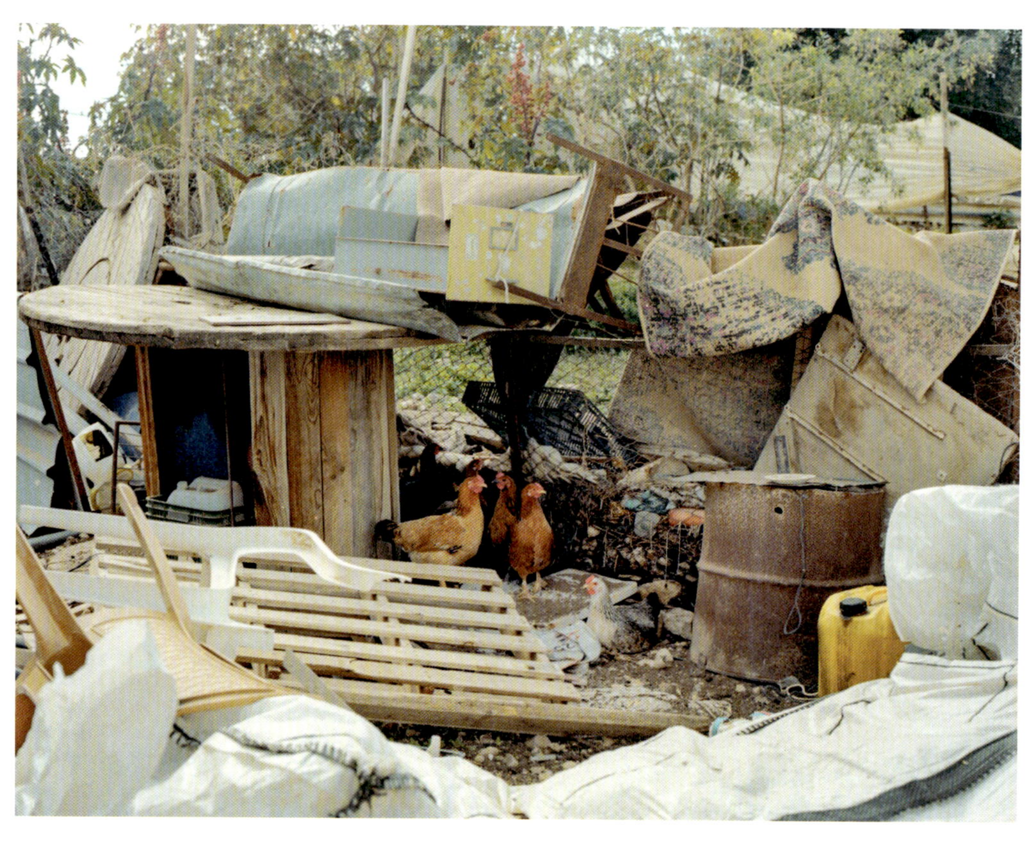

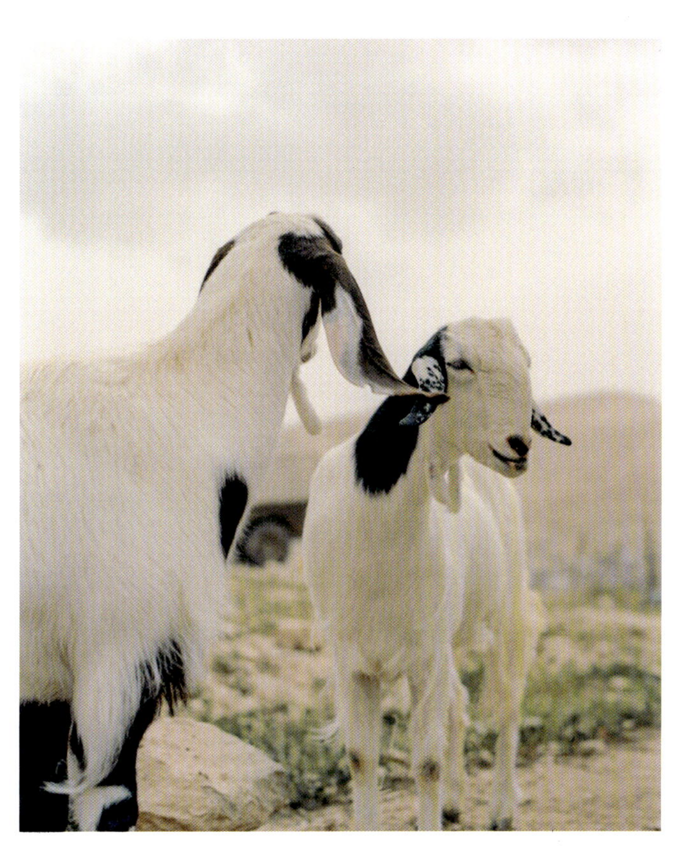

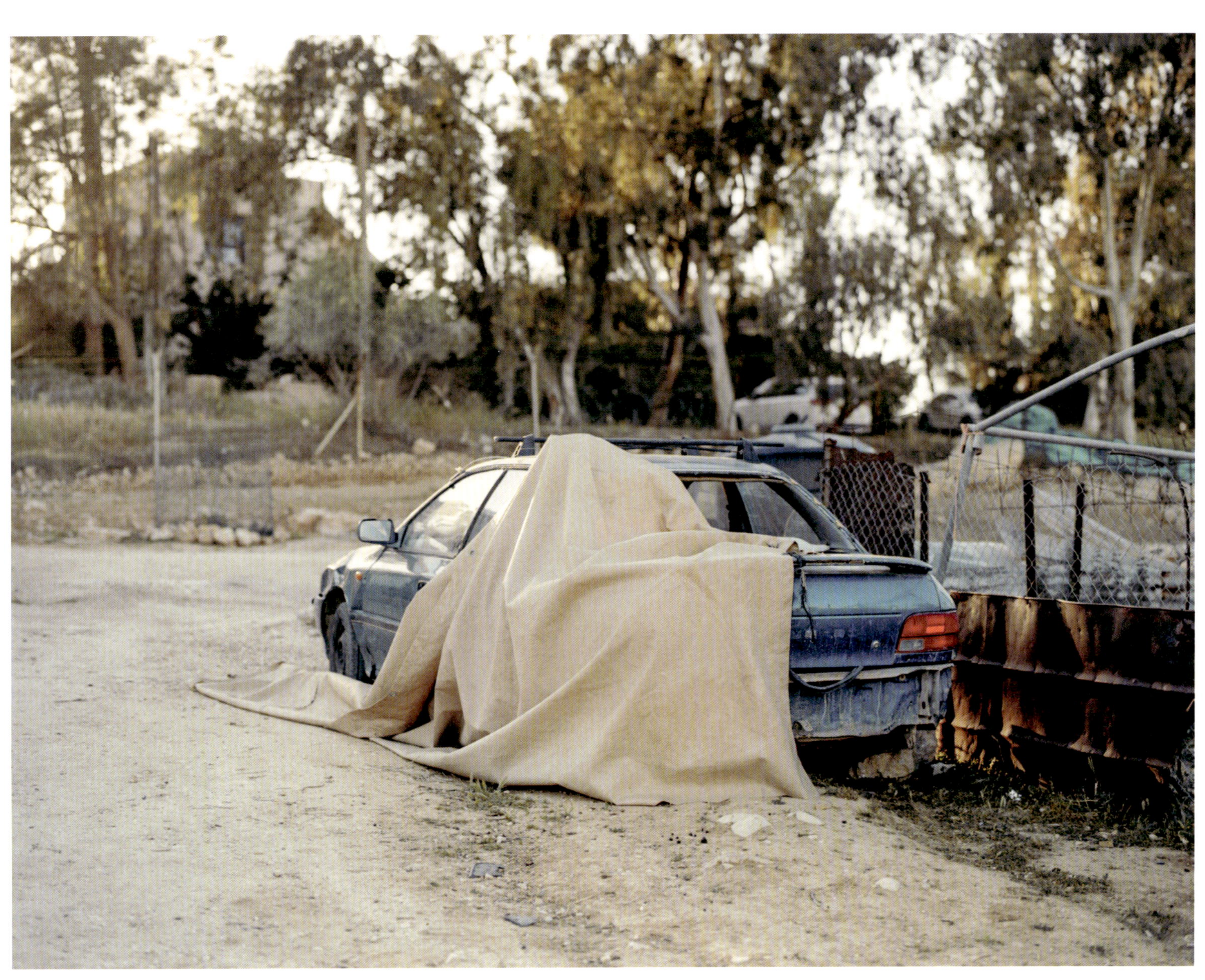

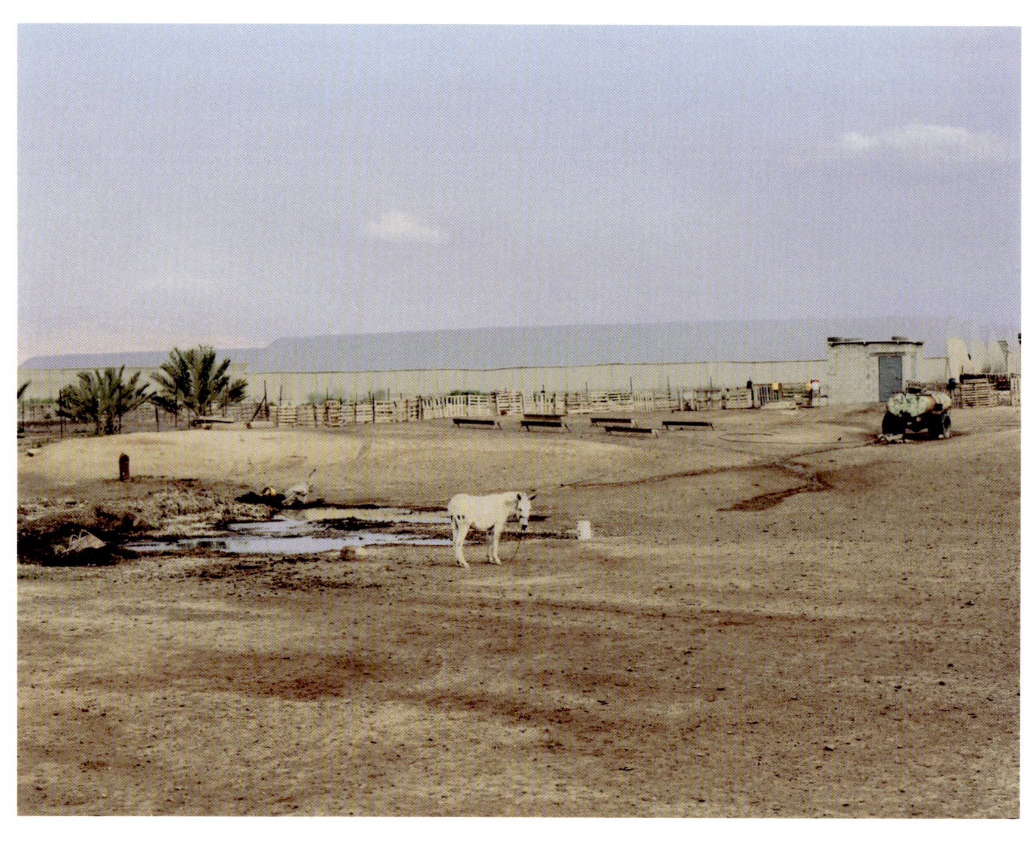

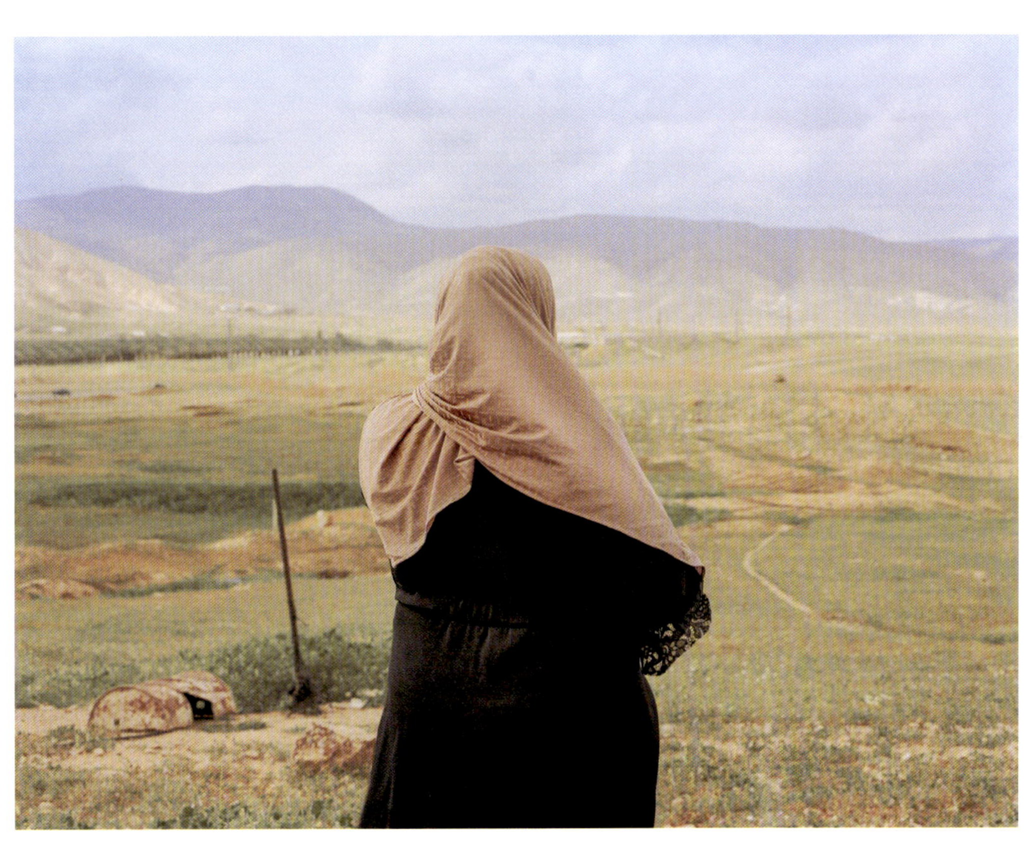

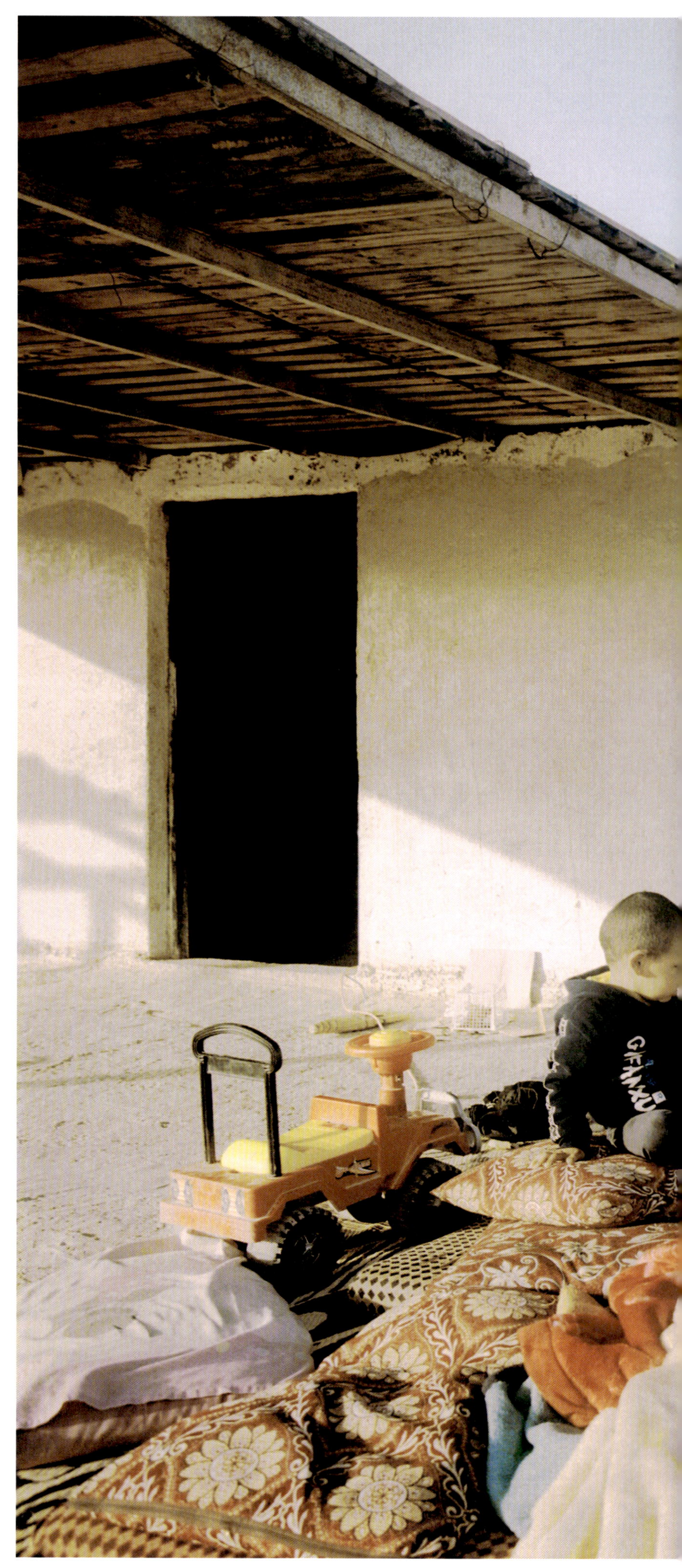

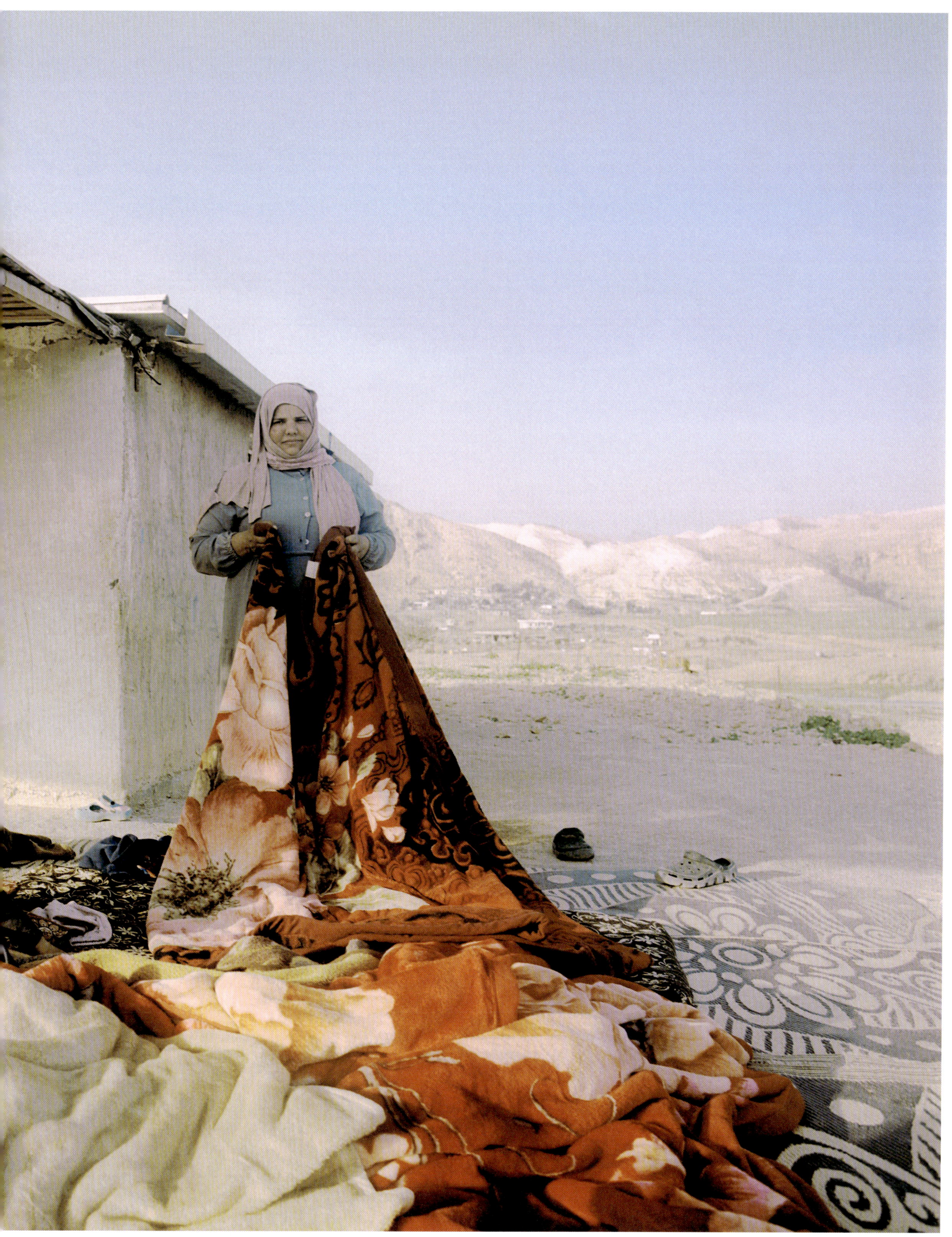

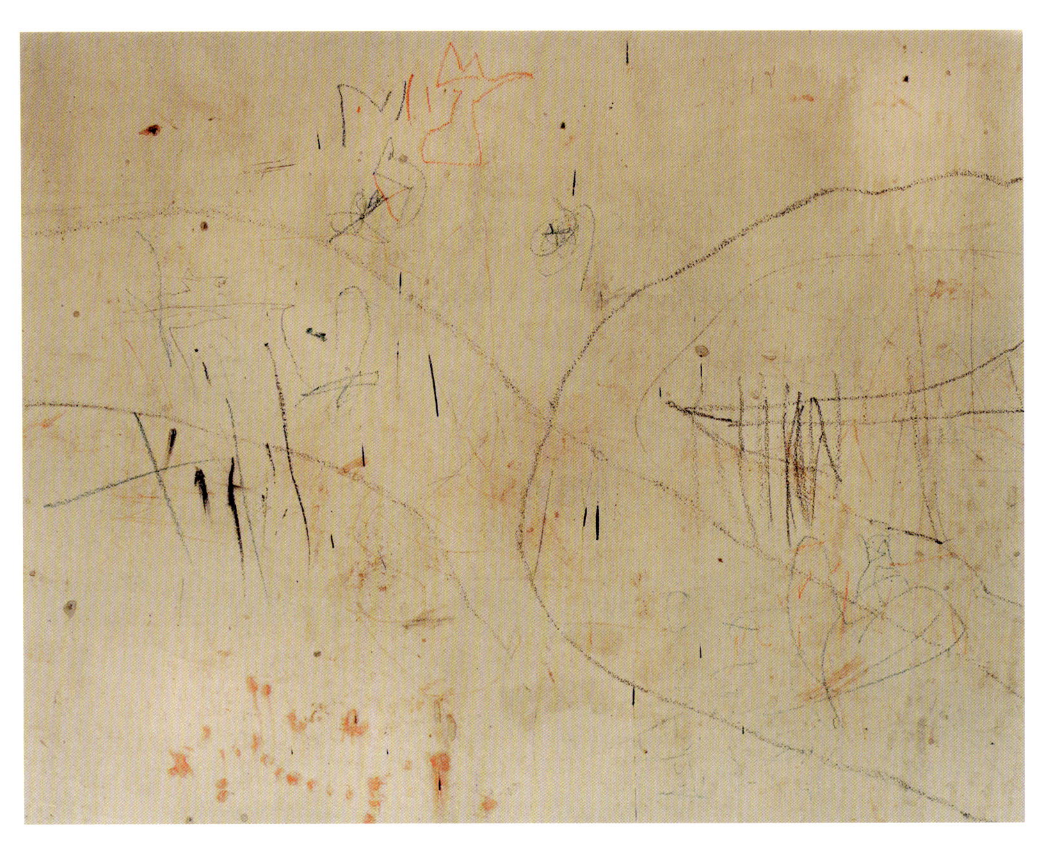

P. 38

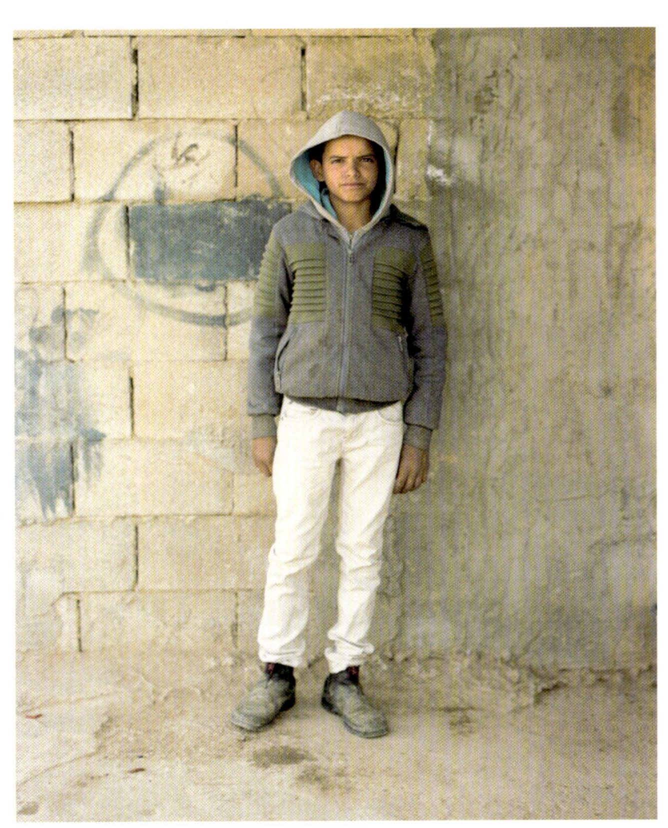

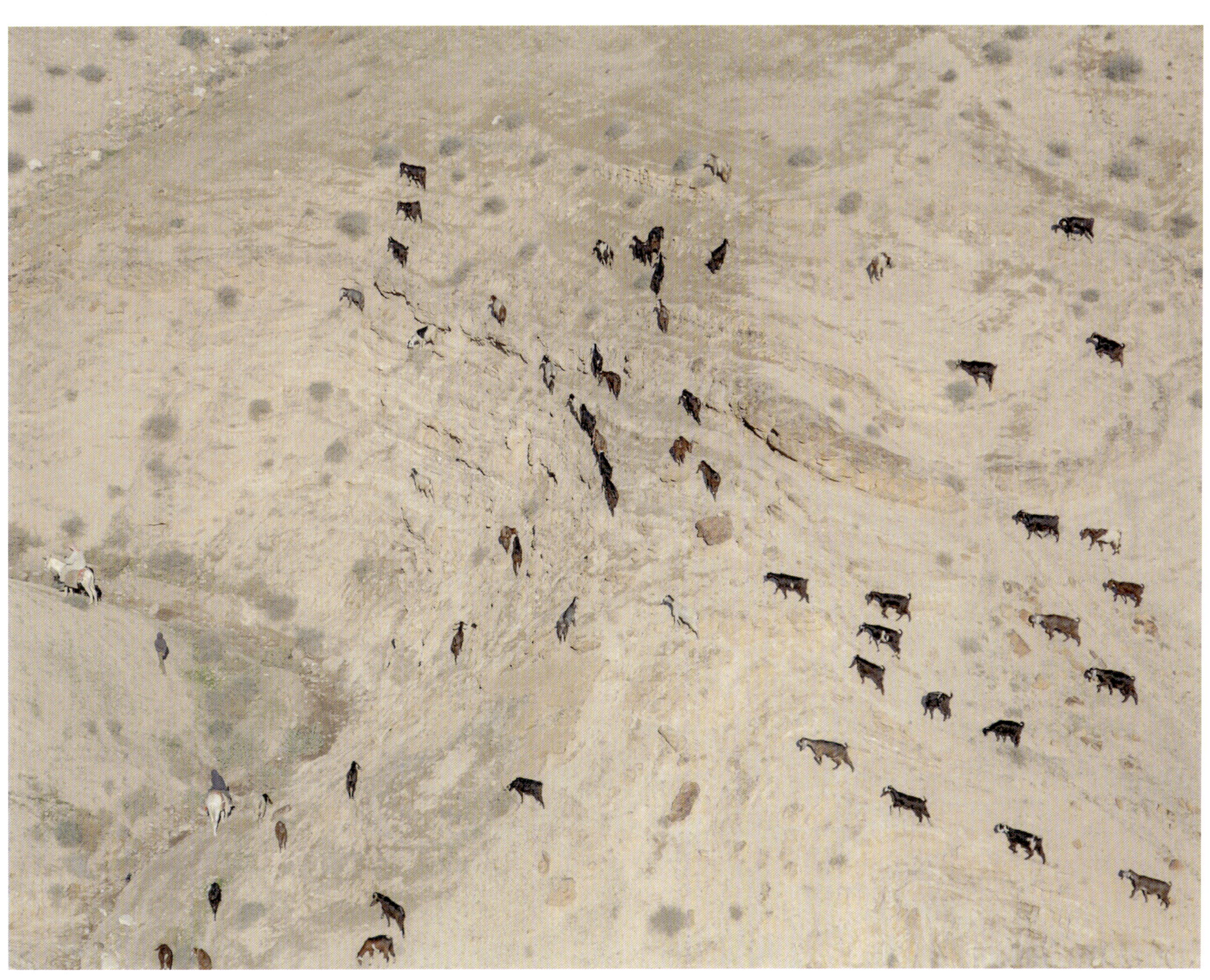

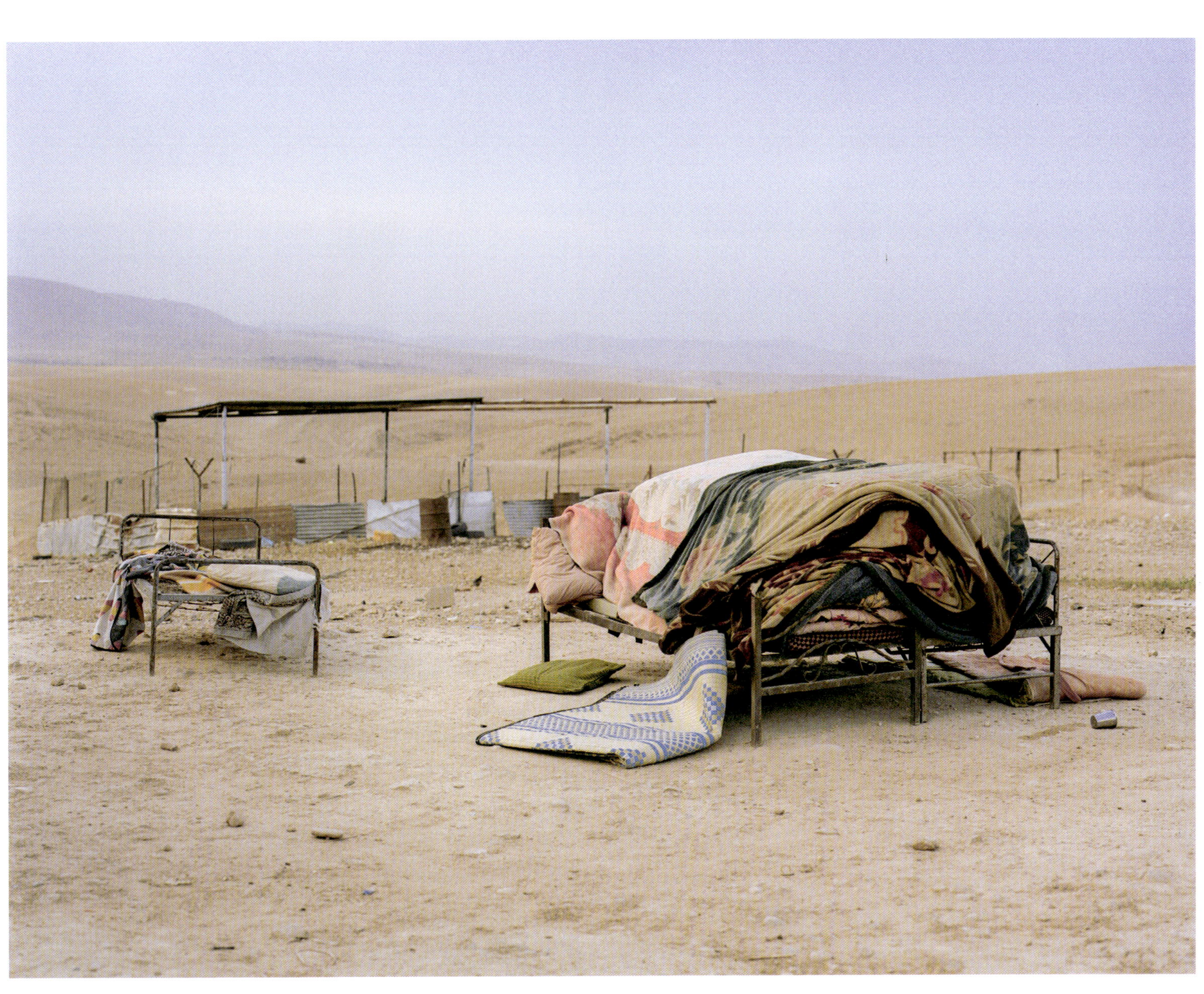

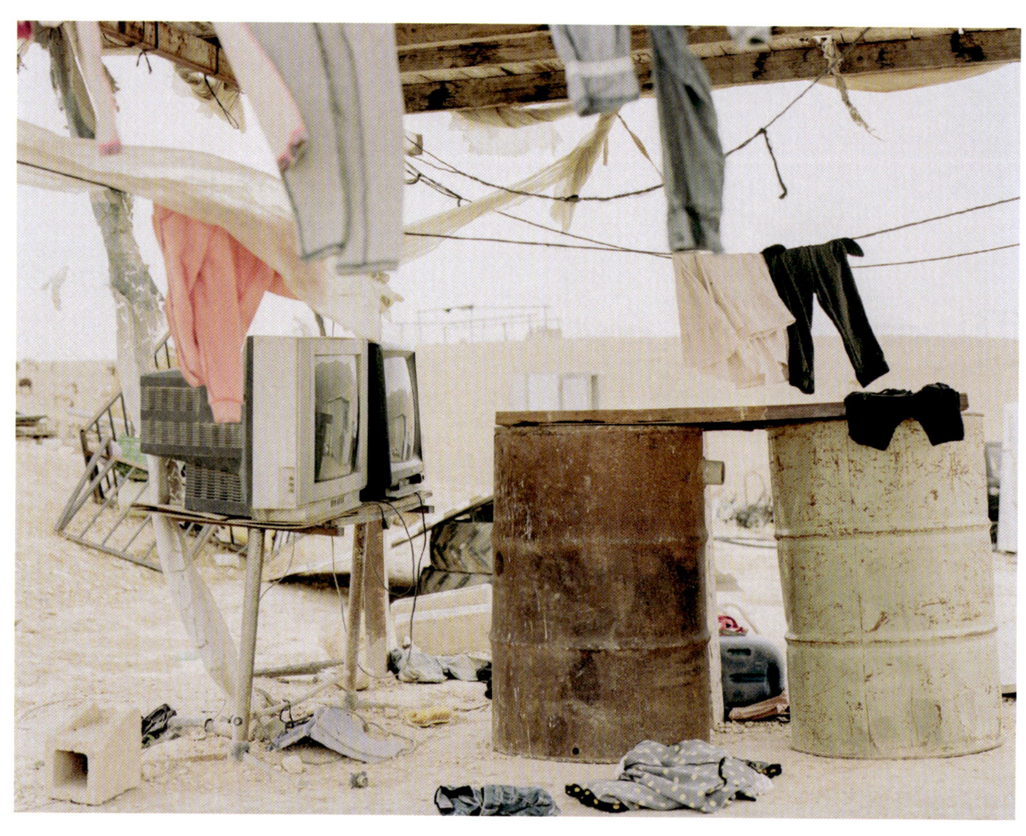

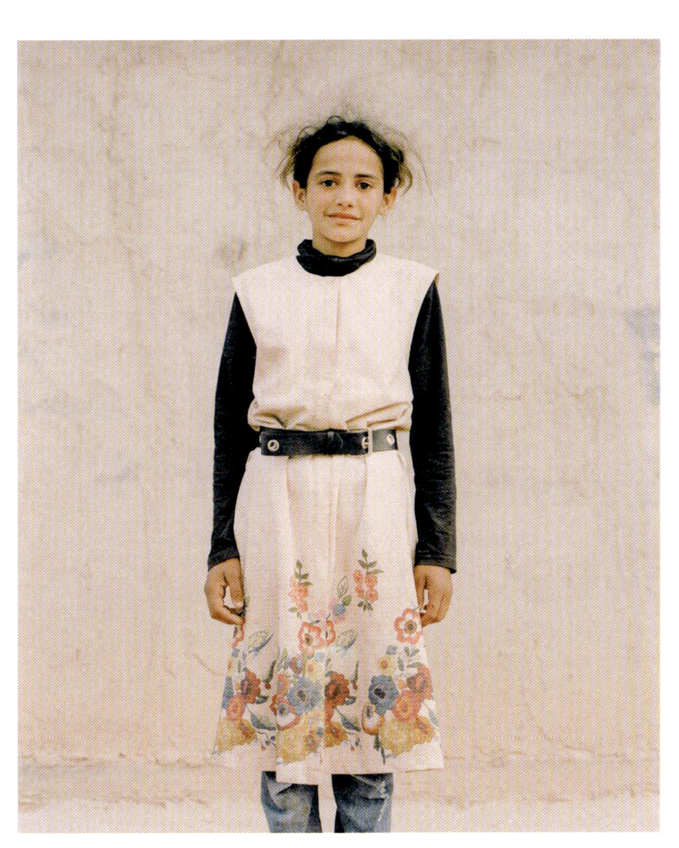

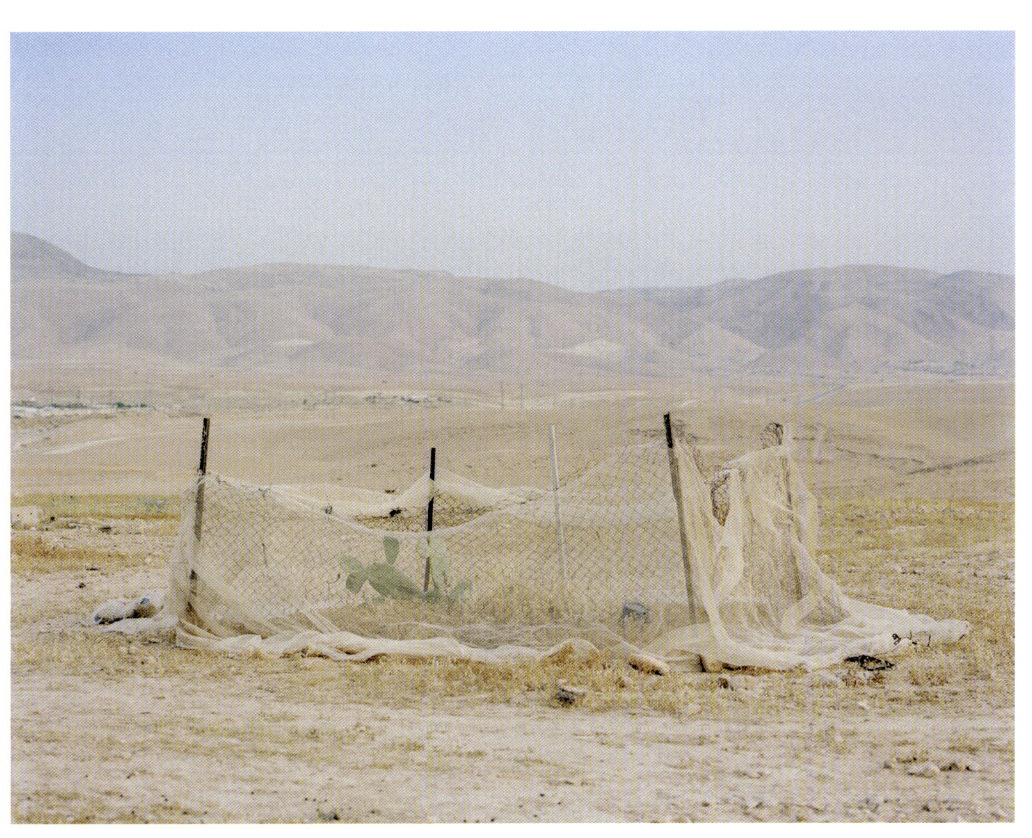

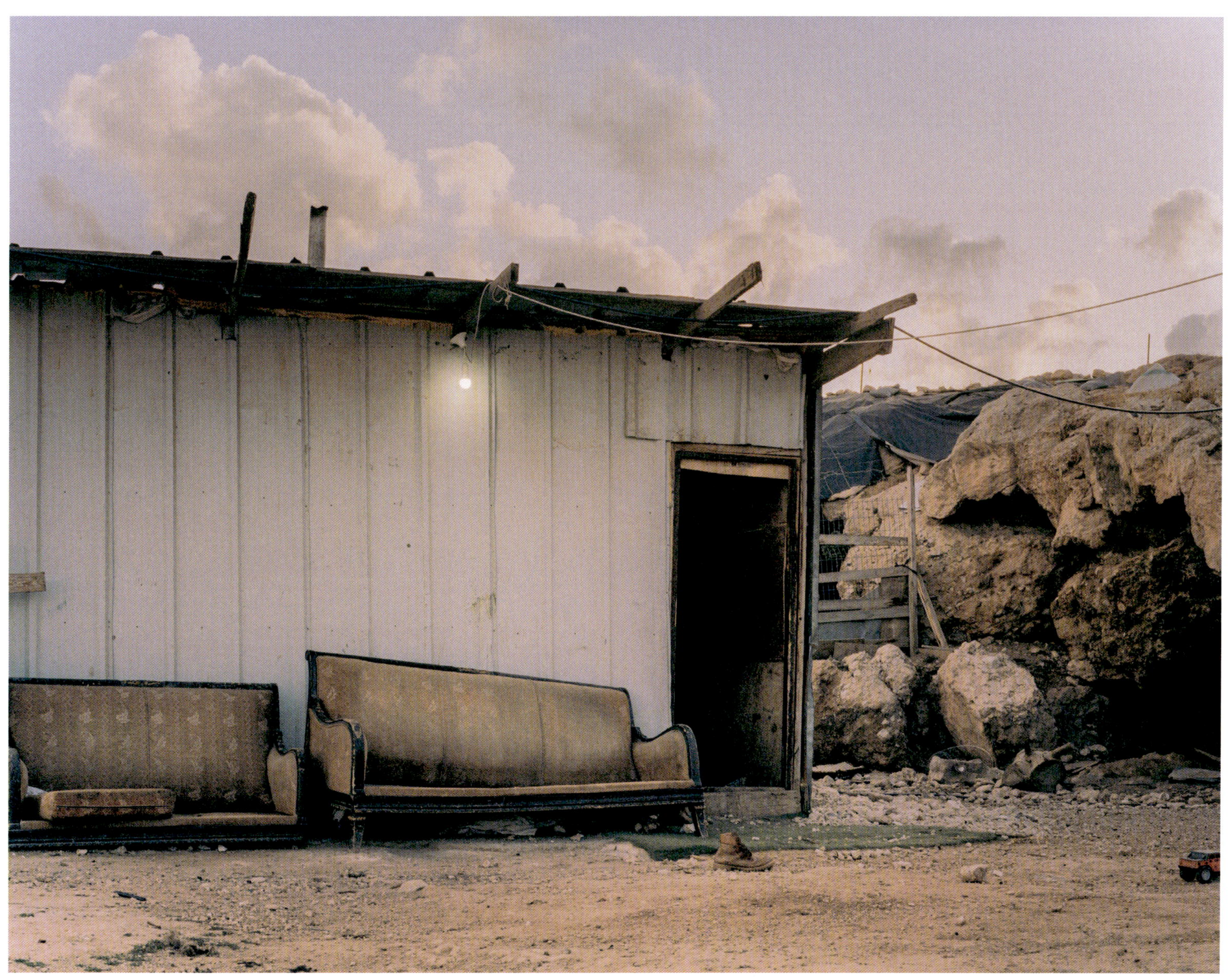

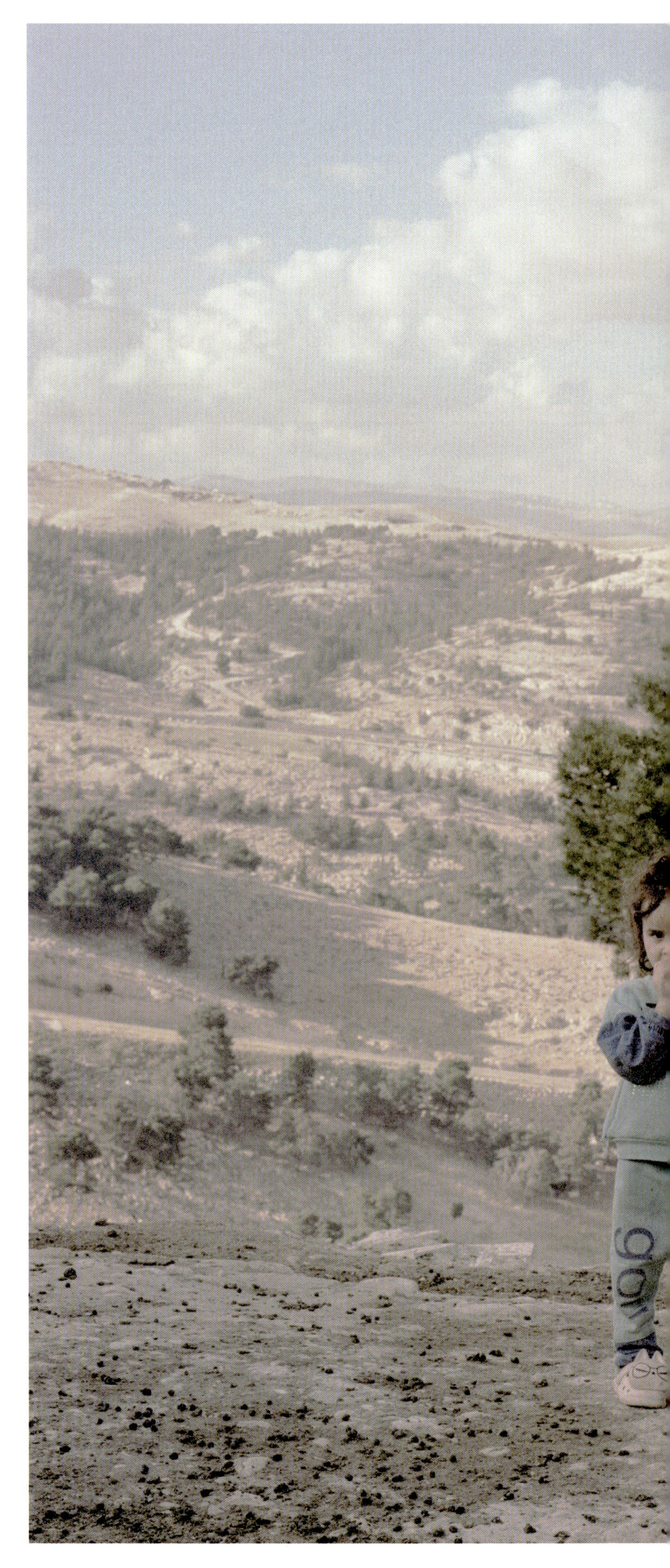

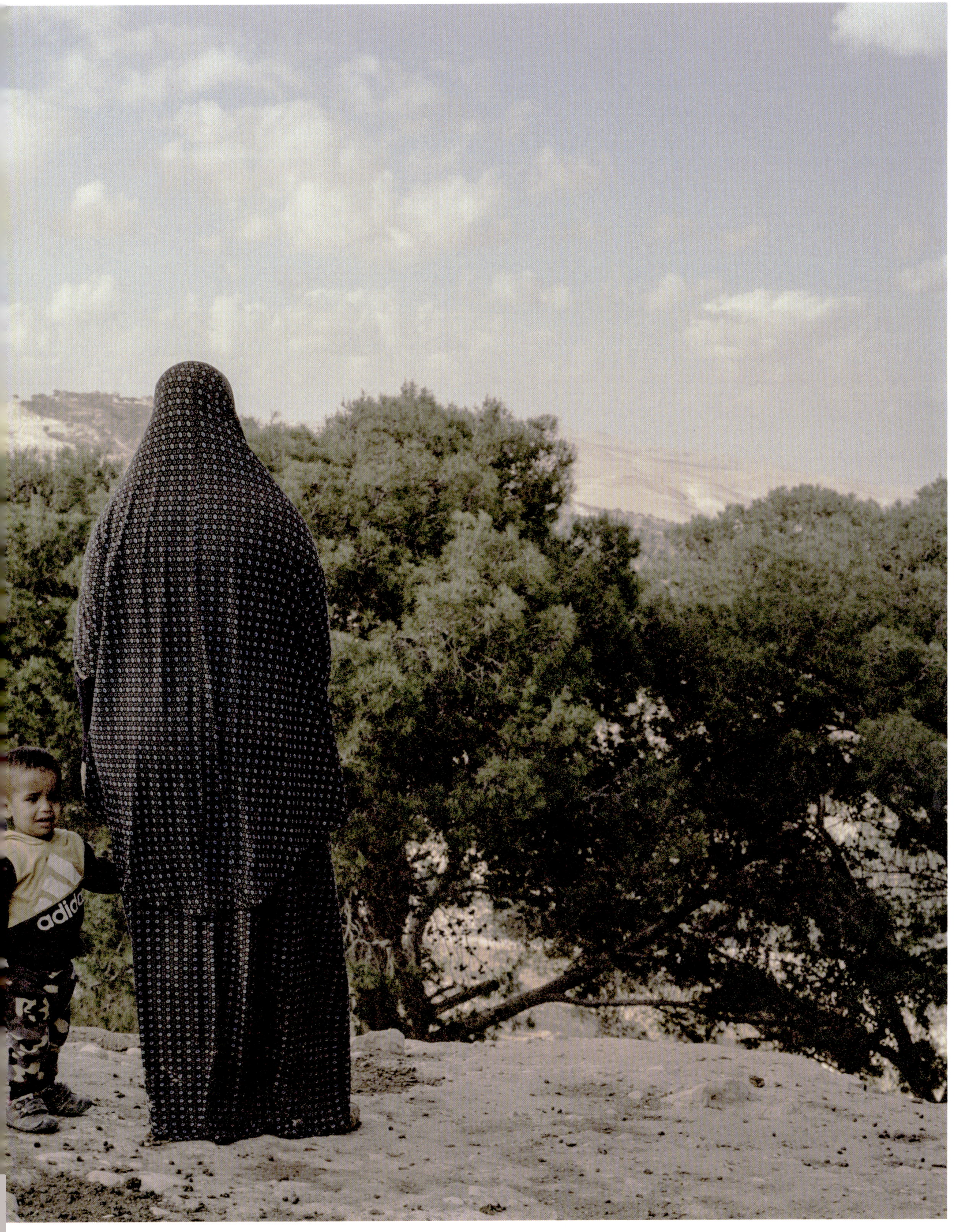

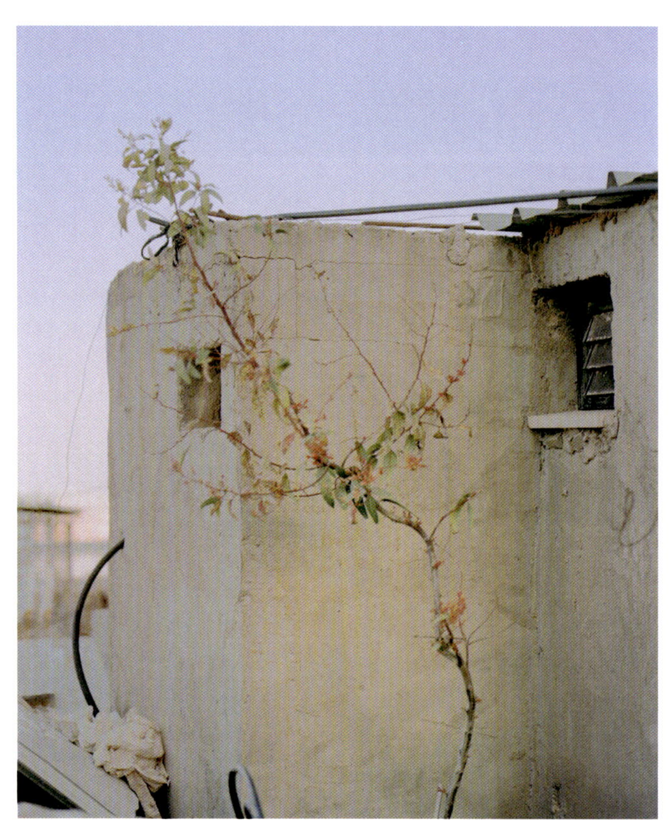

P. 52

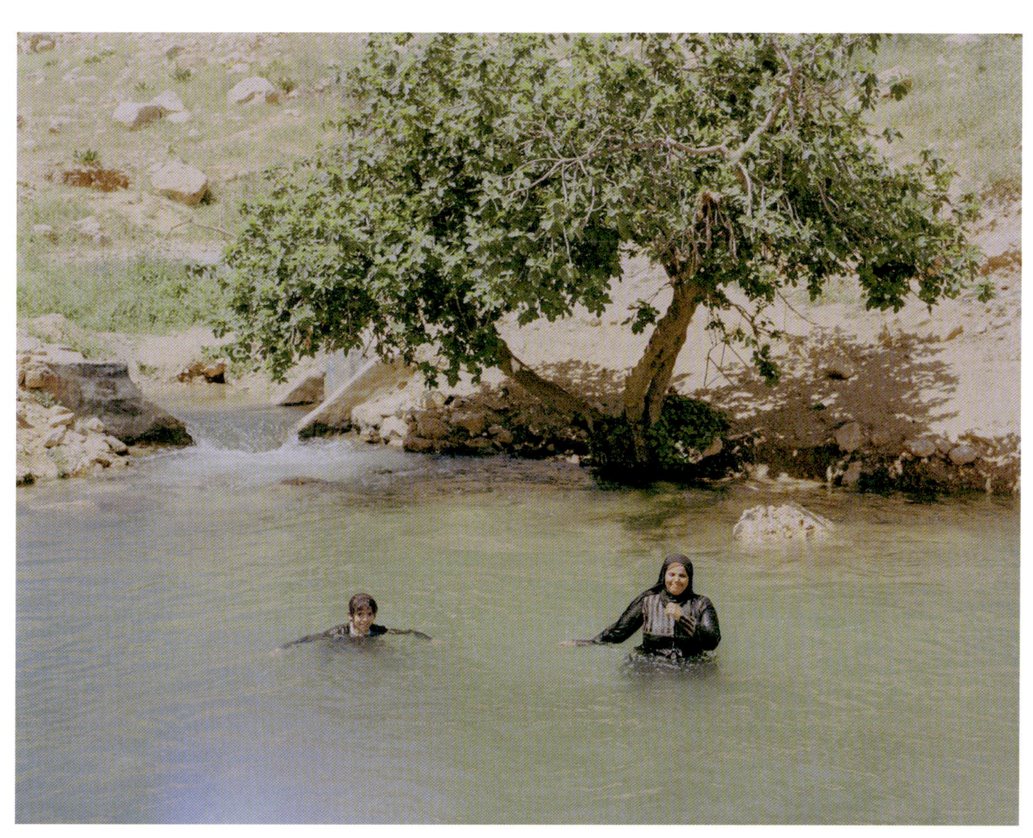

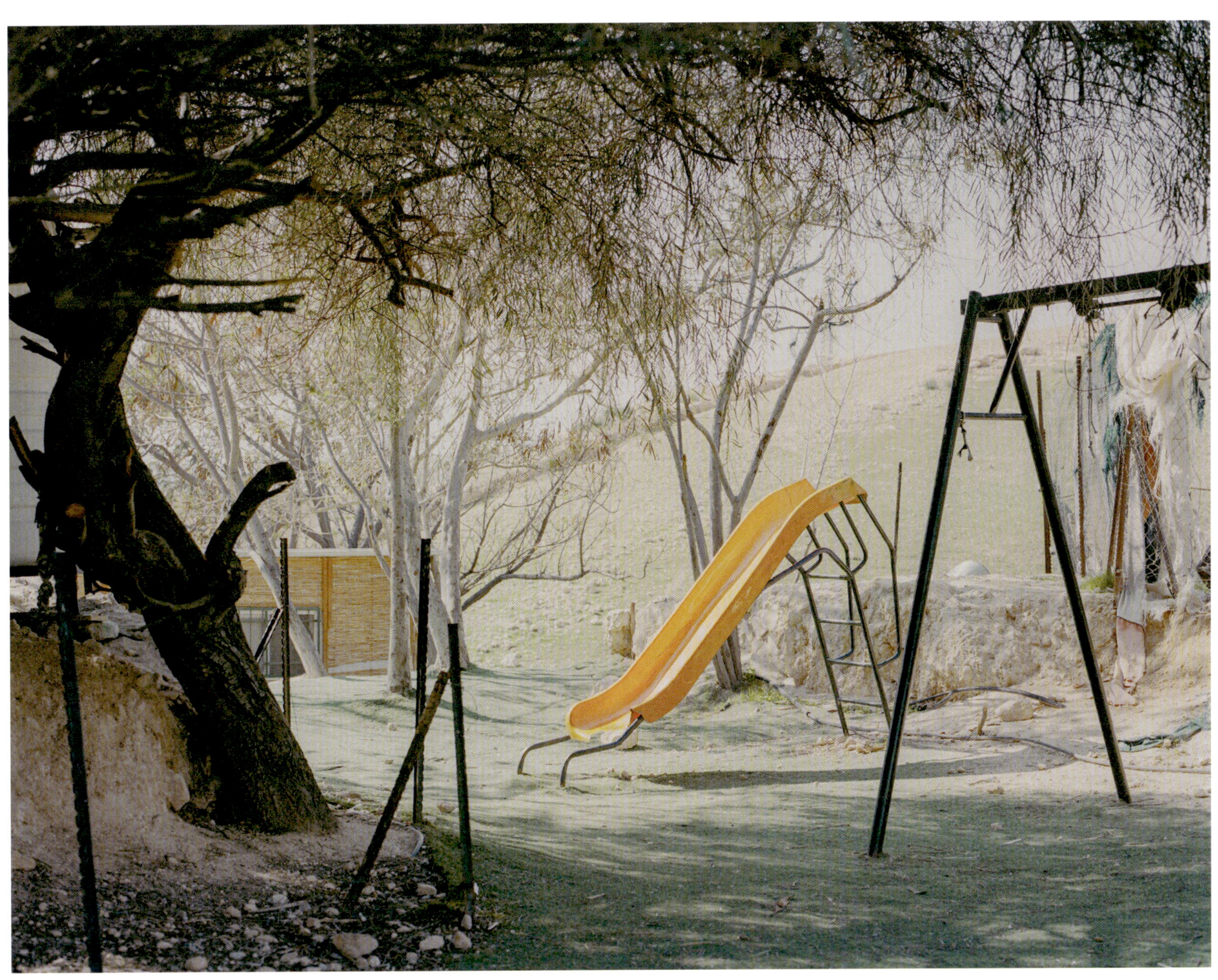

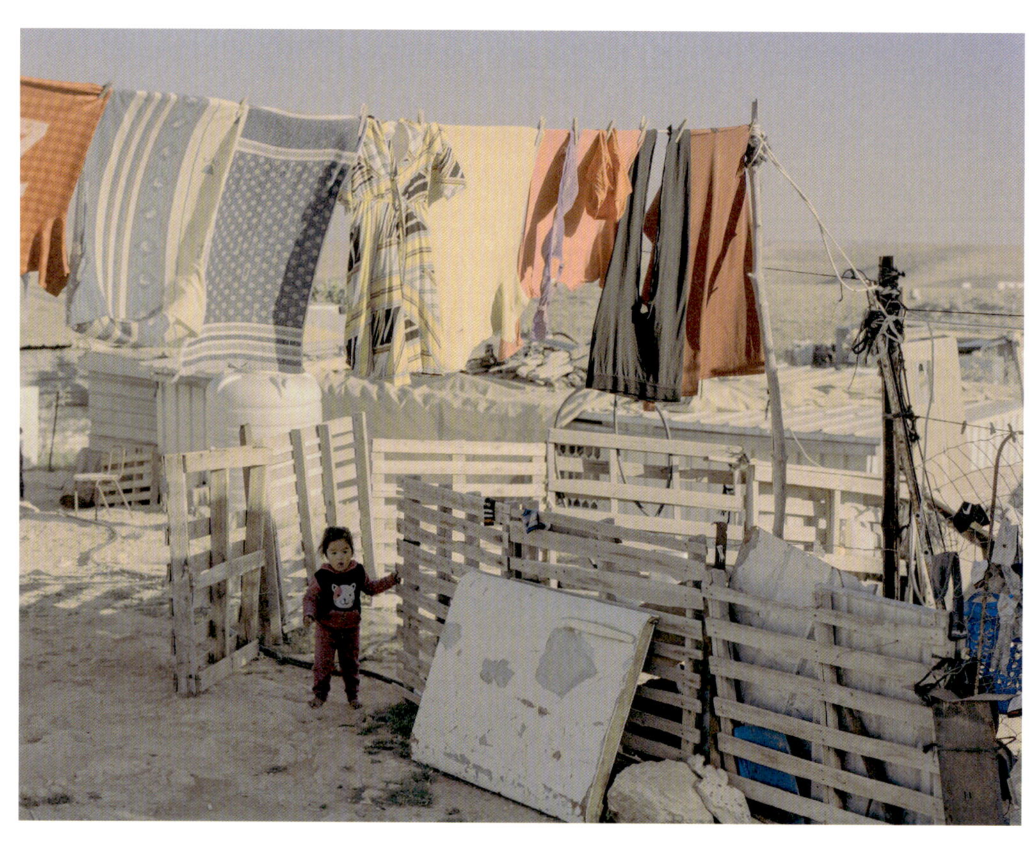

P. 56

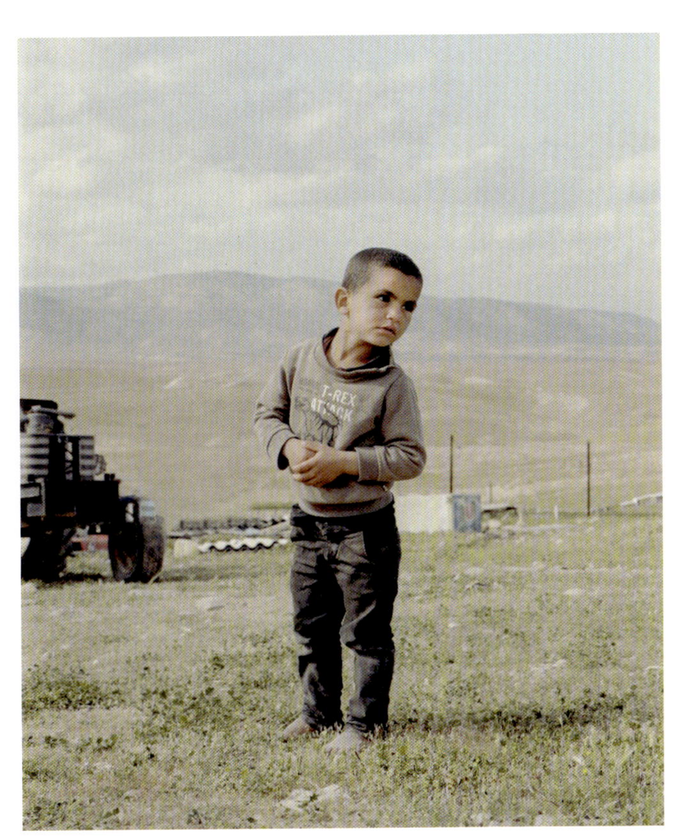
T-REX

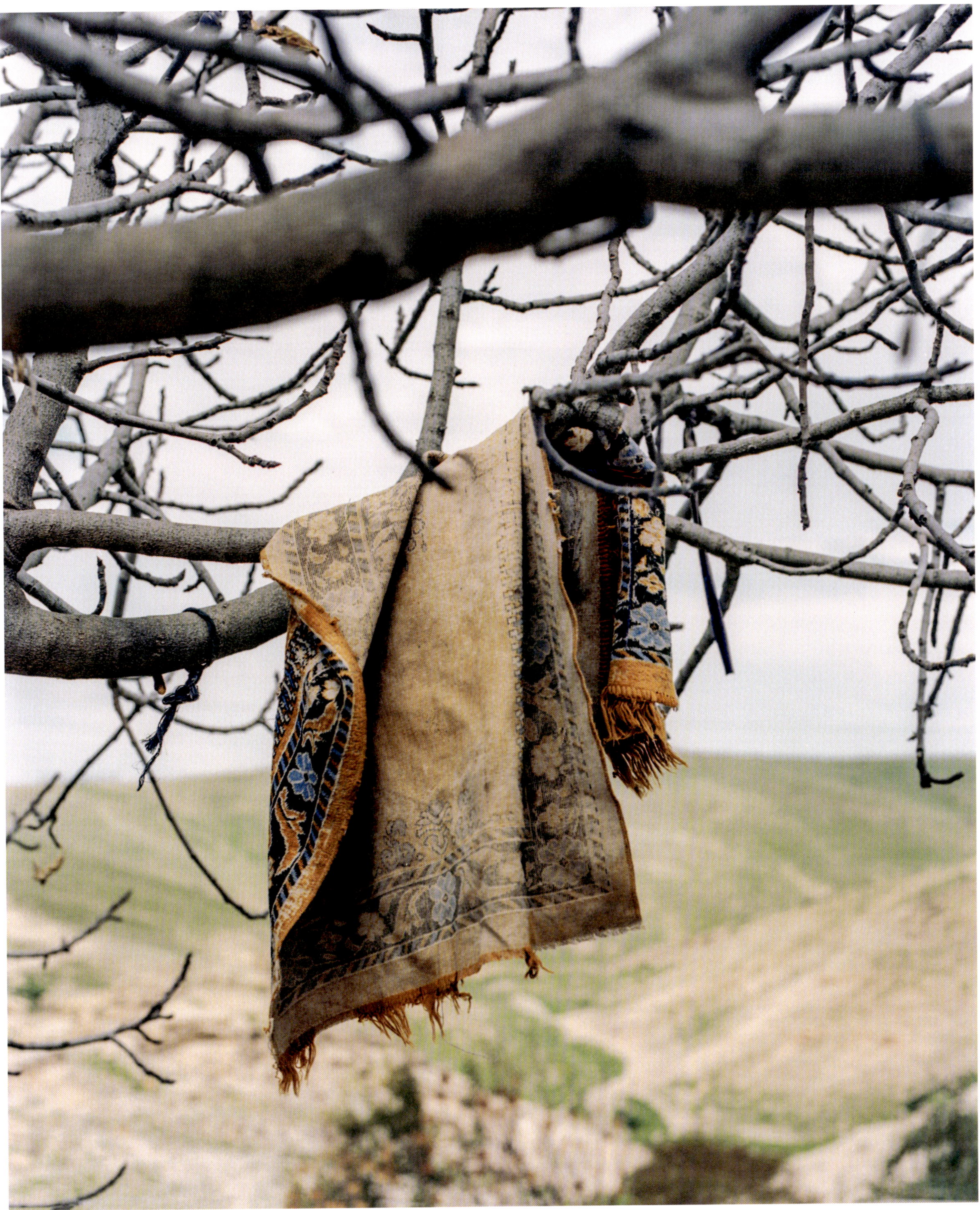

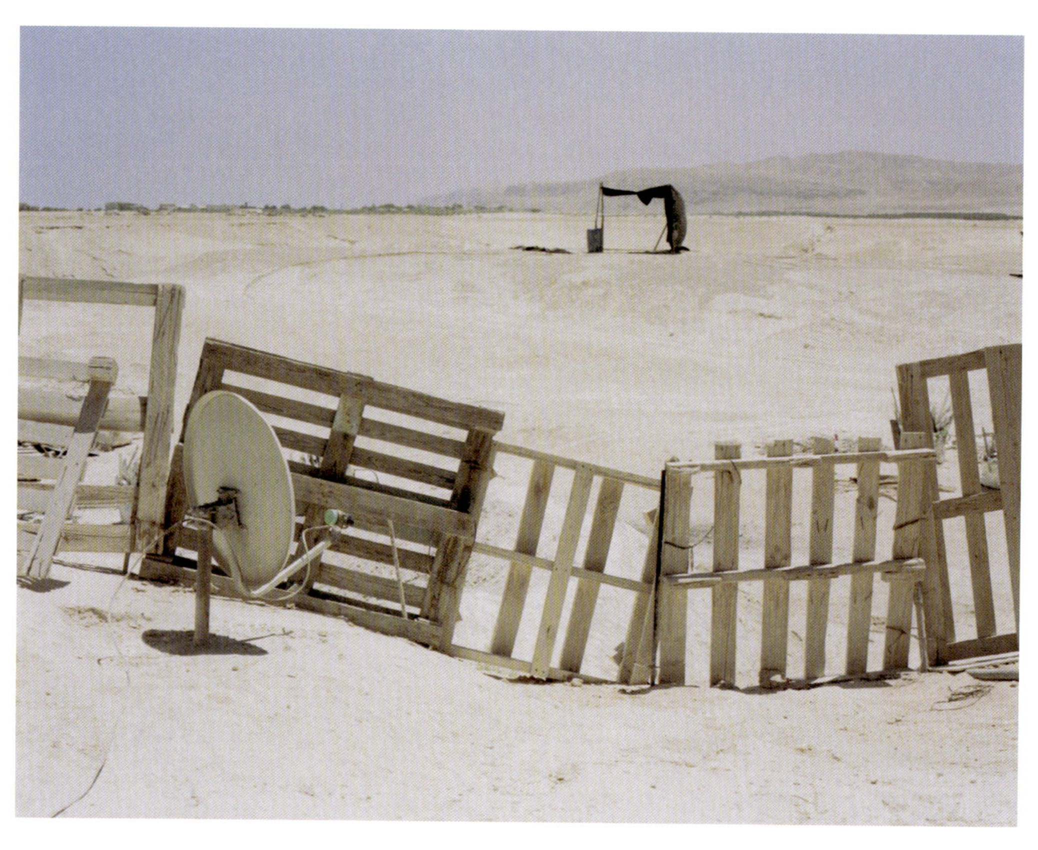

P. 60

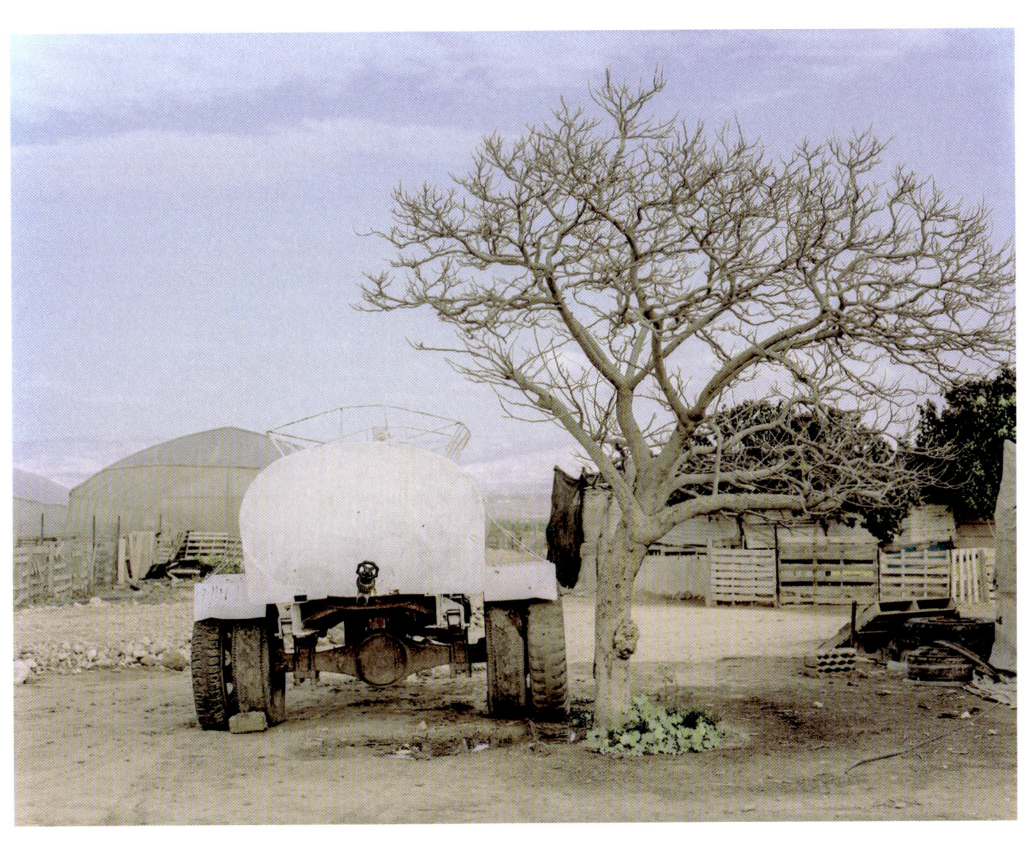

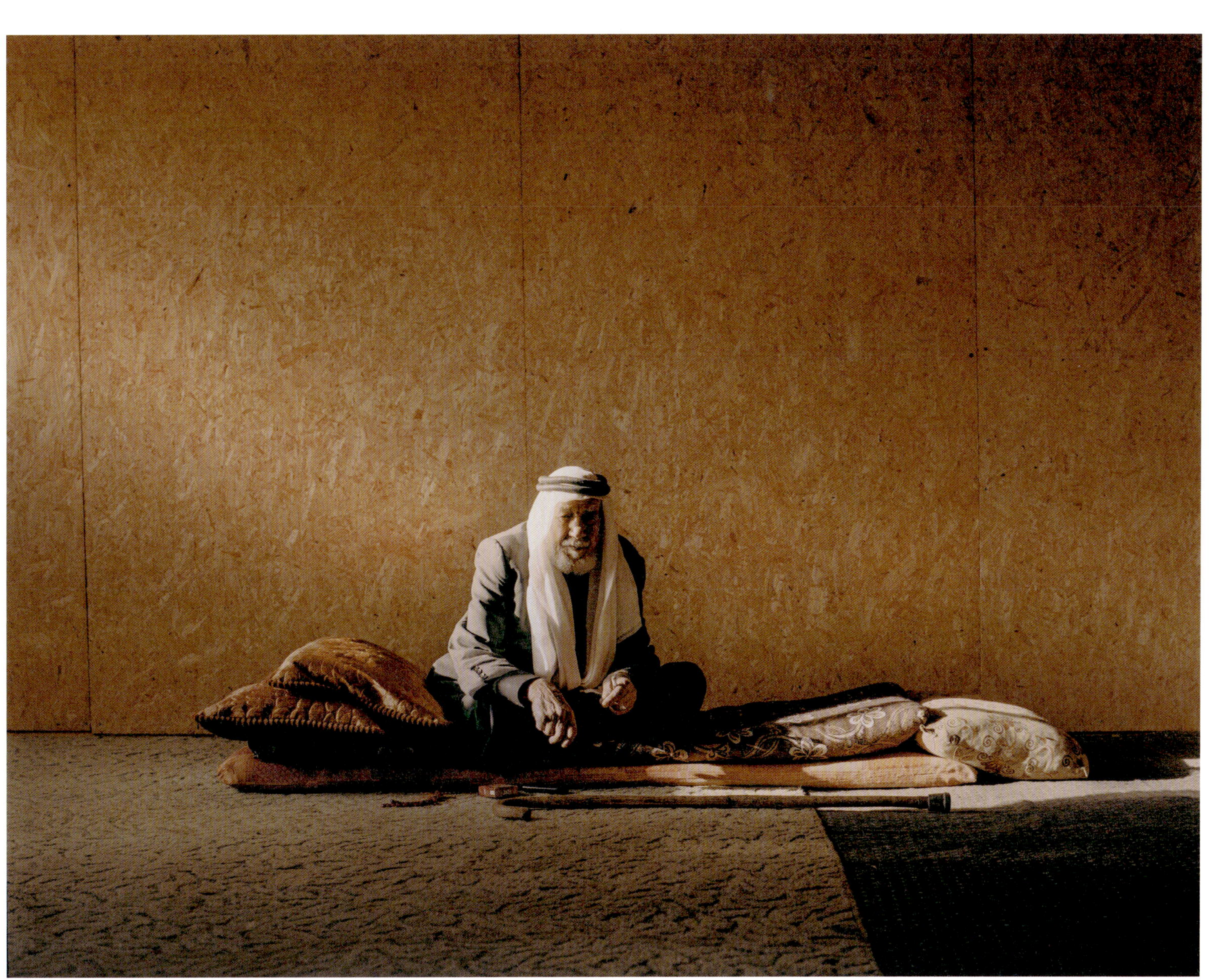

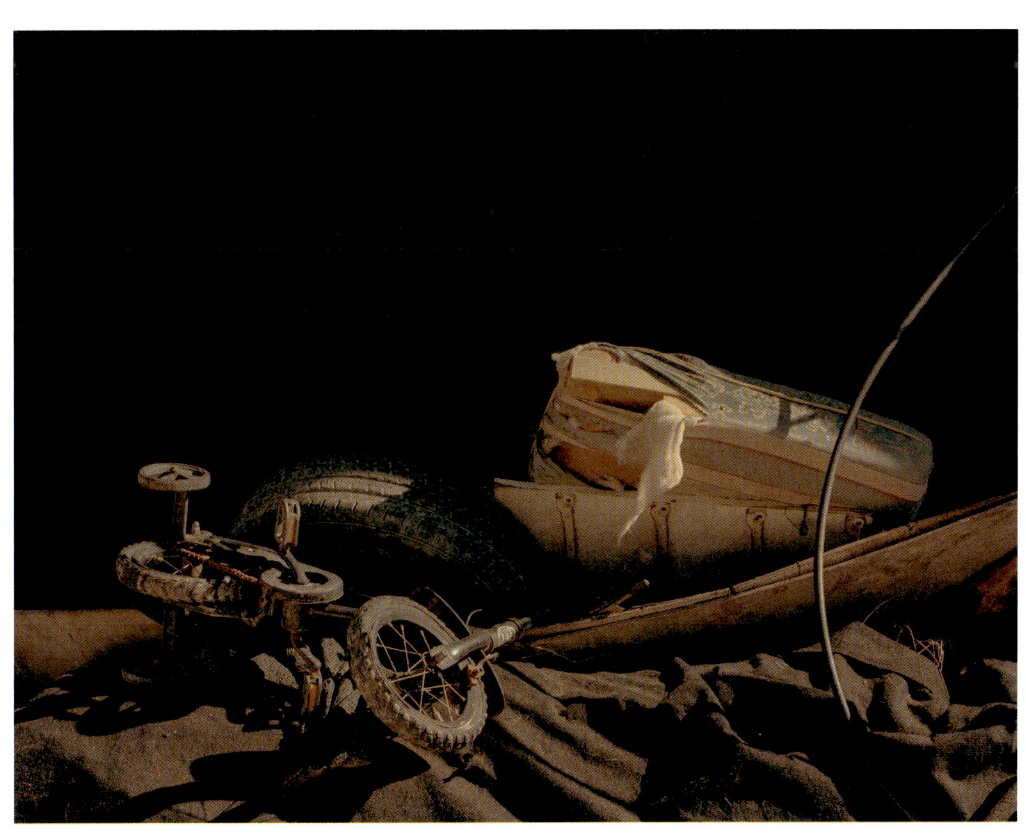

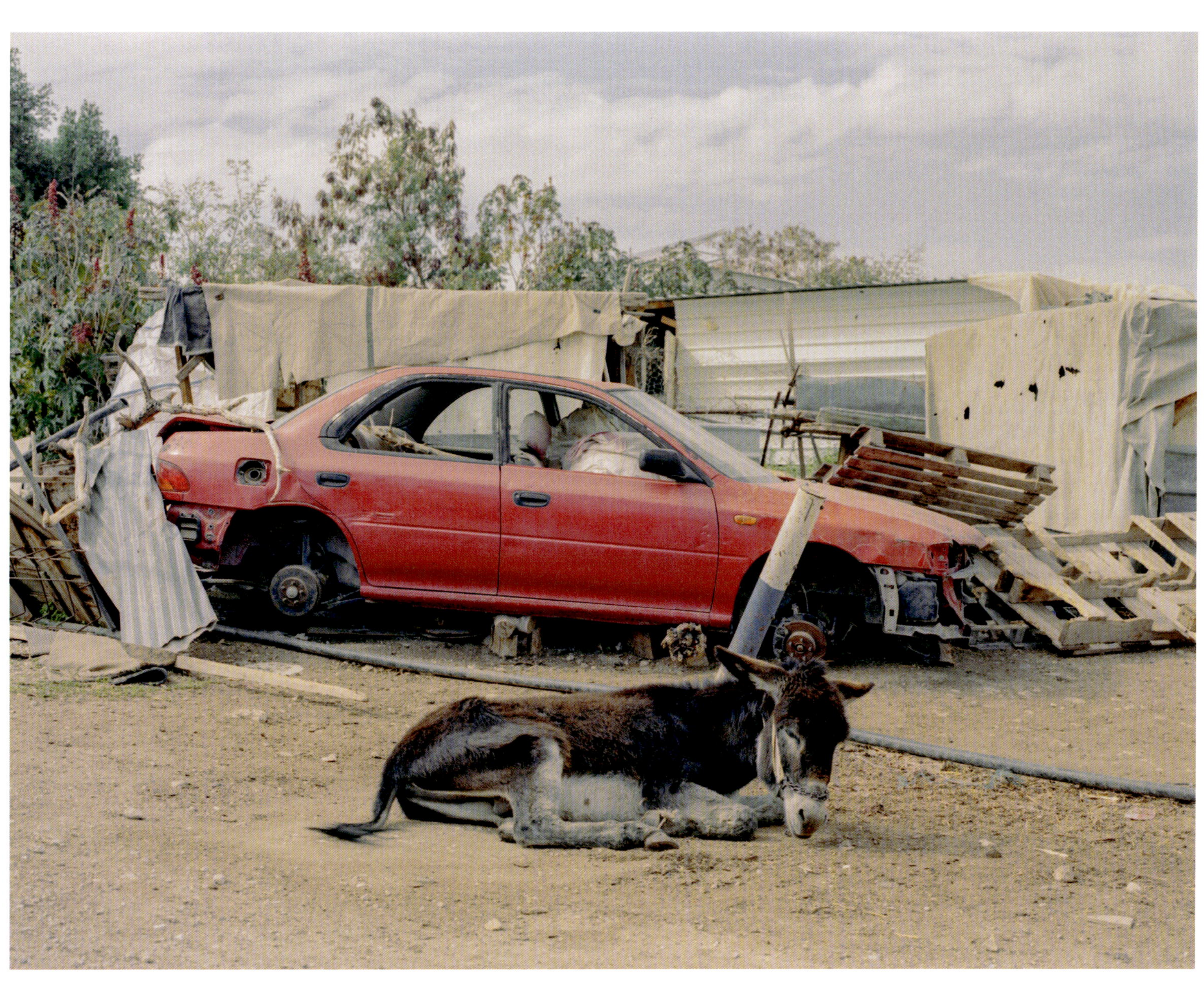

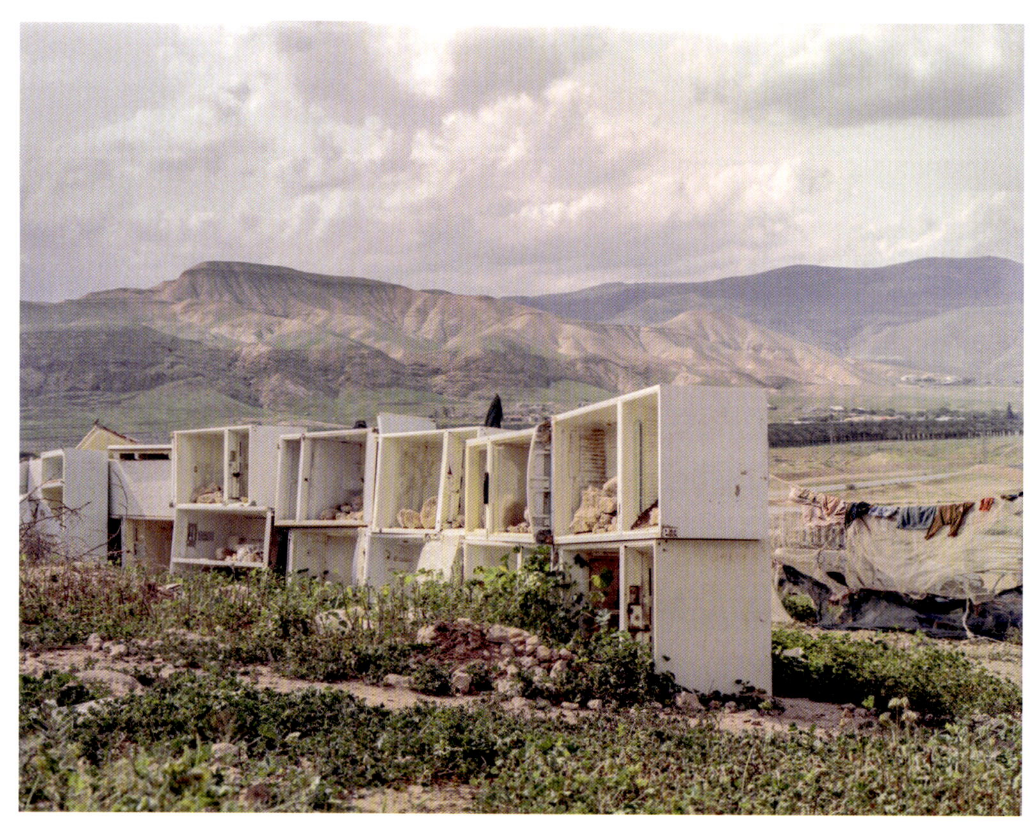

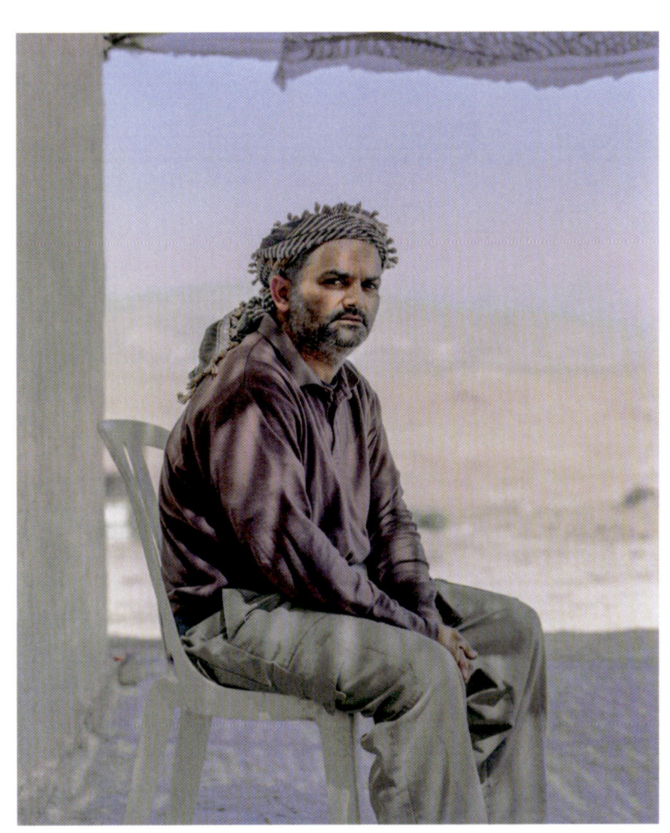

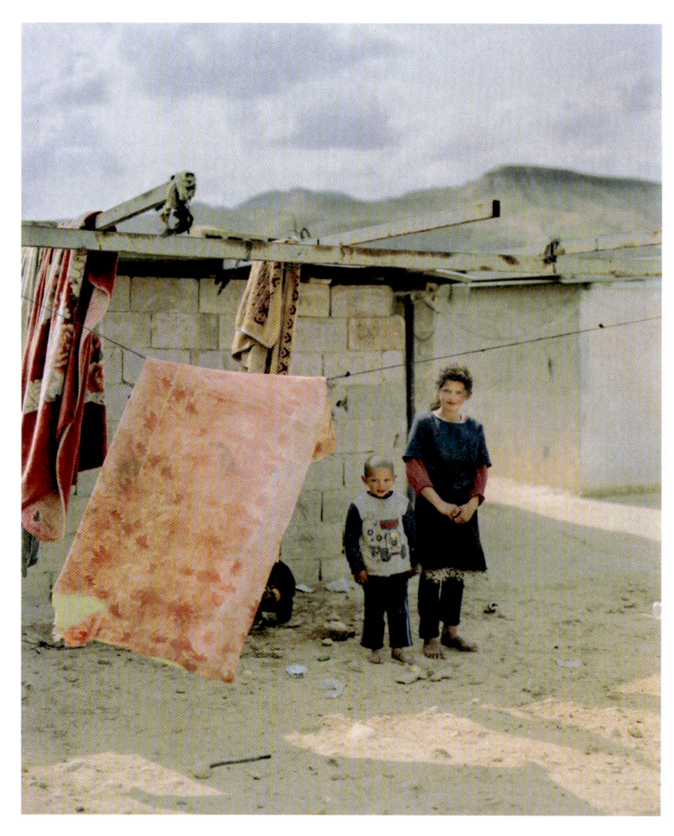

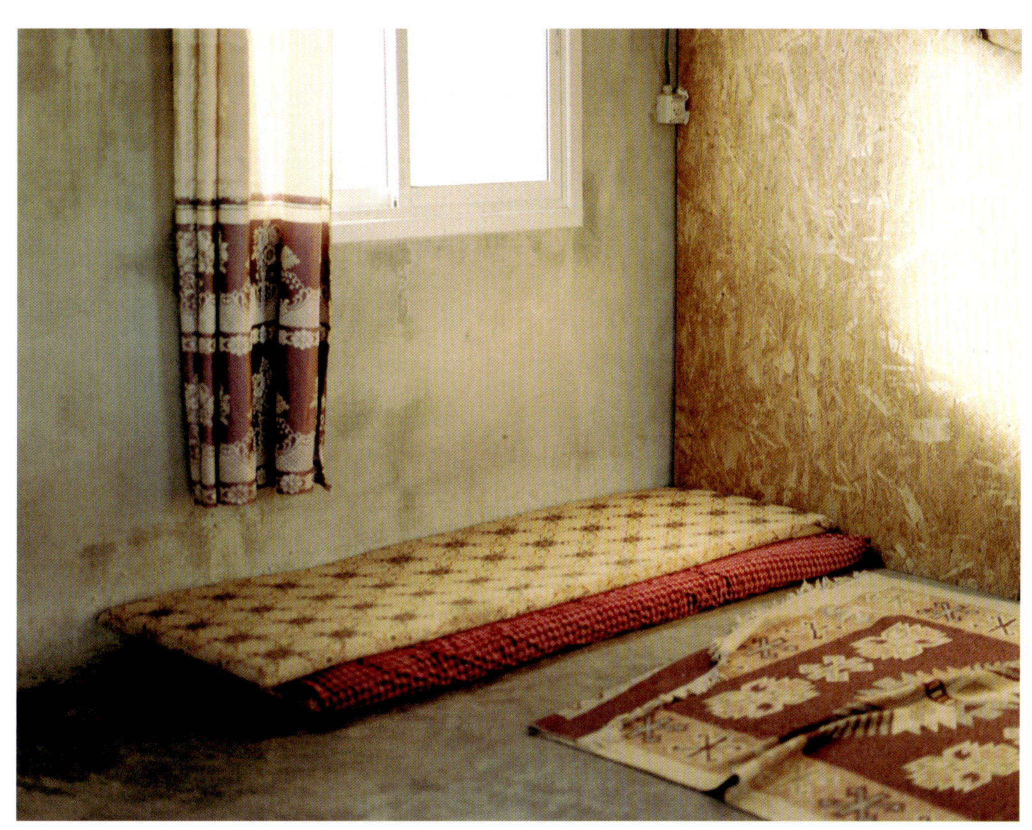

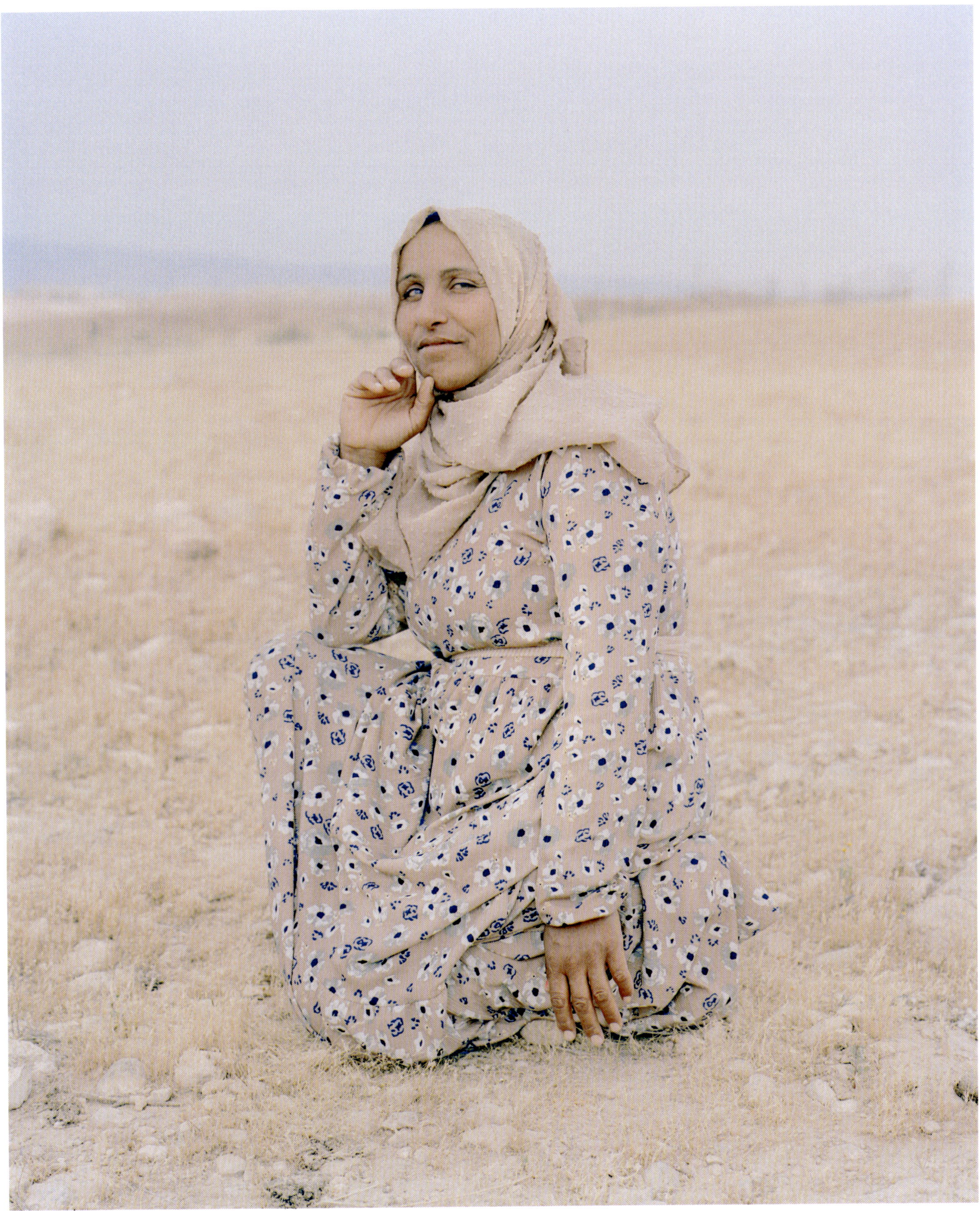

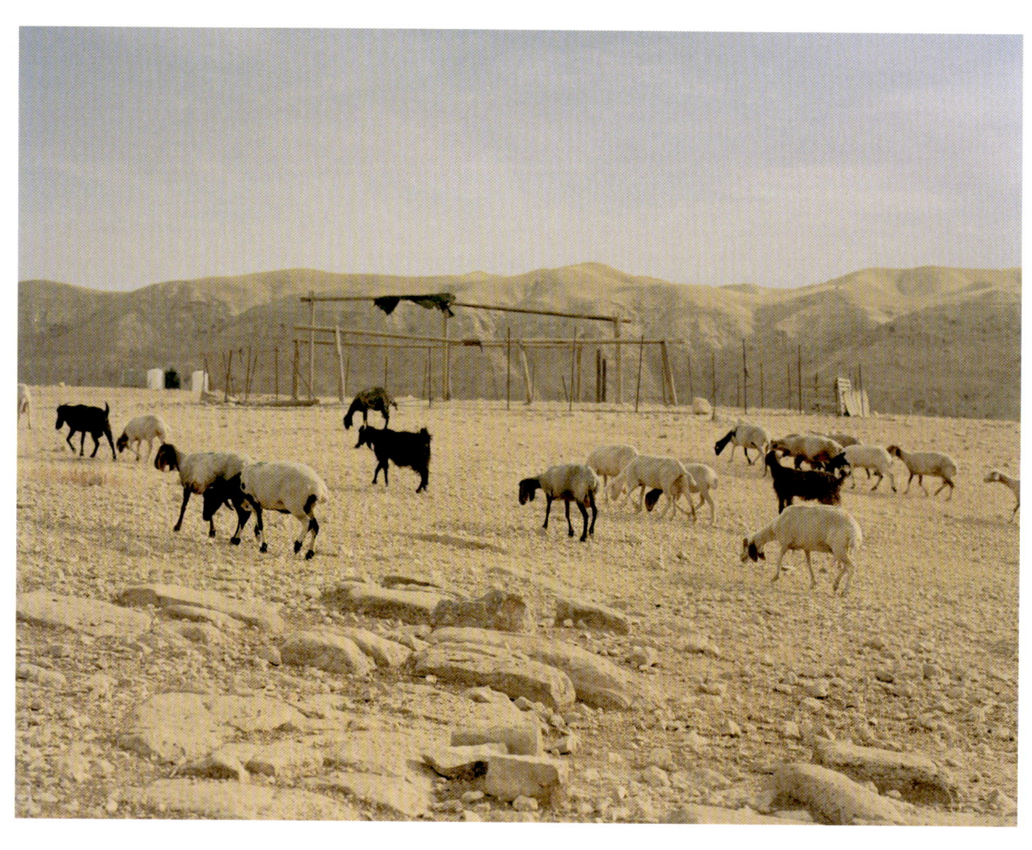

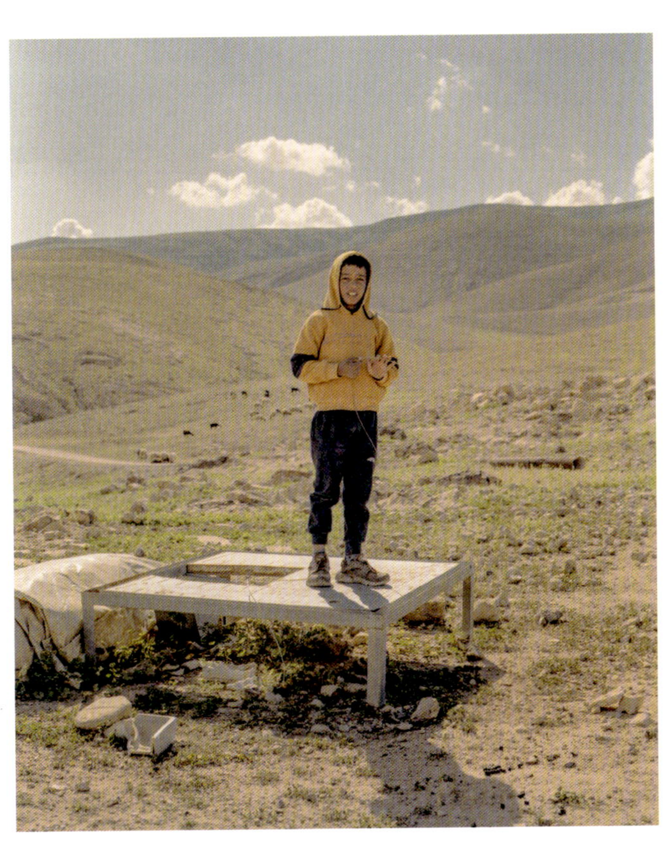

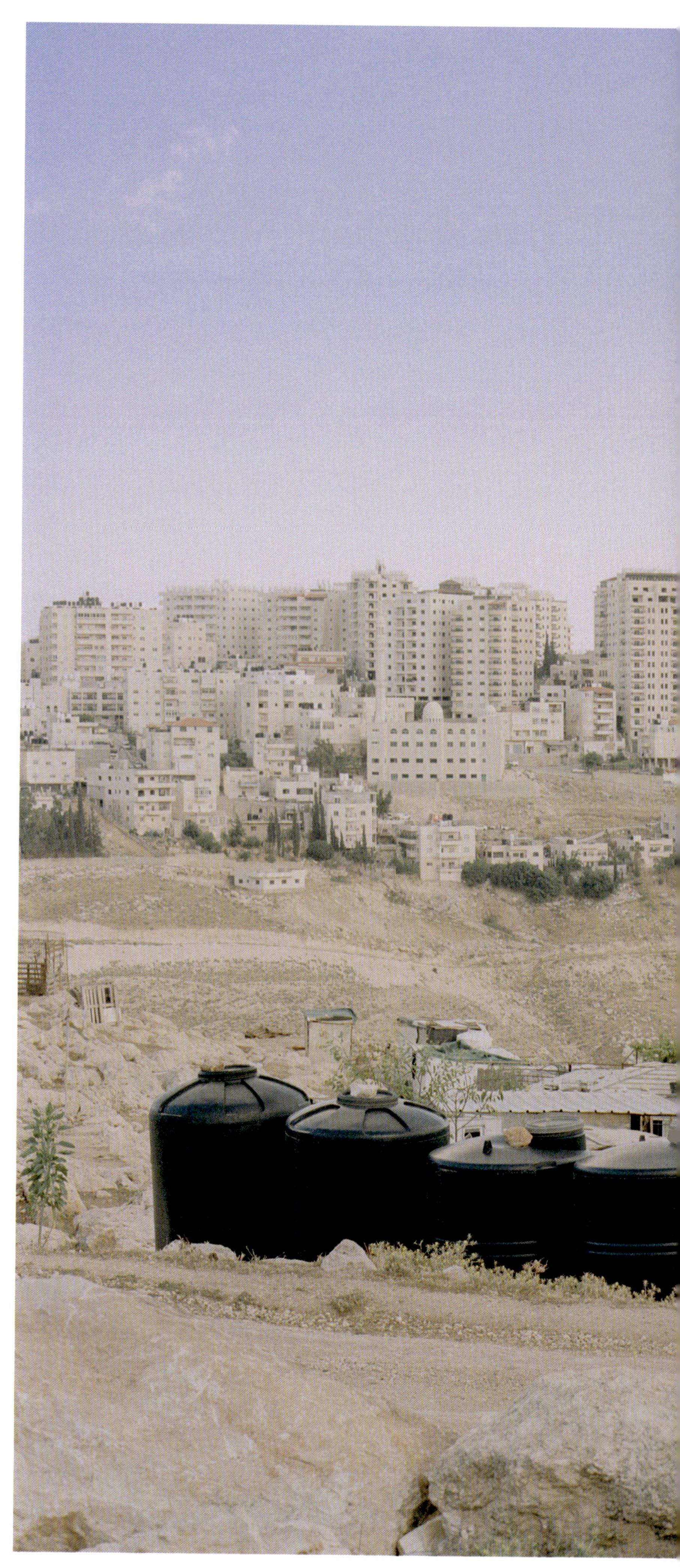

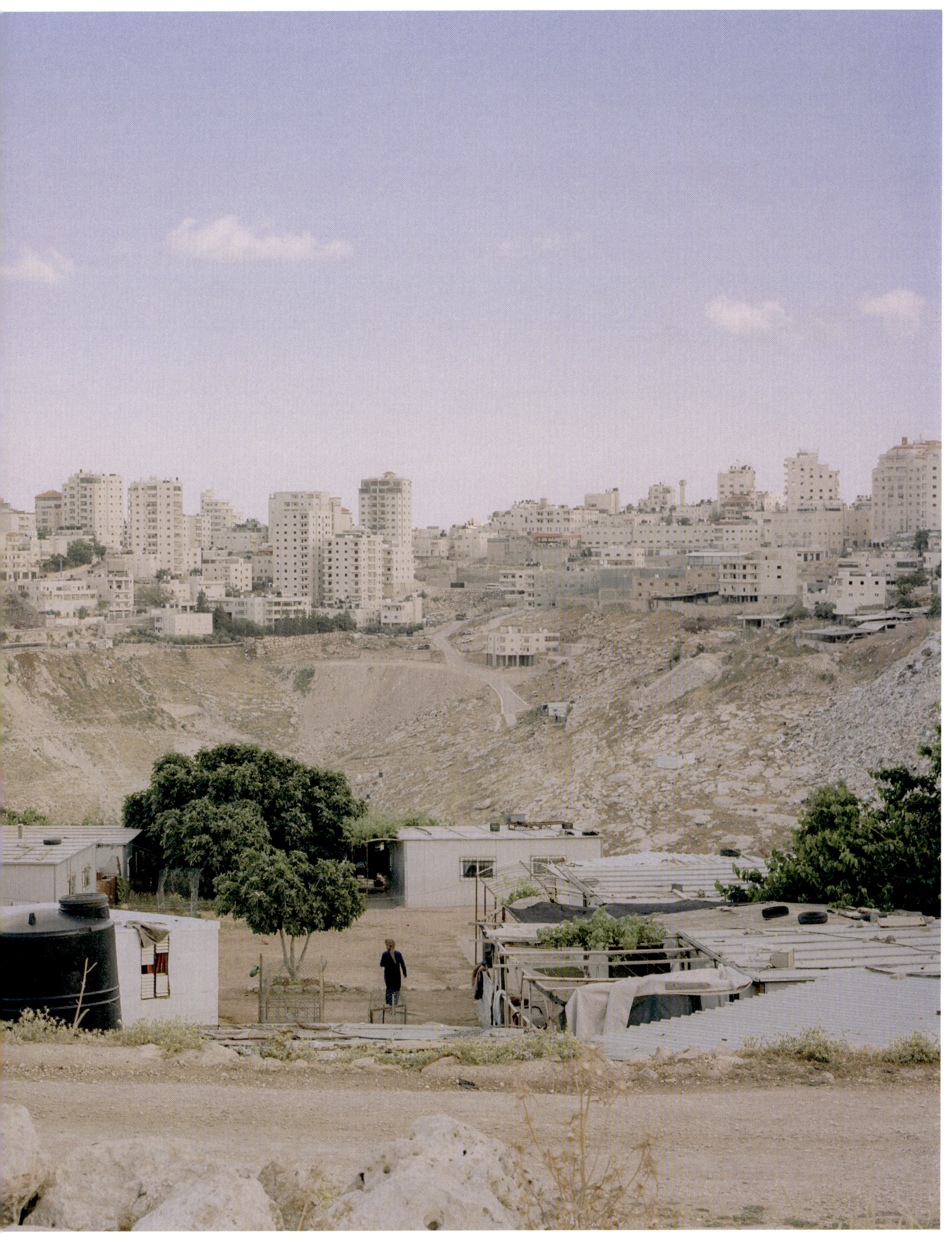

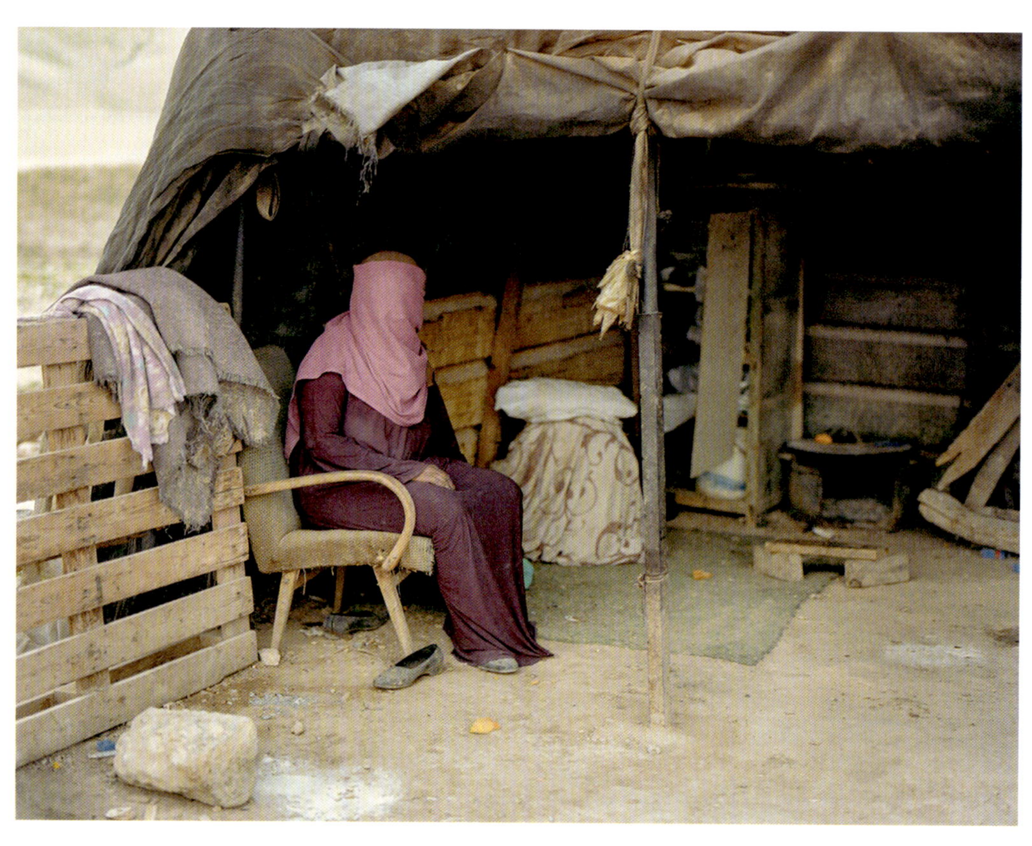

P. 78

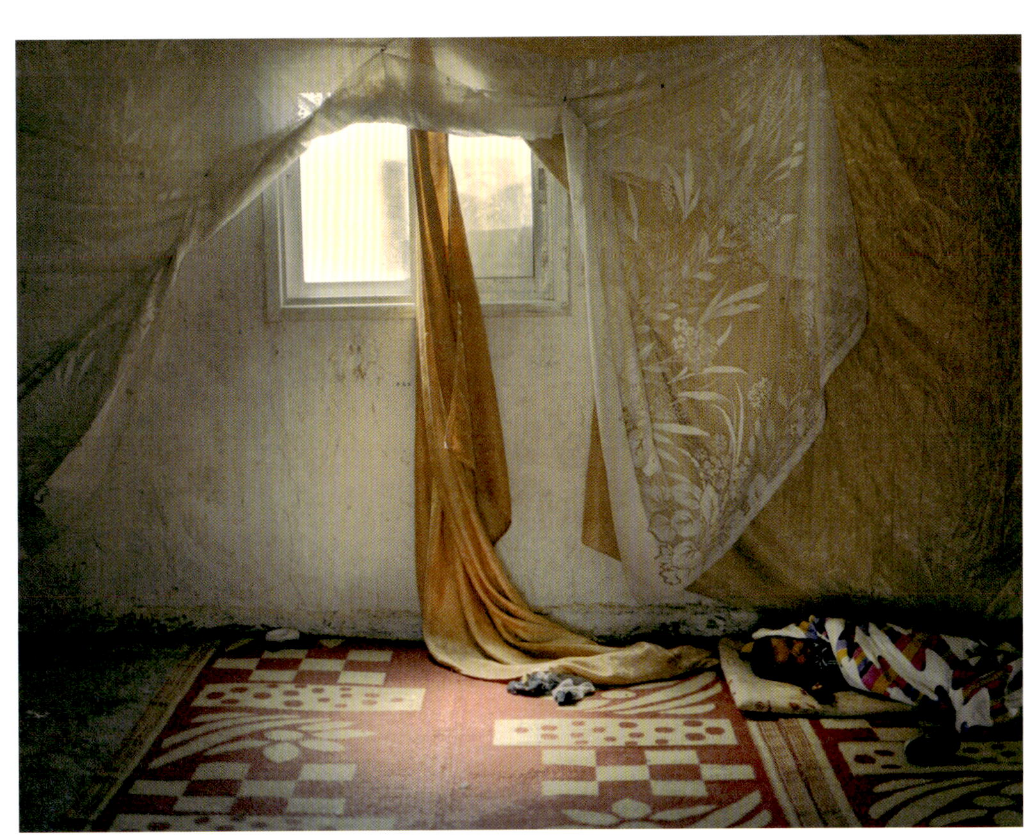

P. 80

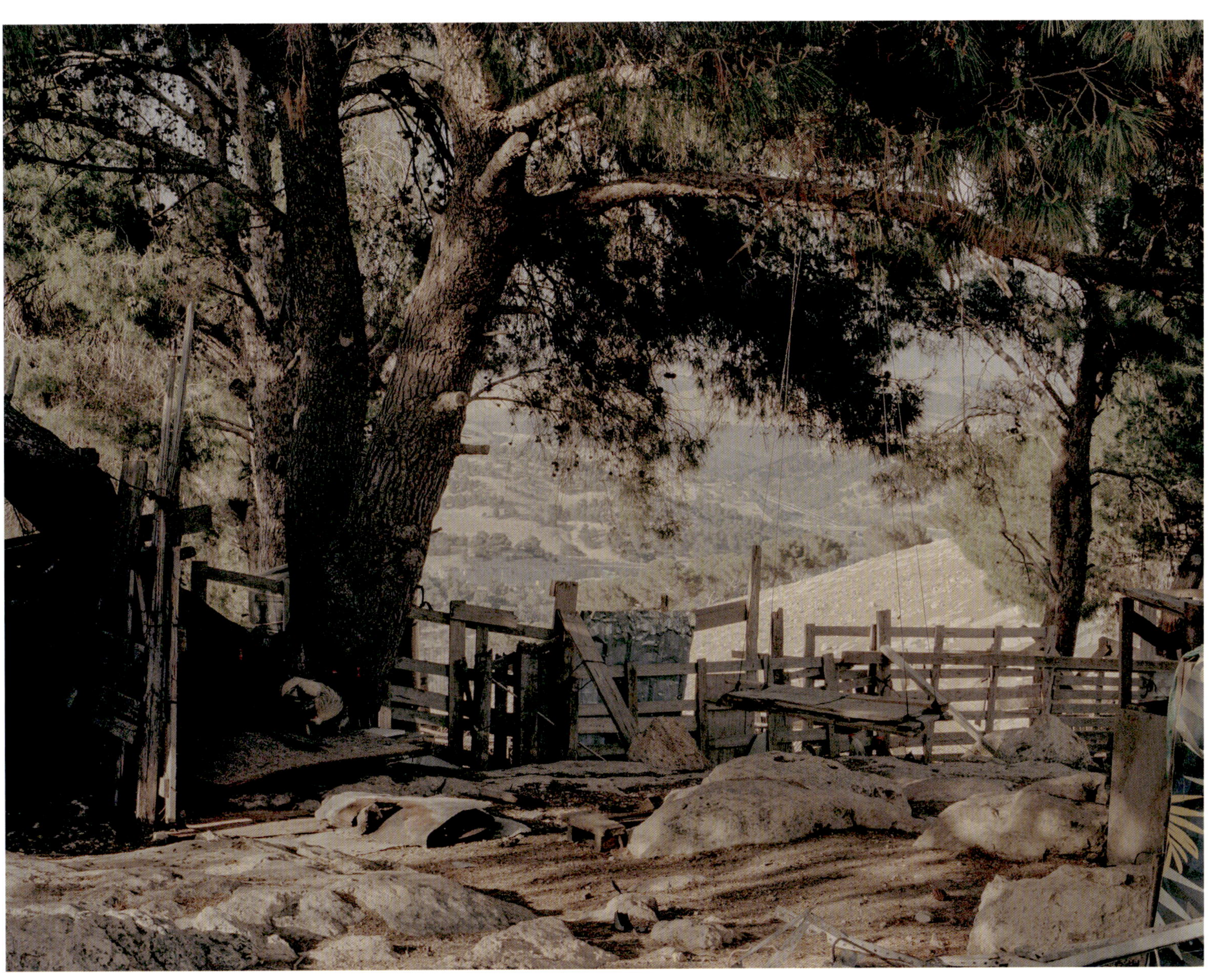

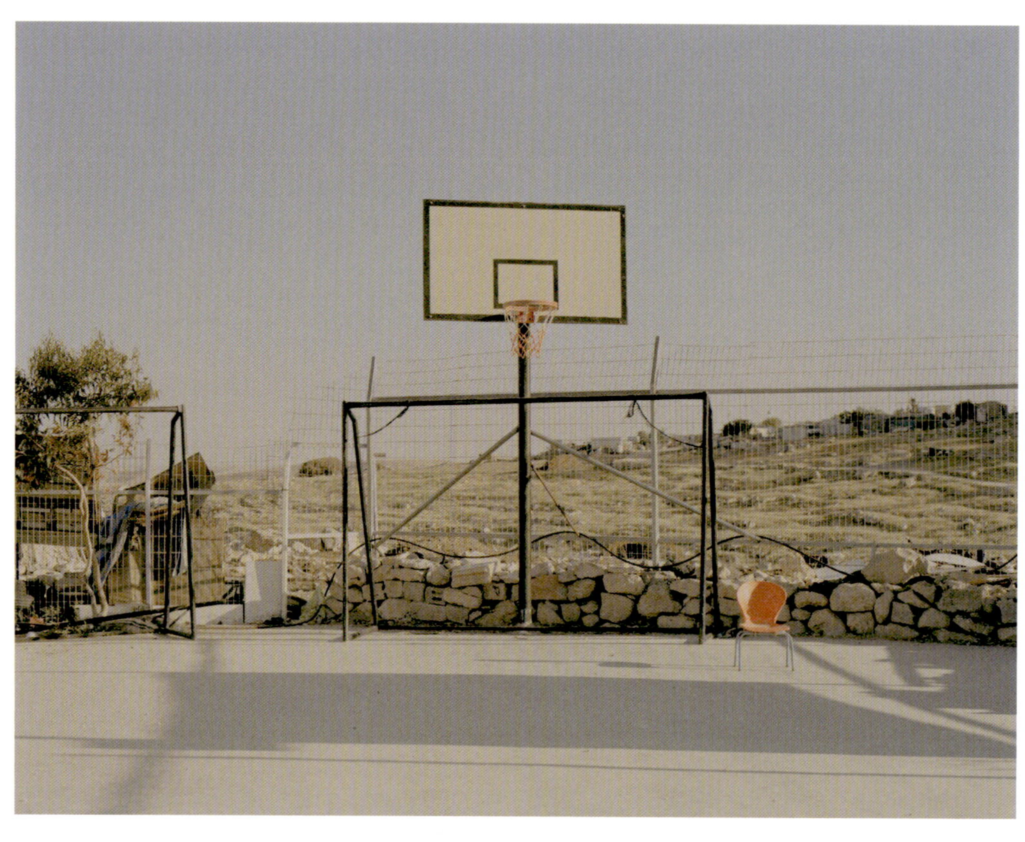

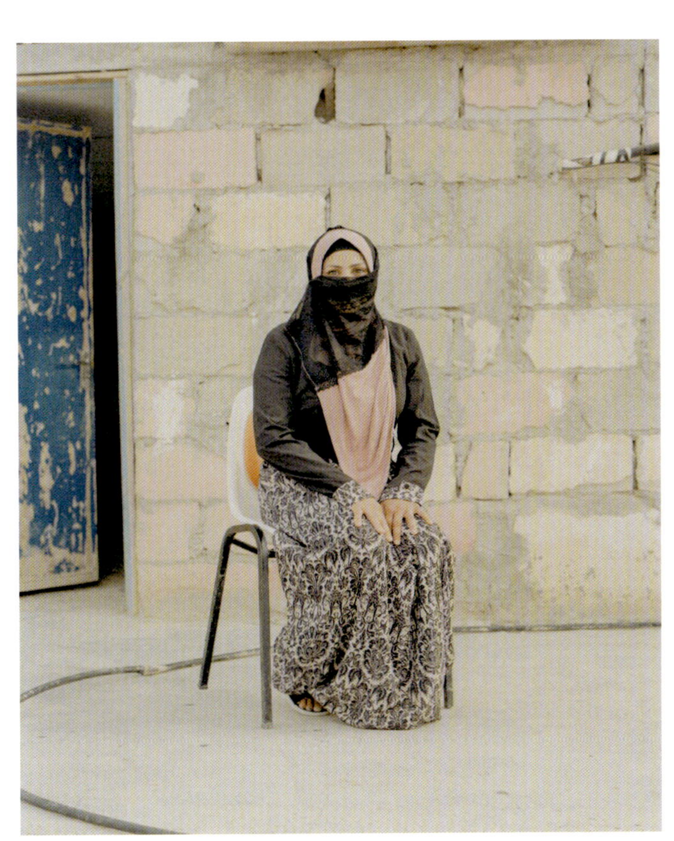

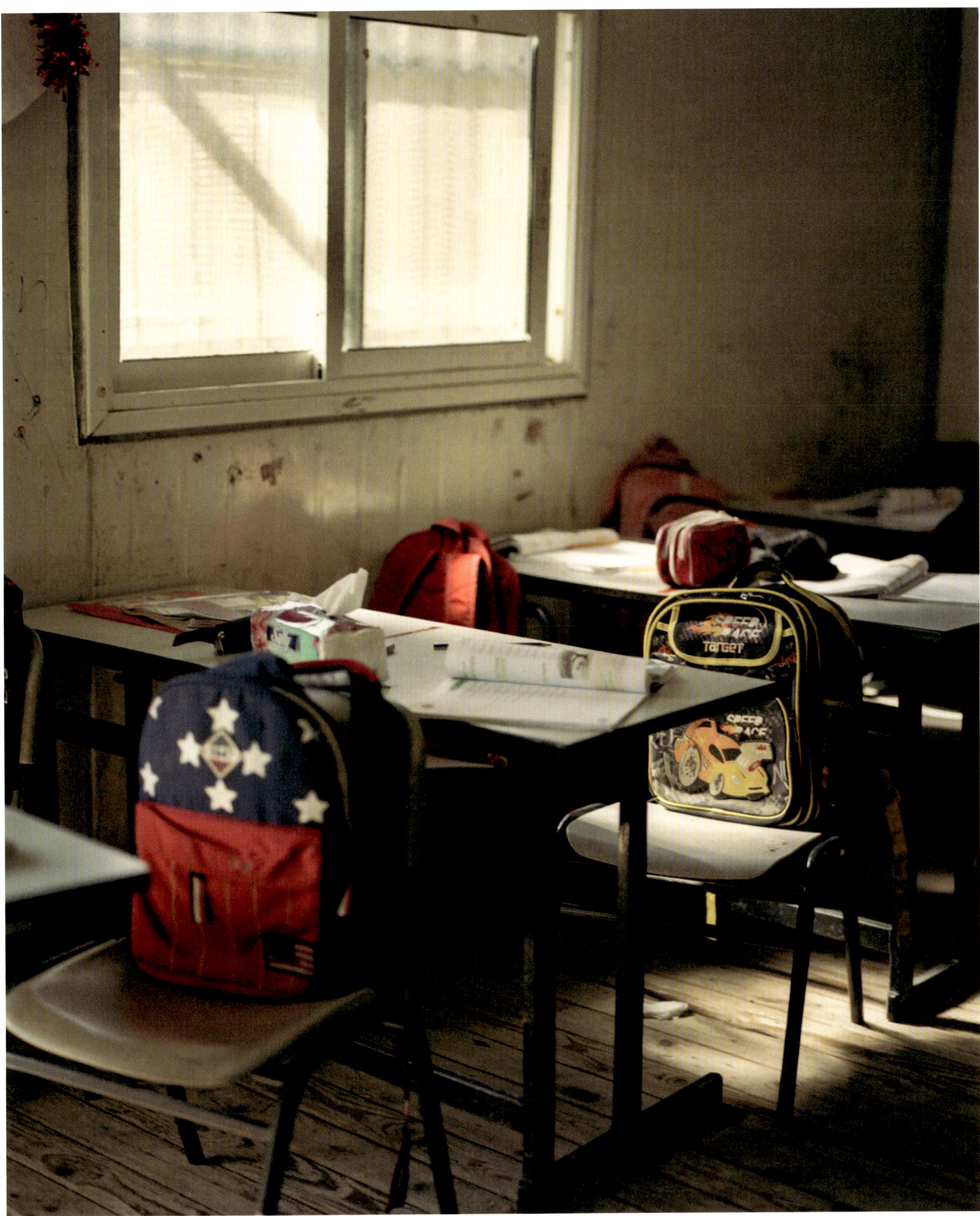
Target
SPEED RACE

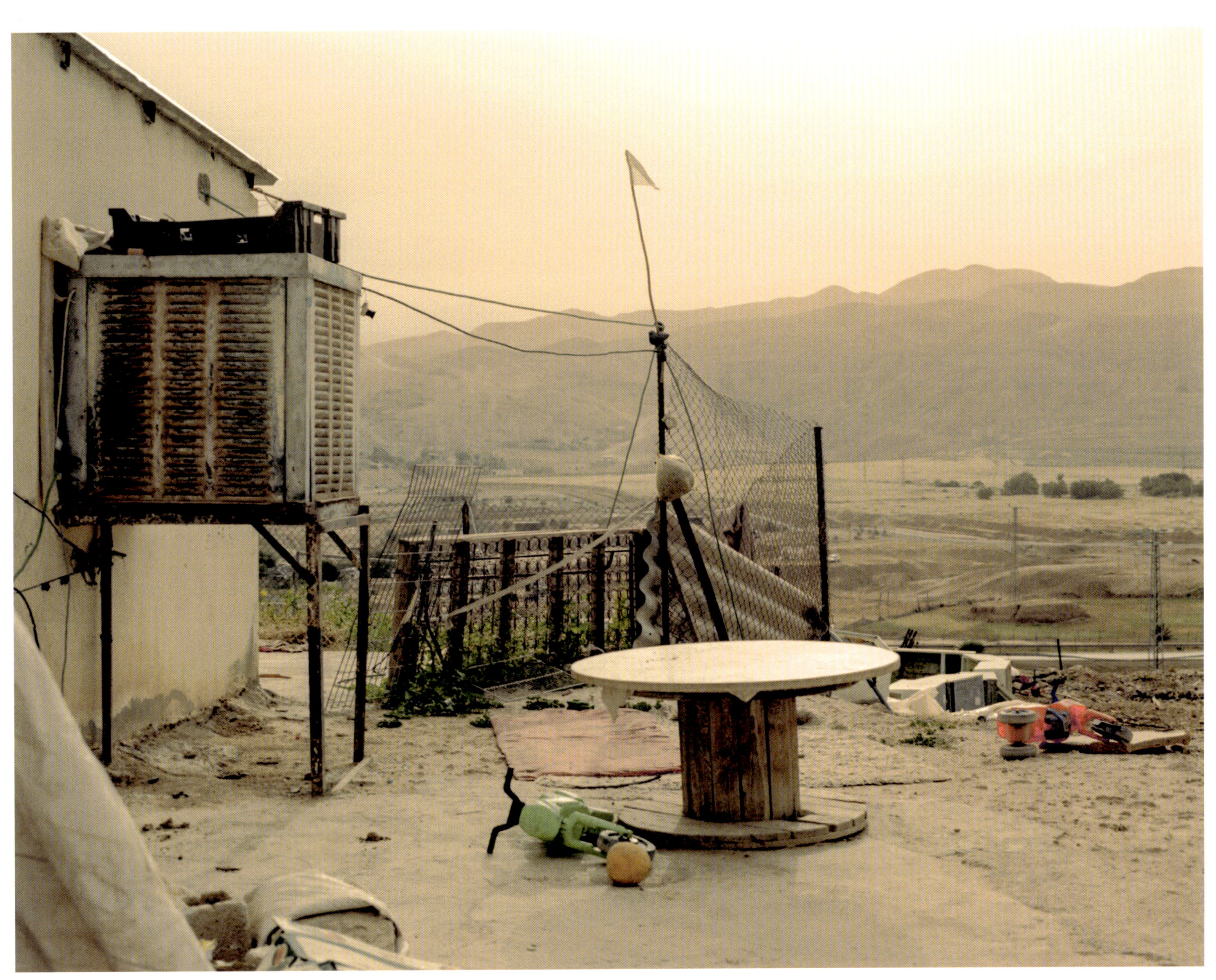

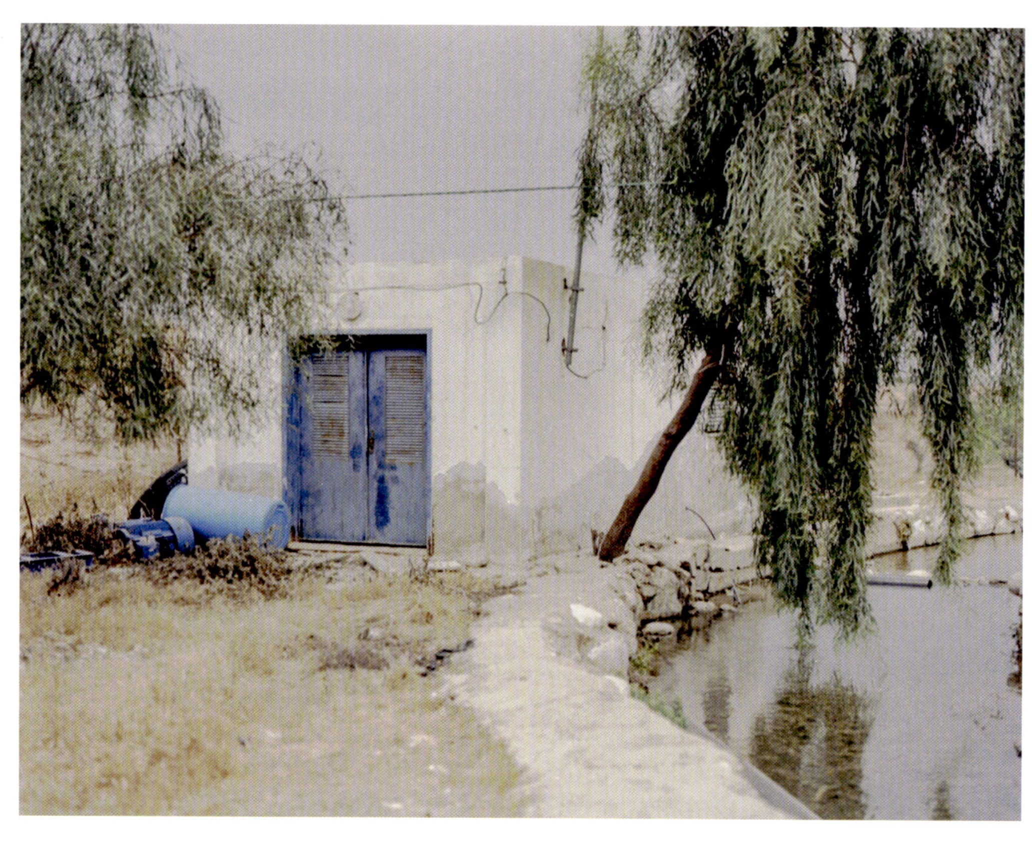

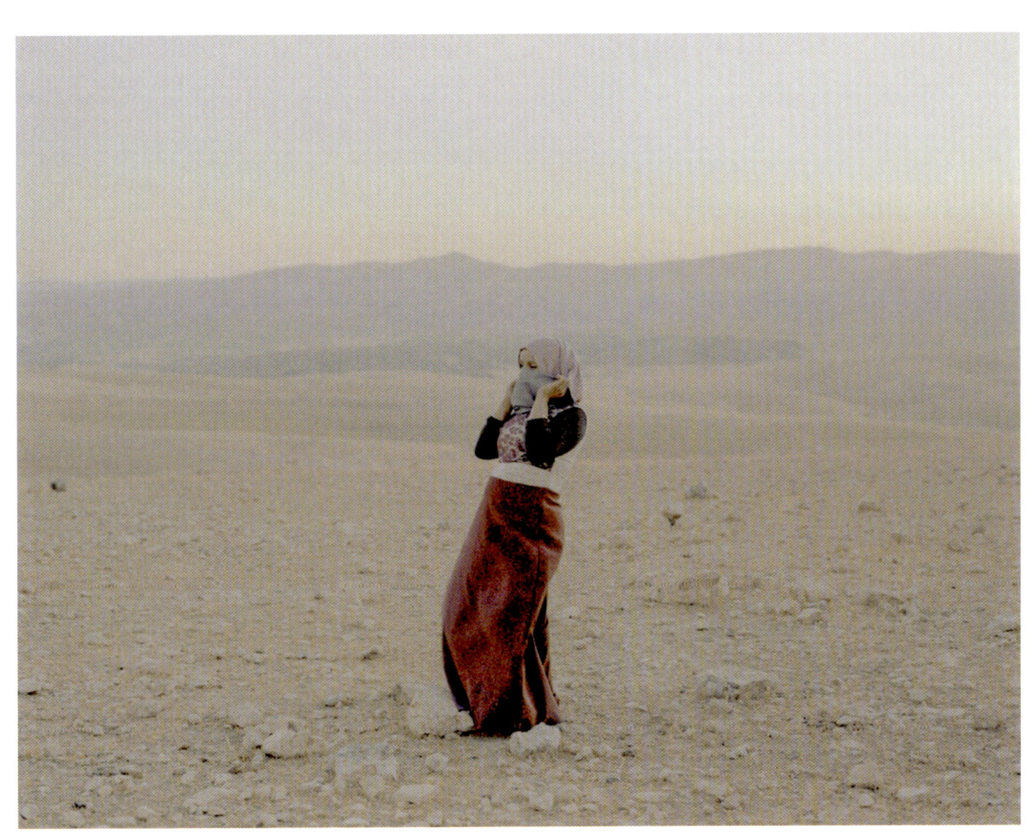

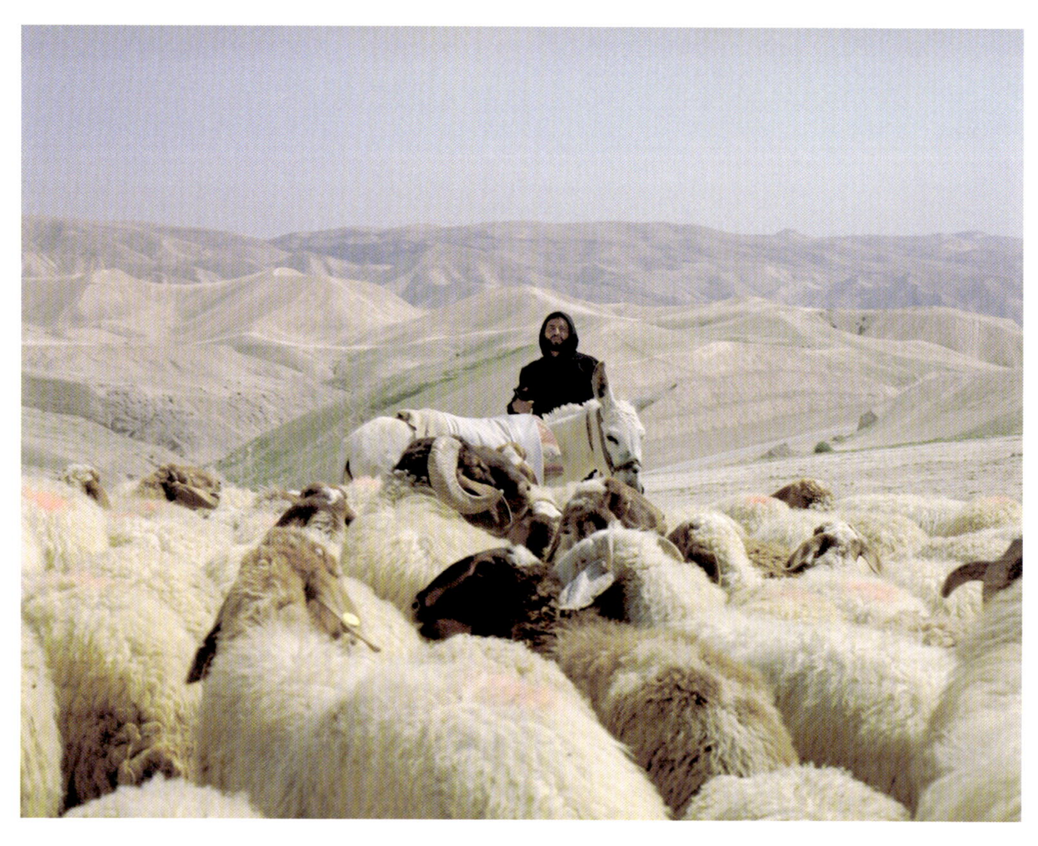

P. 90

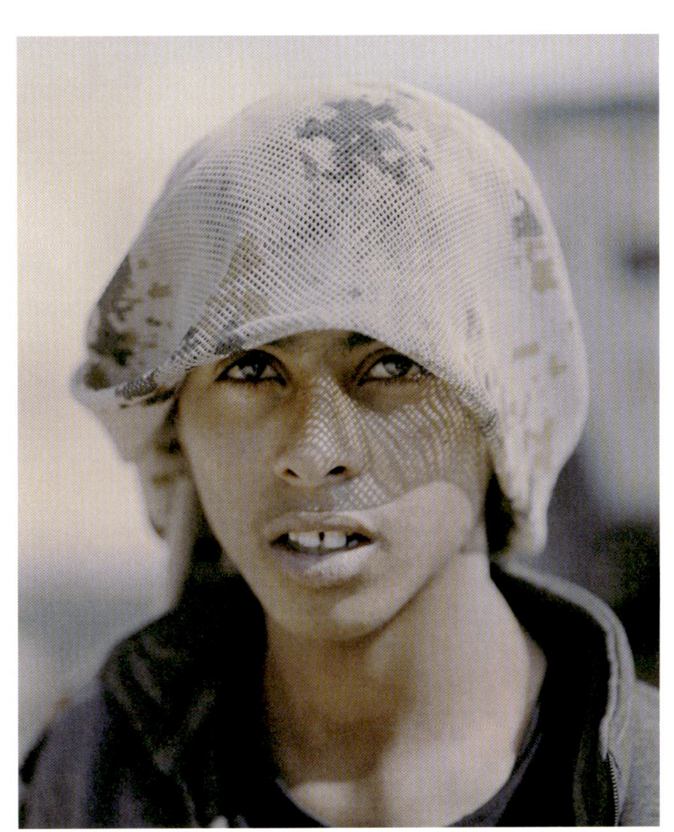

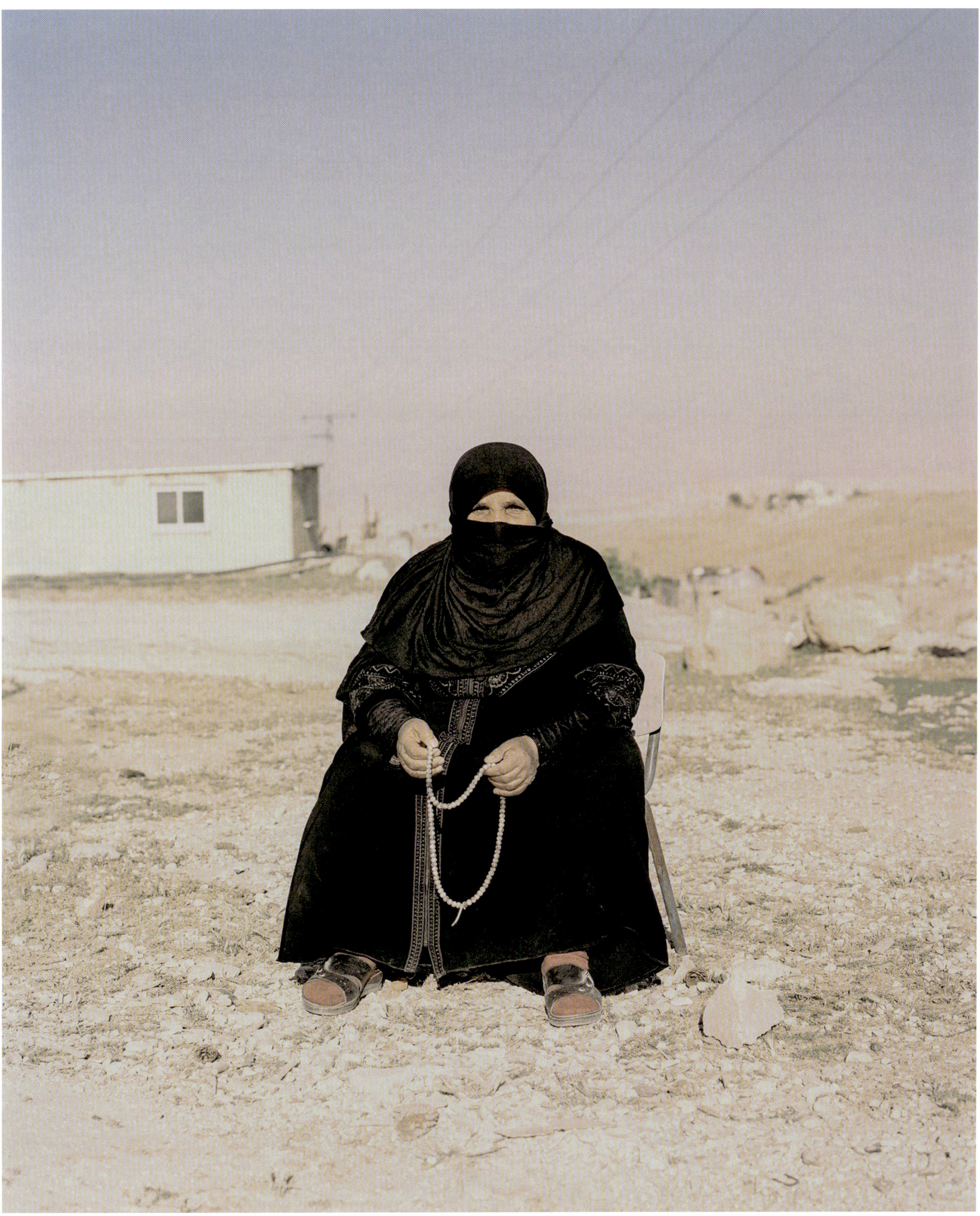

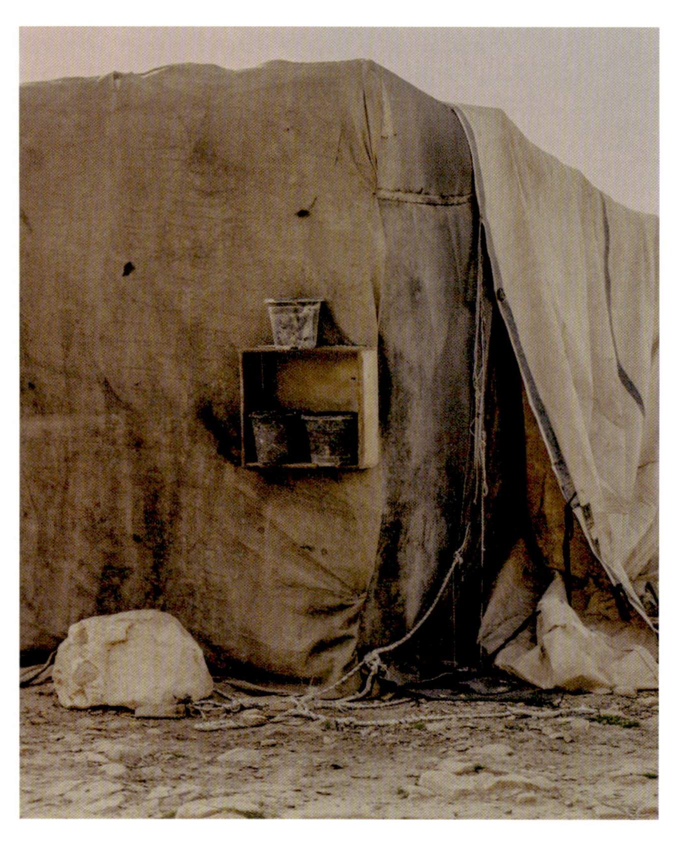

P. 94

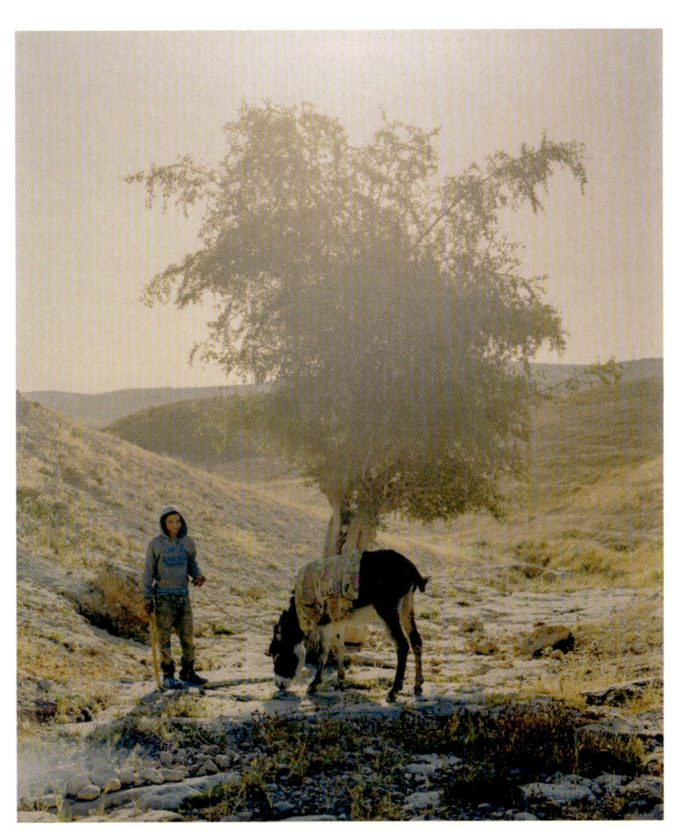

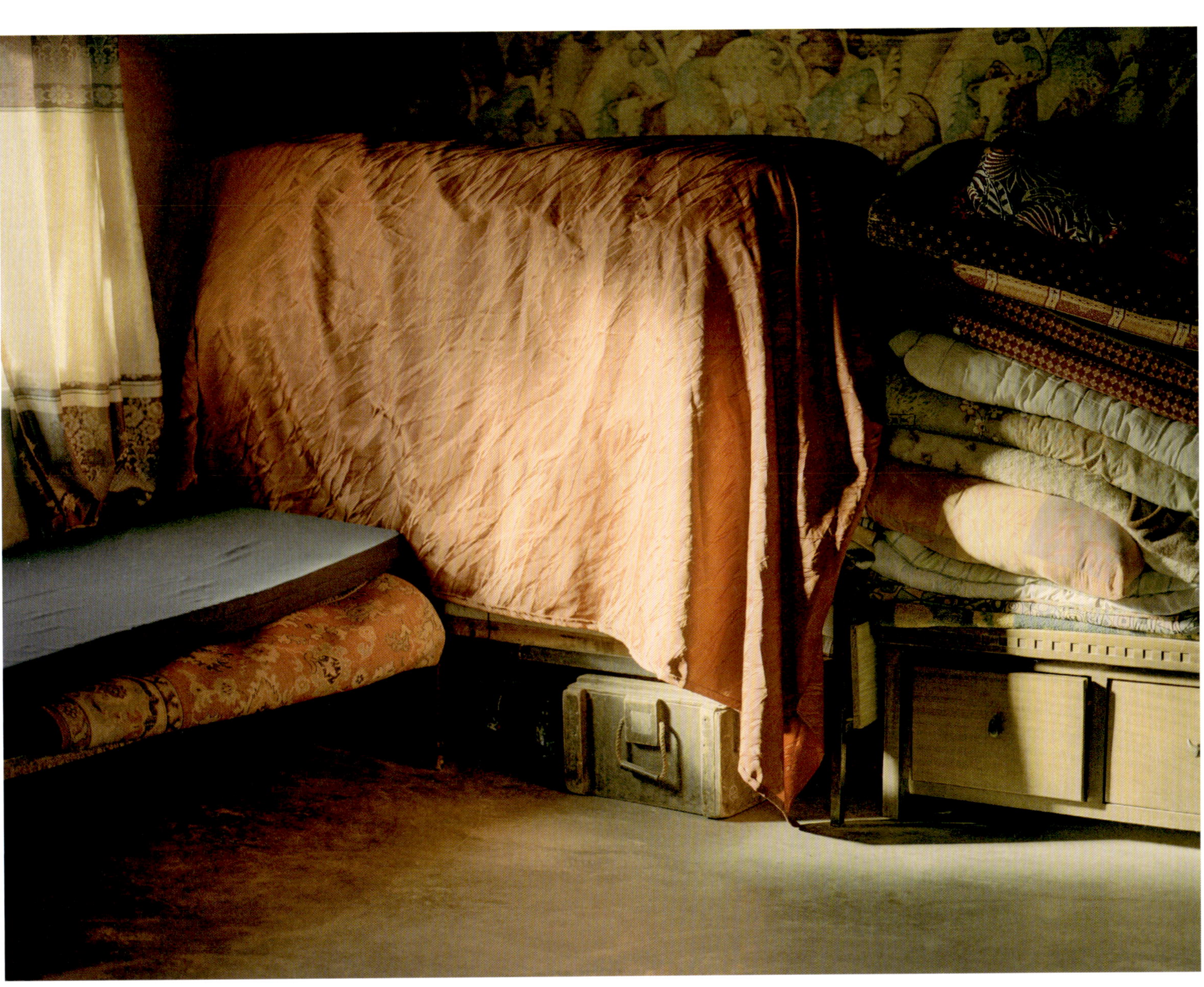

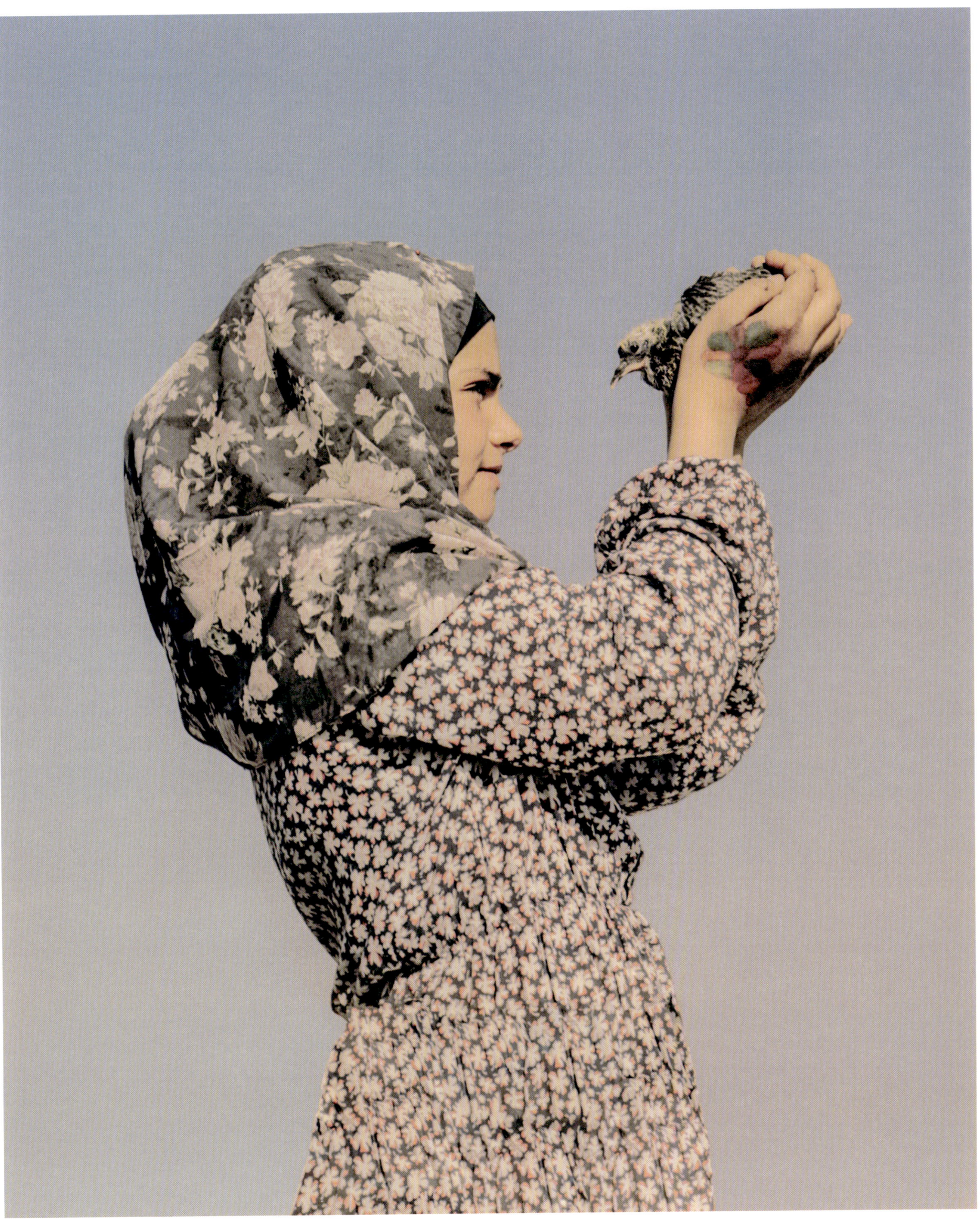

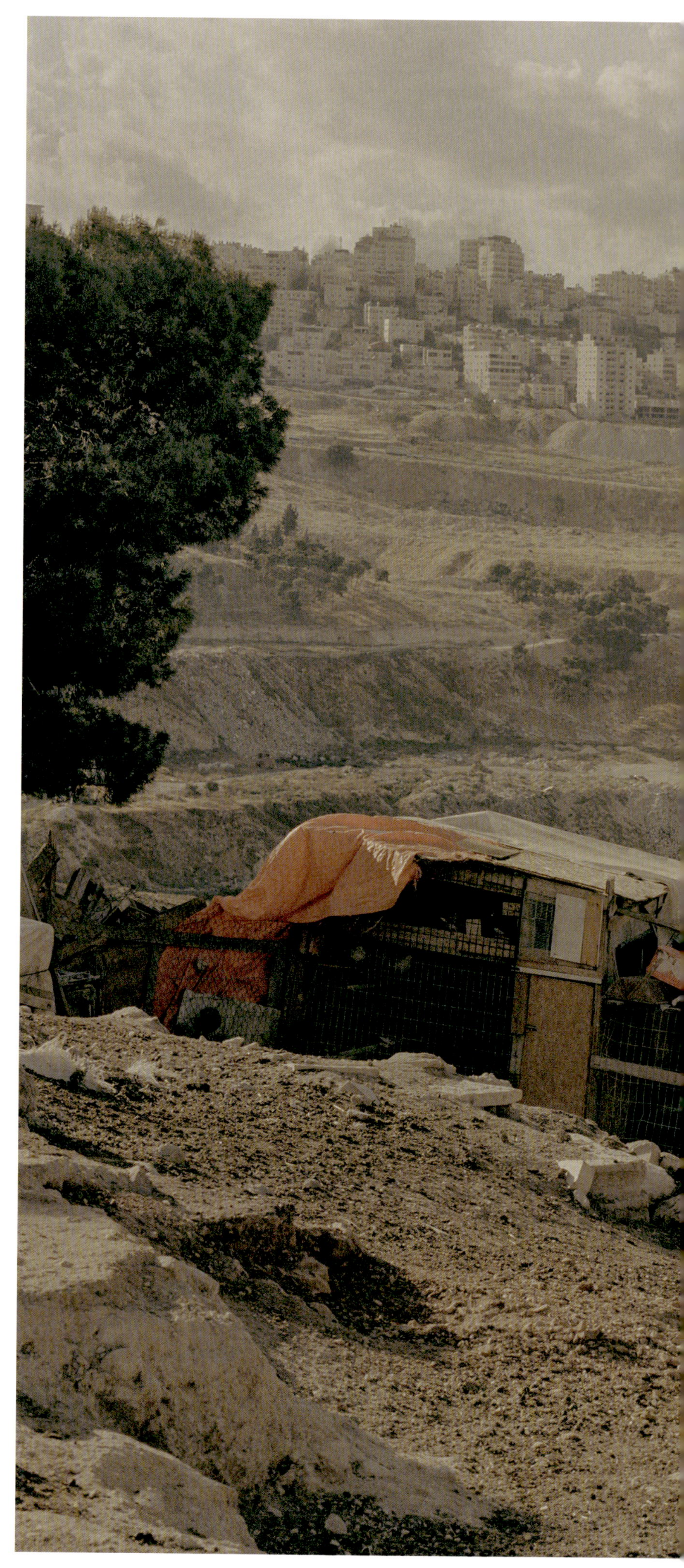

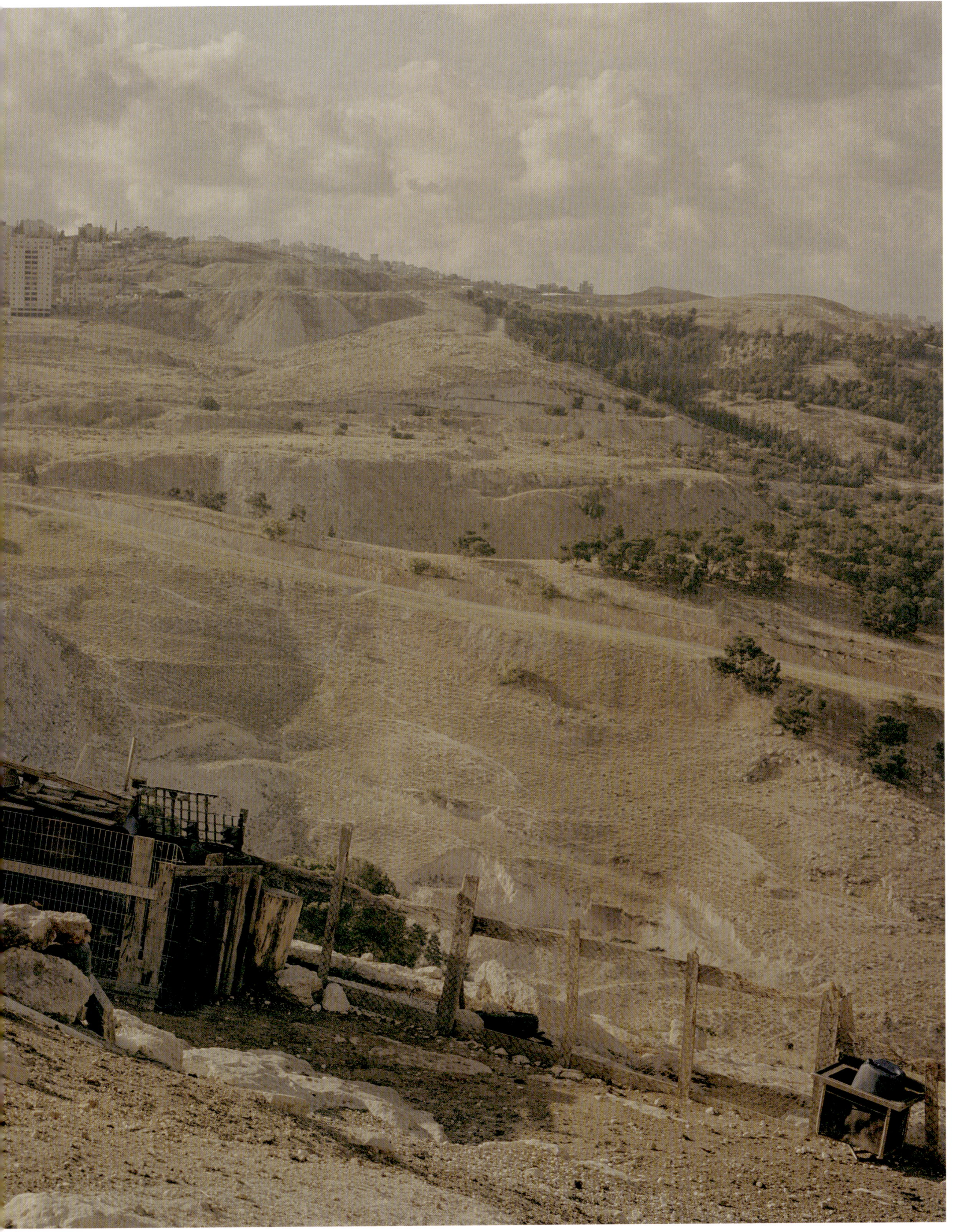

Thank you.

Saqer, Nadia, Ismail, Tariq, Ahmad, Sameer and all the Bedouins who accompanied me on my journey, Dewi Lewis for publishing, Lucia L. Fišerová and Lucia S. Bláhová for editing the book, Jaroslav Prokop, Jan Jindra, Magdalena Jo Umkehrer, Ian Parry Photojournalism Grant, Miki Kratsman and Yaakov Israel for their inputs during my process, family and friends for their support. I would also like to thank everyone else involved in the process of making the book.

In particular, I would like to thank Tomas Bata University in Zlin, which supported the project by FMK IGA scholarship.

Tomas Bata University in Zlín

Born of sand and sun

First published in the United Kingdom
in 2023 by Dewi Lewis Publishing
8 Broomfield Road, Heaton Moor
Stockport SK4 4ND, England
www.dewilewis.com

ISBN: 978-1-911306-98-6

Design & Layout: Magdalena Jo Umkehrer
Translation: Petra Luptáková
Editors: Lucia Fišerová & Lucia Sekerková
Print: EBS, Verona, Italy

Font: Nimbus Sans & IvyOra Display
Paper: GardaPat Kiara

Two Journeys

A Companion to the *Giinaquq: Like a Face* Exhibition

Published by Alutiiq Museum and Archaeological Repository

215 Mission Road, Suite 101
Kodiak, AK 99615
http://www.alutiiqmuseum.org

Author: Koniag, Inc., in collaboration with the Alutiiq Museum and Archaeological Repository and Château Musée, Boulogne-sur-Mer, France

Printed in China
ISBN 10: 1-929650-04-3
ISBN 13: 978-1-929650-04-0

The paper used in this publication meets the minimum requirements of American National Standard for Information Sciences – Permanence of Paper for Printed Library Materials. ANSI/NISO Z39.48—1992(R2002).

Mask photography by Will Anderson
All other photos by Will Anderson except:
Landscape photography on pages 1, 5-6, 25-26 and 64 by Sven Haakanson Jr.
Photo of Perry Eaton Page 46 by Sven Haakanson Jr.
Photo on page 49 by Lena Amason
Group photo on page 89 by Château Musée staff
Designed by Color Brand International
Art Director: Sasha Sagan
Designers: Leaf Lam, Kimi Wong
Text by Patty Ginsburg

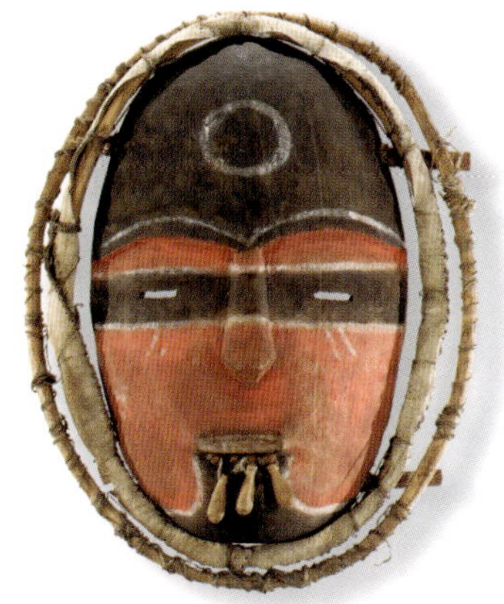

TWO JOURNEYS

A Companion to the *Giinaquq: Like A Face* Exhibition

Koniag, Inc.
In collaboration with the Alutiiq Museum and
The Château Musée

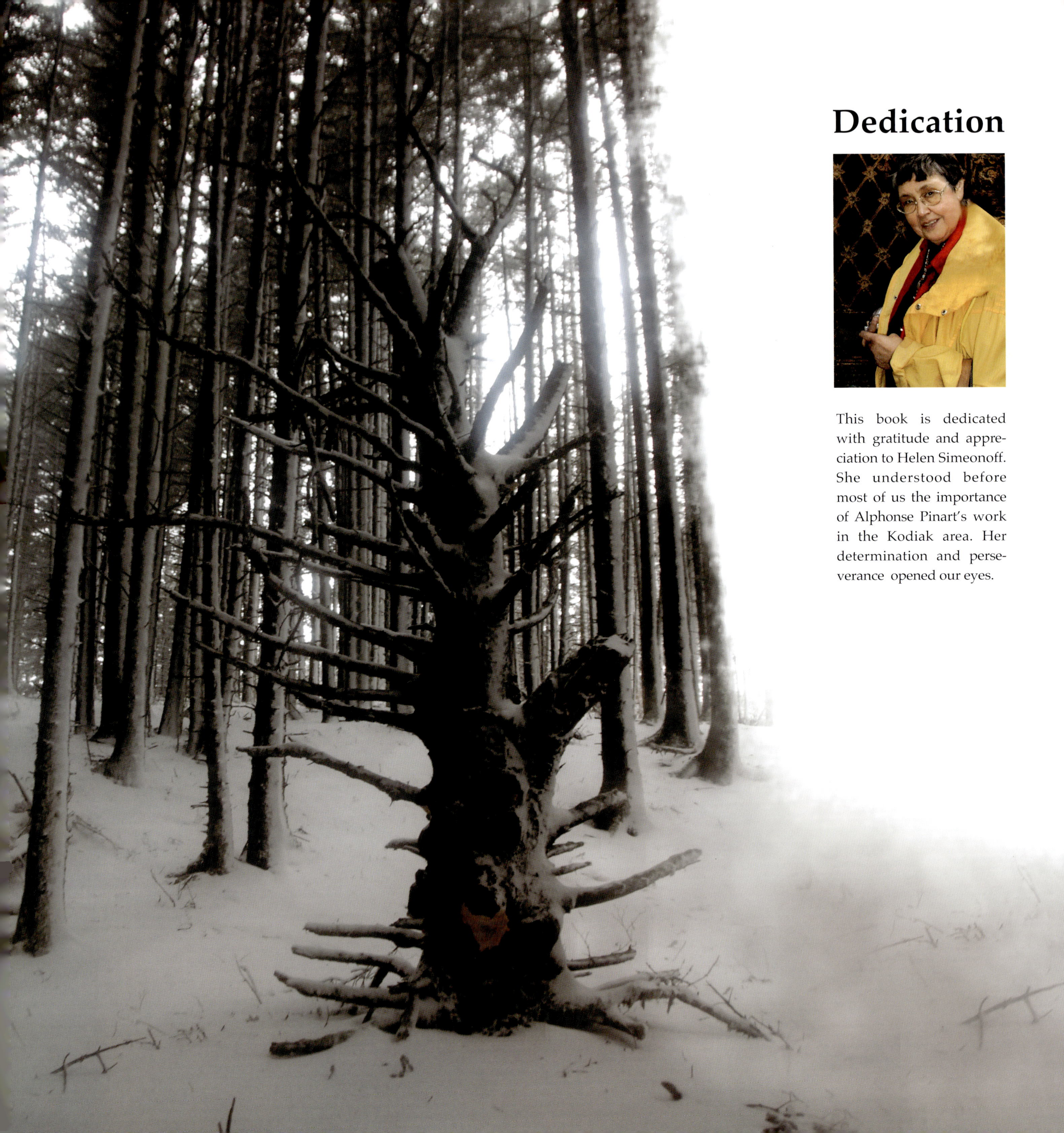

Dedication

This book is dedicated with gratitude and appreciation to Helen Simeonoff. She understood before most of us the importance of Alphonse Pinart's work in the Kodiak area. Her determination and perseverance opened our eyes.

Foreword

Growing up in Kodiak in the 1960s, I sometimes found myself in one of the downtown gift shops that catered to the tourist market. The shops sold curios, postcards, t-shirts, and the occasional mask or paddle that appeared to be hand crafted by an Alaska native. Since Kodiak Island is predominately Alutiiq, it was always puzzling to me that the only native artwork sold in the local shops was of Tlingit design. Why was there no artwork from our own history and culture?

In retrospect, there are a couple of logical answers to my childhood question. To the best of my knowledge, there were no artists of Alutiiq descent producing or selling traditional native art. Perhaps more significantly, very little was known about the distinct style of art historically produced by the Alutiiq people. With the clarity of hindsight 40 years later, the lack of Alutiiq art on those shop shelves reflected a profound scarcity of information about traditional Alutiiq culture. How the picture has changed in a few short years!

Giinaquq: Like A Face is an exhibition of 34 masks and one bowl from a collection held by the Château Musée in Boulogne-sur-Mer, France. The exhibit is the culmination of years of effort by the staff of the Alutiiq Museum and Archaeological Repository. Even before this exhibit, the Museum was the focal point of the region's cultural reawakening through initiatives such as its Alutiiq Language program. However, the Like A Face exhibit rises to another level by providing an unprecedented opportunity for the Alutiiq people and others in the community to learn from one of the most significant collections of Alutiiq art in the world today.

"Two Journeys — A Companion to the *Giinaquq: Like A Face* Exhibition" is the back story of the masks that comprise this exhibit. The title "Two Journeys" is both literal and figurative. On the literal level, it chronicles how the collection came to reside in a museum in France and the efforts of Dr. Sven Haakanson Jr. and the Alutiiq Museum to exhibit a portion of the collection in Alaska. This book also recounts the story of how a small group of Alutiiq artists were able to travel to France and study this remarkable collection in its entirety.

On another level, "Two Journeys" documents the path of the Alutiiq people in their effort to rediscover the mask form as part of their culture. Perhaps no other region in Alaska was more profoundly impacted by early contact with explorers from Russia and other parts of the world. As a result, the Alutiiq culture and language were nearly extinguished. The opportunity to view and study these masks helps us understand the significant role the mask form played in Alutiiq society.

Finally, "Two Journeys" attempts to inspire and inform people of Alutiiq descent who desire to study the unique style of masks that originate from the Koniag region. Unlike other publications with photographs of Alutiiq masks, "Two Journeys" contains multiple views of each object in an attempt to provide a more complete perspective of the distinct Alutiiq style.

While studying photographs from various angles is a tremendous advantage, it is no substitute for seeing the actual masks for oneself. The value of being able to examine the pieces and study them up close was the underlying reason for organizing the Alutiiq artists' trip to France in 2006. It is also one of the reasons for bringing a portion of the collection through the *Giinaquq: Like A Face* Exhibition from France to the United States.

In bringing the exhibit to Alaska, Dr. Haakanson and his staff at the Alutiiq Museum have accomplished extraordinary work in a relatively short time. It is also important to note the critical role the staff at the Château Musée played in allowing the Alutiiq community to reconnect with these rare and important examples of our culture. At every point along the way, the staff at the Château Musée made every effort to ensure the success of the *Giinaquq: Like A Face* Exhibition, enabling the Alutiiq community to view the beauty of this collection first hand. It is remarkable that two relatively small institutions like the Alutiiq Museum and the Château Musée have been able to plan and execute such an ambitious project.

The 2006 trip by the Alutiiq artists' group has already borne fruit as reflected in the work of these artists. In stark contrast to the gift shops of the 1960s, the gift shop at the Alutiiq Museum now has a wonderful selection of art for sale made in the distinct style of the Alutiiq culture. I hope that "Two Journeys" and the *Giinaquq: Like A Face* Exhibition will have a similar impact on other talented Alutiiq people and lead to even more artwork that reflects and builds on our traditional style.

However, this book and the related exhibit are not only about art. They are about a people separated from many elements of their culture. They are about the opportunity to reconnect with some of the few items that still exist from a time nearly forgotten. This exhibit is a watershed moment in the journey of the Alutiiq people to rediscover their culture.

Whether you are an active participant or a casual observer of this remarkable process, I hope you see the value in the effort and recognize the historical significance of the moment.

by Will Anderson
President, Koniag, Inc.
May 2008

Preface

A Shared History:

Alphonse Pinart, the Alutiiq People and the Château Musée

by Sven D. Haakanson, Jr. and Anne Claire Laronde

All people explore their history. A sense of the past is among the handful of cultural characteristics that anthropologists consider universal. Like marriage, music or a belief in the supernatural, a desire to understand history is found in every human society. When Alphonse Pinart traveled to the Kodiak Archipelago in 1871, he forever linked the histories of the French and Alutiiq peoples and created unique opportunities for mutual understanding and collaboration through the exploration of history.

This photographic companion to the *Giinaquq: Like A Face* exhibition tells the story of Alphonse Pinart, the Alutiiq people and the Château Musée. It illustrates how the residents of two small fishing communities on nearly opposite sides of the world — Boulogne-sur-Mer, France, and Kodiak, Alaska — joined forces to shed light on each other's pasts and in doing so are creating a brighter future. Beyond differences in language and culture, our communities found a common love of history.

For the French, the Pinart collection represents an important piece of national heritage. It reflects a period of scientific inquiry when scholars like Pinart left the comfort of their homes to record the world's people. Their research documented societies at the threshold of irrevocable cultural change and now offers a window through the oppressive fog of colonialism. The efforts of Pinart and others of his time represent a major contribution to human knowledge. This is the gift the French share with Alutiiqs – access to a large, well-preserved archive of Alutiiq culture.

For the Alutiiq people, the Pinart collection represents ancestral knowledge. It is not just a set of beautiful objects, but a storehouse of information. The items in the collection were made in traditional ways and each preserves specialized knowledge. Studying the collection is like being an apprentice to an Alutiiq master – it reveals long forgotten details about the daily lives of Alutiiq people, the materials and the tools they employed. This is the gift Alutiiqs bring to the French. By combining their cultural knowledge with clues held in the objects, Alutiiqs are helping the French understand Pinart's collections more fully, placing them in a more meaningful cultural context.

The collection is also a testament to the tenacity of both peoples. During two world wars, in the midst of unfathomable destruction, the curators of the Château Musée saved Pinart's treasures. More than 300 Kodiak Alutiiq objects survive today because of the unwavering commitment of the French to preserving art and history. The collection's presence in the 21st century demonstrates how much the French value their history. Similarly, the persistence of Alutiiq culture in the modern world reflects incredible fortitude. Until recently, Alutiiq history has been suppressed. But with access to collections, a new exploration is under way. Alutiiq history is again informing the present and shaping the future.

We encourage you to enjoy *Giinaquq: Like A Face* with both the excitement and reverence our communities bring to it. Alutiiq and French collaborators have accomplished much more than arranging photography and signing loan agreements; they have developed a lasting respect for our shared history. This respect will bring the Pinart collection to life for many future generations. The project is the continuation of a cultural exchange that began many years ago, but it is not an end.

Quyanaa – Our thanks to the many people who have assisted with the *Giinaquq: Like A Face* project. They include the Honorable Frédéric Cuvilier, mayor of the city of Boulogne-sur-Mer and a deputy of the national parliament, the Honorable Claude Allan, deputy mayor of culture and heritage for Boulogne-sur-Mer, Sarah Froning, Philippe Girot, Stéphane Delpierre, Francis Donval, Céline Ramio, Eneline Guette, Will Anderson, Perry Eaton, Nick Alokli, Valen Bishop, Peter Boskofsky, April Laktonen Counceller, Ruth Dawson, Dixie Deo, Jennifer Dickinson, Jim Dillard, Carol Duncan, Walt Ebell, Clare Fulp, Tanya Glaspell, Mary Haakanson, Erica Hill, Doug Inga, Tanya Inga, Suzi Jones, Sarah Kennedy, Rose Kinsley, Dennis Knagin, Gary Knagin, Julie Knagin, Jeff Leer, Marnie Leist, Ivan Lukin, Anne-Claire Laronde, Levia Lew, Patty Mahoney, Marti Murray, Alfred Naumoff, David Nicholls, Robert Patterson, Rick Pelasara, Florence Pestrikoff, Gordon Pullar, Mark Rusk, Katie St. John, Patrick Saltonstall, Teri Schneider, Helen Simeonoff, Speridon Simeonoff, Herman Squartsoff, Tricia Squartsoff, Amy Steffian, Andy Teuber, Céline Wallace, Jack Wick, Pat Wolf and the Bancroft Library.

Timeline

1871-72 Alphonse Pinart spends six months on Kodiak and neighboring islands, collecting stories, recording rituals and myths and gathering artifacts.

1872-73 The Natural History Museum of Paris stages an exhibit of Pinart's Alaska collection.

1875 Pinart gives most of his Alaska collection to the museum in Boulogne-sur-Mer (now the Château Musée), not far from his family home.

1957 French anthropologist Evelyne Lot-Falck writes about the Pinart masks in *Journal de la Société des Americanistes.*

1980s-'90s Anthropologist Dr. Lydia Black of the University of Alaska Fairbanks knows about the Pinart collection through her work on Aleut art and whaling. She tells Alutiiq mask carver Jacob Simeonoff about the Pinart masks. Dr. Black urges doctoral candidate Dominique Desson to focus her dissertation on Alutiiq masks, including the Pinart collection.

1994 Alutiiq artist Helen Simeonoff is in the audience when Desson gives a slide show in Kodiak on the Pinart collection.

1995 Desson completes "Masked Rituals of the Kodiak Archipelago."

2000 After learning all she can about Pinart and saving money, Helen Simeonoff travels to France, spending five days at the Château Musée. Simeonoff's photos and excitement about the Pinart masks spreads to other Alutiiq artists, including Perry Eaton. Eaton makes the first of several trips to France.

2001 Sven Haakanson makes the first of many trips to France as he begins to negotiate a Pinart exhibit in Kodiak.

2002 The Château Musée mounts its first exhibition of the Pinart collection together with a special exhibit on contemporary Kodiak. A small contingent from Kodiak, including Alutiiq dancers, travels to Boulogne for the event. A tentative agreement to bring a Pinart exhibit to Kodiak falls apart.

2002 The Pinart collection travels to Paris for an exhibition set up by the Quai-Branley Museum at the Musée de l'Homme, the first time the pieces have left Boulogne since Pinart donated them in 1875.

2004 Haakanson again seeks to bring the Pinart exhibit to Kodiak. The acting director of Château Musée agrees to consider sending one mask. Haakanson declines.

2005 Anne Claire Laronde takes over at Château Musée. She indicates interest in an Alaska exhibition. With an economic development grant to the Alutiiq Museum, plans begin for 10 Alutiiq artists to study the Pinart collection.

2006 The Alutiiq artists spend three days at Château Musée, studying masks and other pieces in the Pinart collection. The museum director and the deputy mayor of Boulogne agree to support a Pinart exhibition in Alaska.

2007 In November, the papers are signed to cement the arrangements: In May 2008, the Alutiiq Museum will bring 34 of the masks to Alaska for the exhibition *Giinaquq: Like a Face* - Sugpiaq Masks of the Kodiak Archipelago.

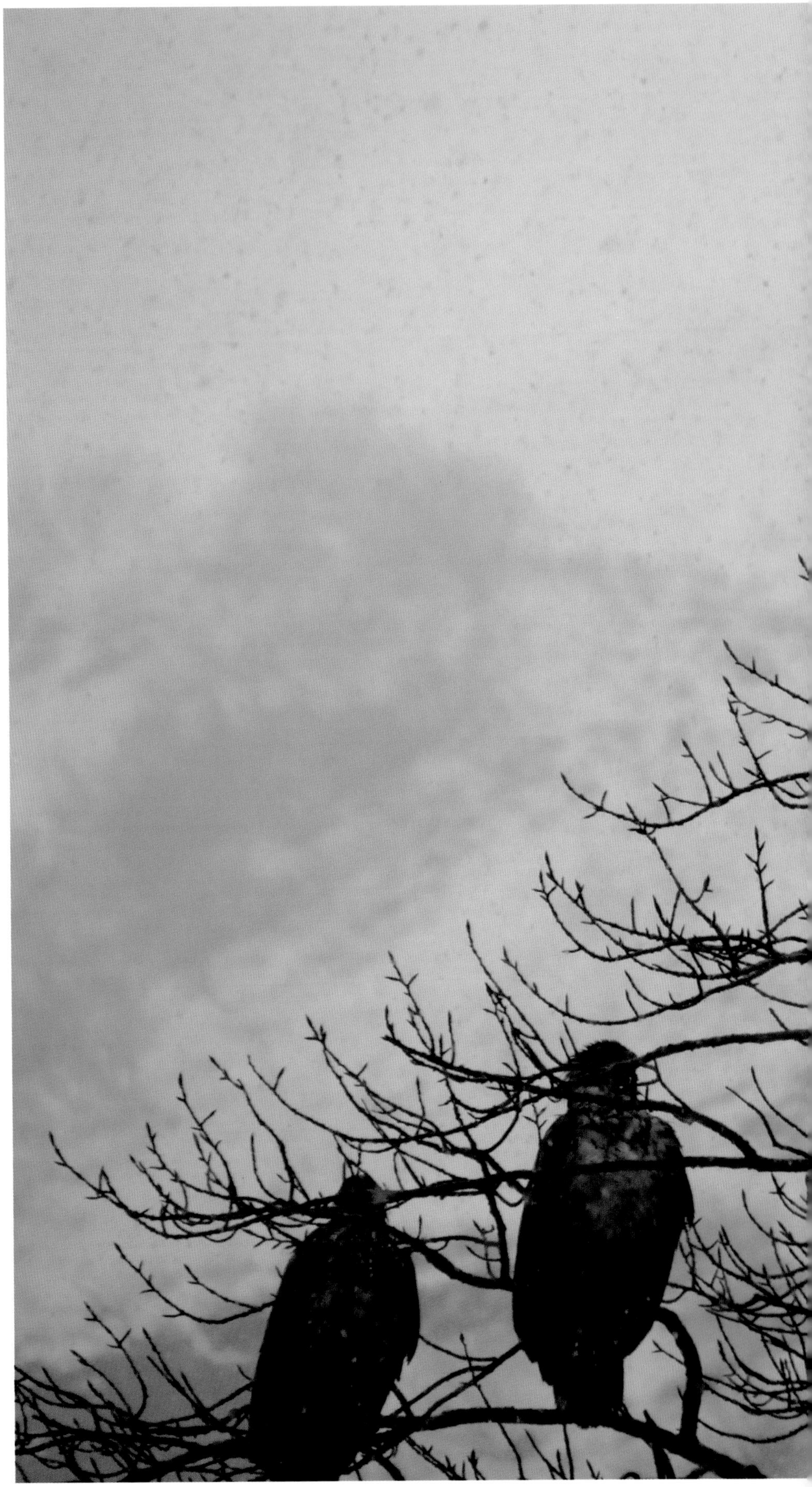

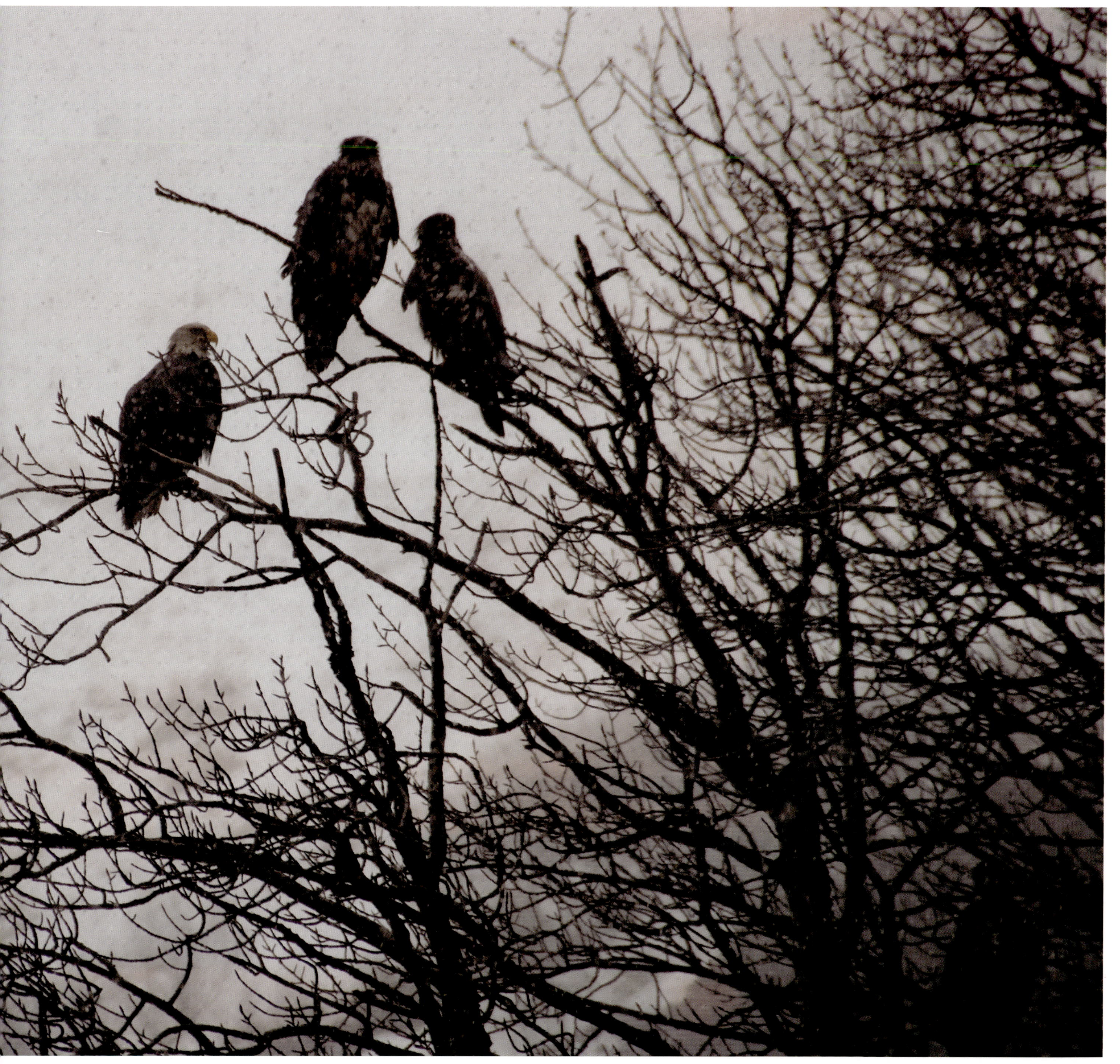

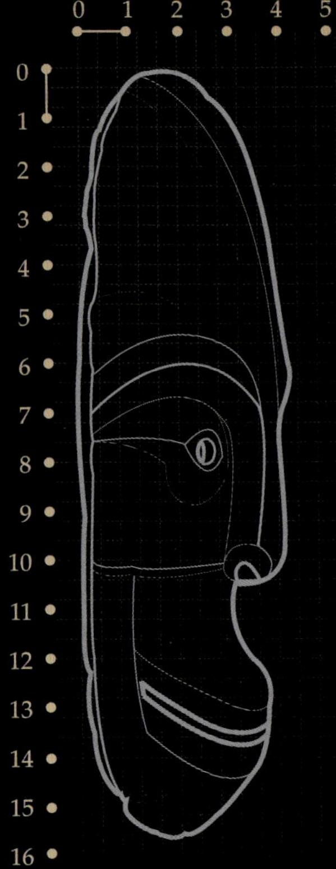

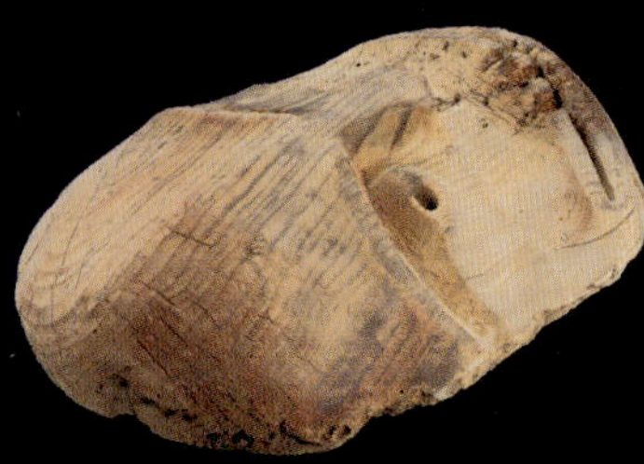

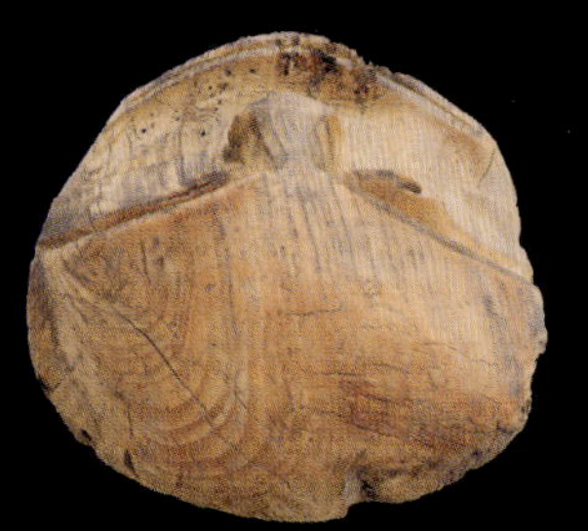

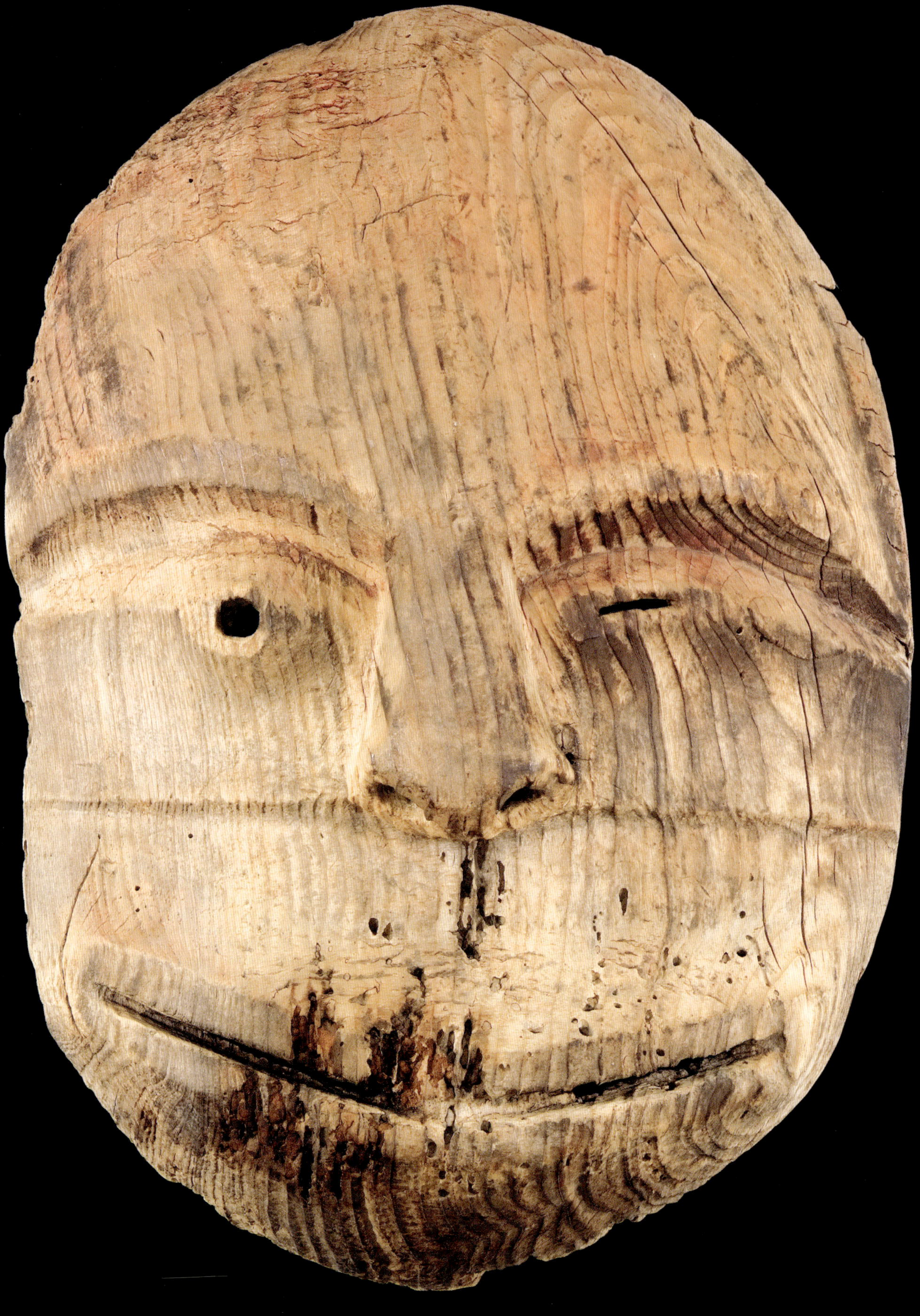

Temciyusqaq "Skeptical one"

H. 40 cm;
W. 29 cm;
D. 11 cm.

H. 15.75 in;
W. 11.42 in;
D. 4.33 in.

Spruce

What struck me was how did they do it? What tools did they use? They had such a nice finish to them. I don't understand how they did it because the finish is so nice. Some masks I saw they used stone. — **Doug Inga**

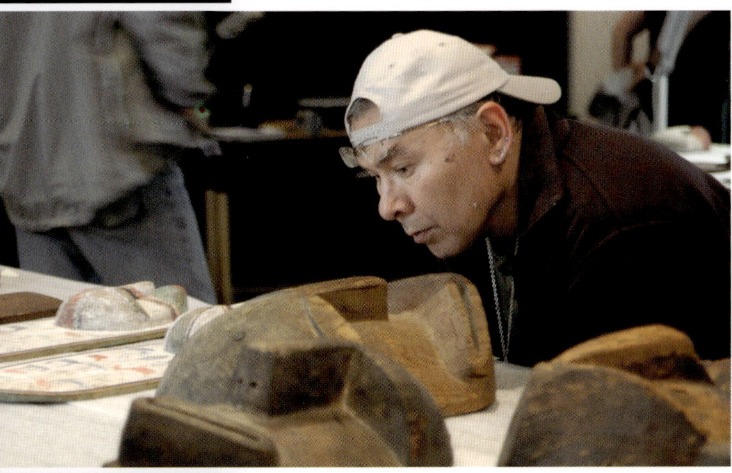

Doug Inga

On April 27, 1871, a 19-year-old Frenchman left San Francisco on a journey of discovery, fueled by a theory, enormous energy, intellectual curiosity and a fair amount of family money. On that spring day, Alphonse Pinart set sail on a salmon schooner headed for Alaska. Over the course of 13 months, the young linguist and ethnographer would spend the biggest portion of his time on the Kodiak Archipelago, learning about the Alutiiq people, recording their rituals and stories and gathering artifacts.

Pinart was born in 1852 to a wealthy family in Marquis, Pas-de-Calais, where his father had founded and owned the local ironworks. Intelligent and curious as a child, Pinart developed an interest in the languages of China and Japan.

When he was just 15, Pinart met the Abbé Brasseur de Bourbourg, a scholar famous at that time for his studies of Mexico. From the Abbé, Pinart learned about the indigenous peoples of America. Pinart began a quest to determine whether the indigenous languages of America would support a theory that the original Americans had come from Asia. There might be patterns in the languages of American Indians that reflected an ancestral link to Asia.

Akagngasqamek Giinaqlek
"Round-Faced One"

H. 35 cm;
W. 27 cm;
D. 10.5cm.

H. 13.78 in;
W. 10.63 in;
D. 4.13 in.

Spruce, remnants of paint

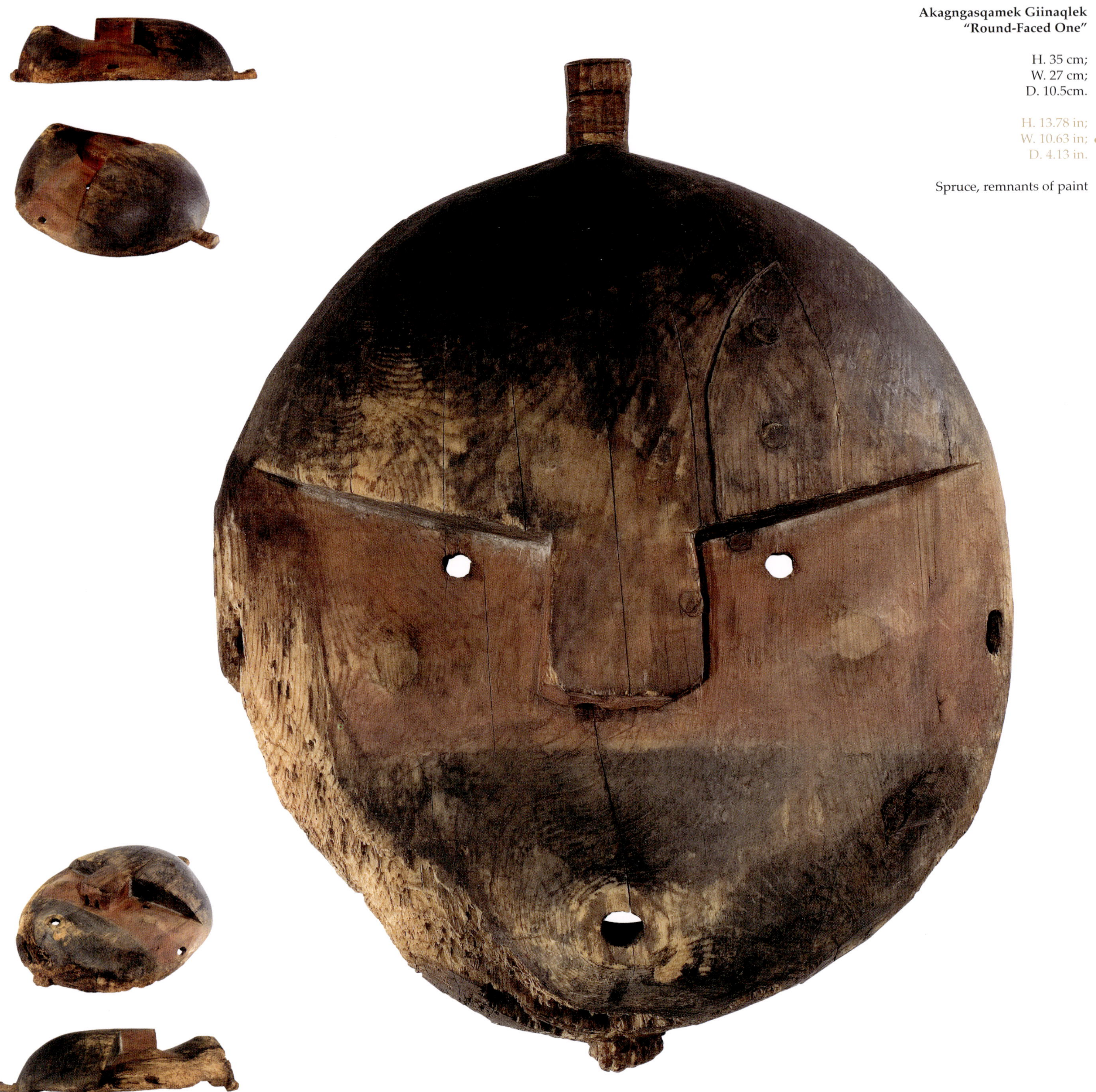

Looking at the pieces, the pictures just don't do them justice. There's definitely more detail, more thought that goes into them, like wrapping the hoops with leather, different details that you can't see in photos. I wasn't expecting them to be that advanced.
— **Gary Knagin**

From San Francisco, Pinart traveled first to the Aleutian Islands, arriving in Unalaska in May. He spent the next three months traveling the Alaska Peninsula and points north, with stops in Nushagak, Nunivak Island and the Yukon River. He continued further north still along the Siberian coast of the Bering Strait before turning south again. Back in Unalaska in August 1871, Pinart decided to travel by kayak to Kodiak. The trip took just over two months and he arrived at Kodiak Island on November 8, 1871. He also kayaked around Afognak and Shuyak Islands in March and April 1872. [1]

The young man's original mission had been to study the linguistics of Native American groups, but Pinart was keenly interested in the people and cultures he encountered. He was most interested in their worldview and belief system, which he feared would soon disappear if not documented and preserved. The old ways were being abandoned, a legacy of the Russian occupation. The United States' purchase of Alaska from Russia in 1867 did not change the fact that the Russian imprint had become a permanent and major part of Alutiiq society and culture.

The Russian occupation had brought enormous changes to the Alutiiq people. Their numbers decimated by smallpox and other diseases, they were forced to serve the commercial interests of Russian traders, and cultural and religious assimilation turned the Alutiiqs away from their traditional ways. An important part of Pinart's mission was to collect and record remnants of the culture while it was still possible to do so.

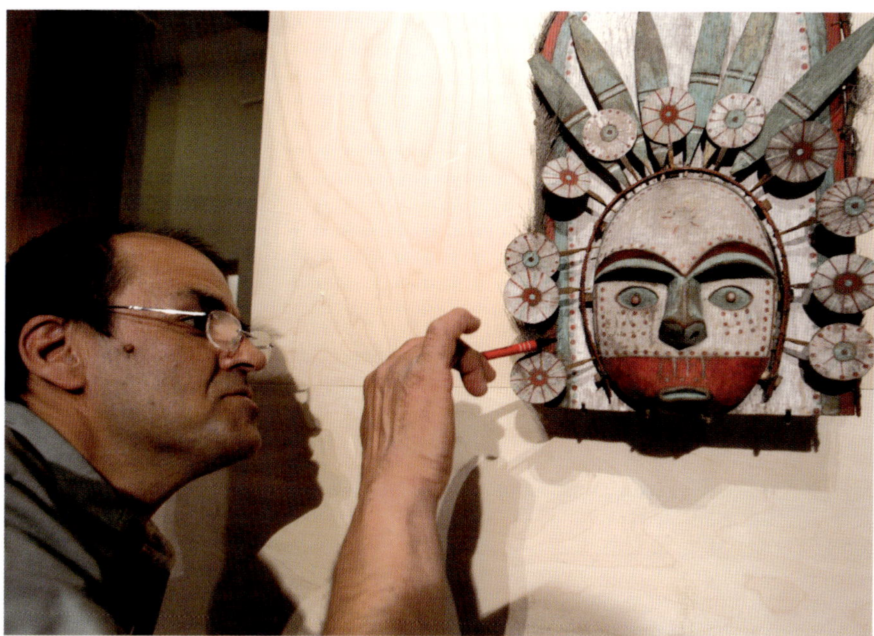

Gary Knagin

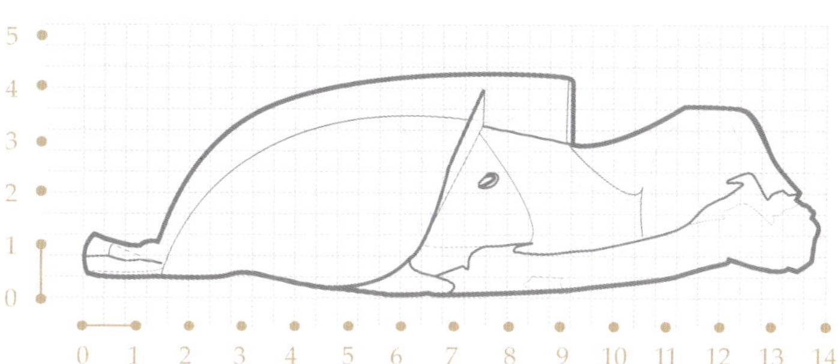

In the six months Pinart was on the Kodiak Archipelago, he spent time in Afognak, St. Paul Harbor (now Kodiak) and Eagle Harbor, south of Kodiak. He gathered and recorded stories, learned about various rituals, transcribed the Alutiiq language and collected items used in rituals and everyday life. He collected about 80 masks and other items such as beaded headdresses, bowls, paddles, model kayaks and open boats and bows and arrows.

I carved a hunting hat. It took two and a half years. You have to teach yourself patience. They had patience.
— **Alfred Naumoff**

Pinart left Kodiak in the spring of 1872 and headed south for a brief rest in San Francisco before turning back north to Sitka. When he returned home to France in late 1872, Pinart was well received. The Natural History Museum of Paris staged an exhibit of his Alaska artifacts; journals published his articles and speeches. The Société de Géographie (1874) awarded him its annual gold medal for the world's most important discovery in geography reported in 1873. [2] In 1875, Pinart donated most of his collection to a small regional museum, now the Château Musée, in Boulogne-sur-Mer, near his birthplace.

Pinart was not the first Westerner to explore and document the Kodiak Archipelago, but his writings and descriptions of ritual, worldview, beliefs and culture were extraordinary. His work preserves for contemporary Alutiiqs a window, a doorway into their ancestry, heritage and culture.

In her 1995 thesis for the University of Alaska Fairbanks, Dominique Desson explained what made Pinart's work so special. Continued on P. 18

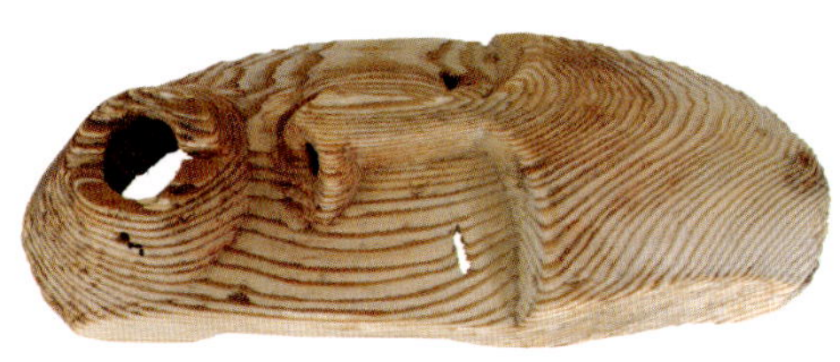

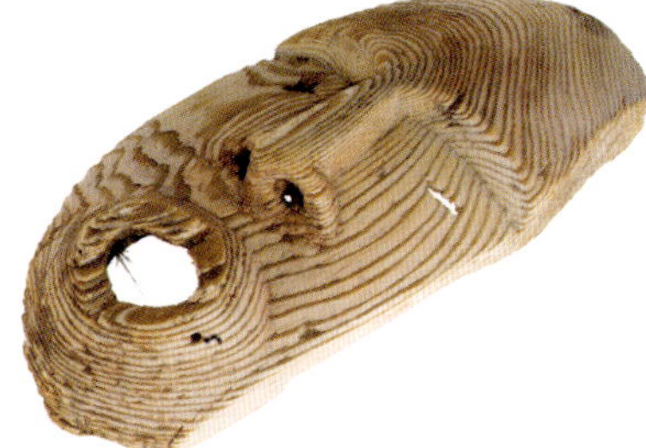

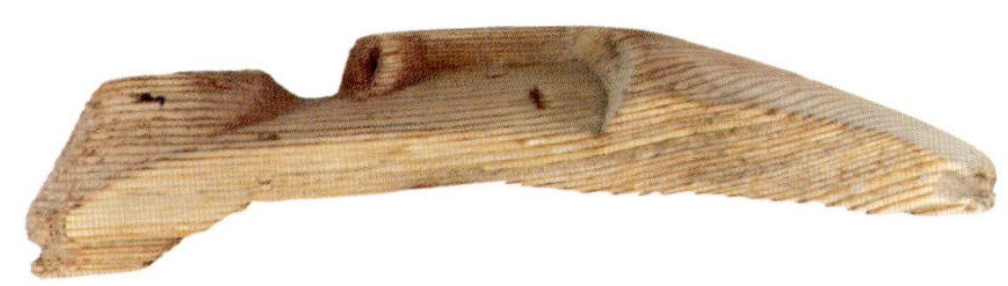

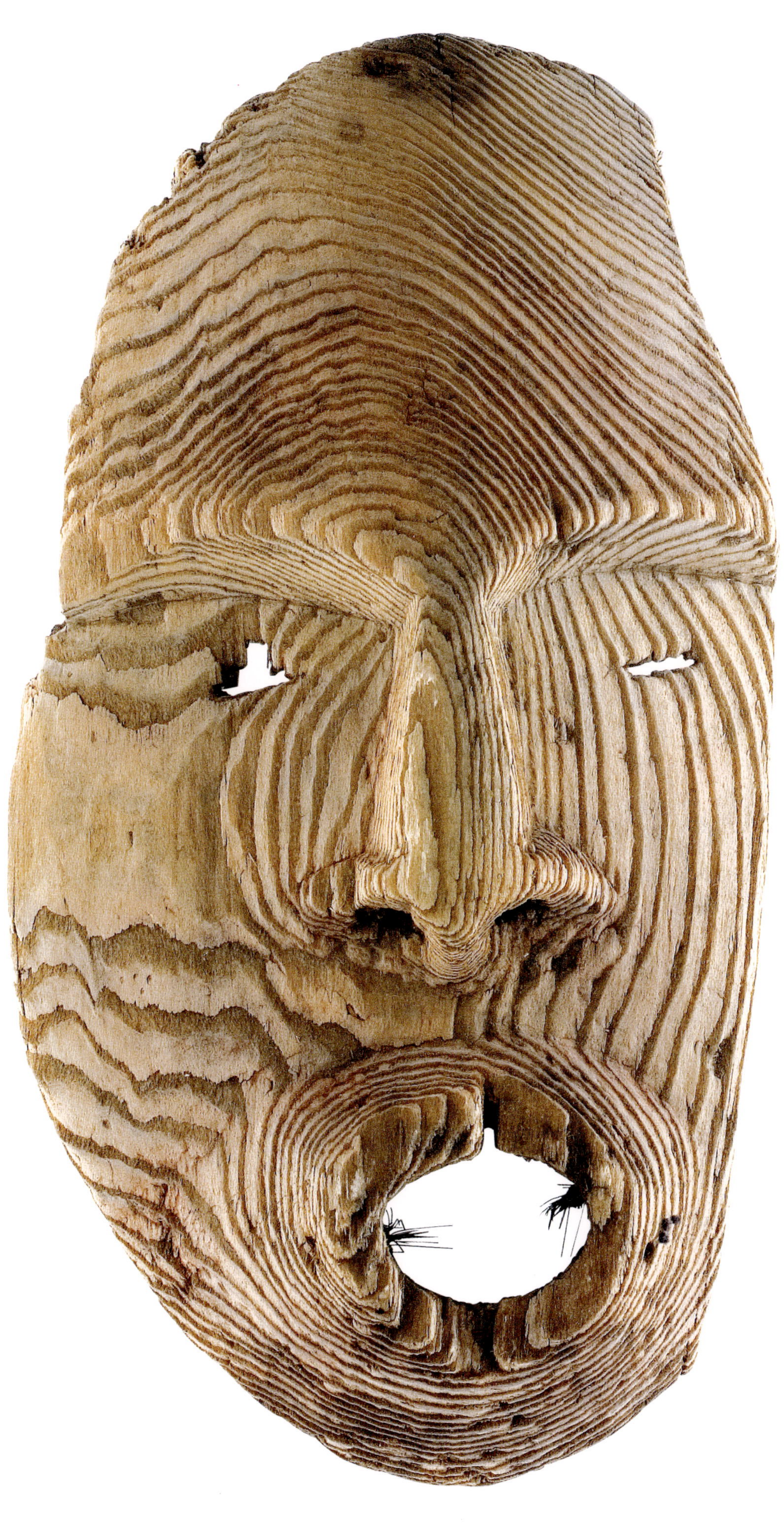

Aitauwasqaq
"Open-Mouth One"

H. 30.5 cm;
W. 16 cm;
D. 8 cm.

H. 12.01 in;
W. 6.3 in;
D. 3.15 in.

Douglas Fir, remnants of paint, baleen

Tupasqaq "Surprised One"

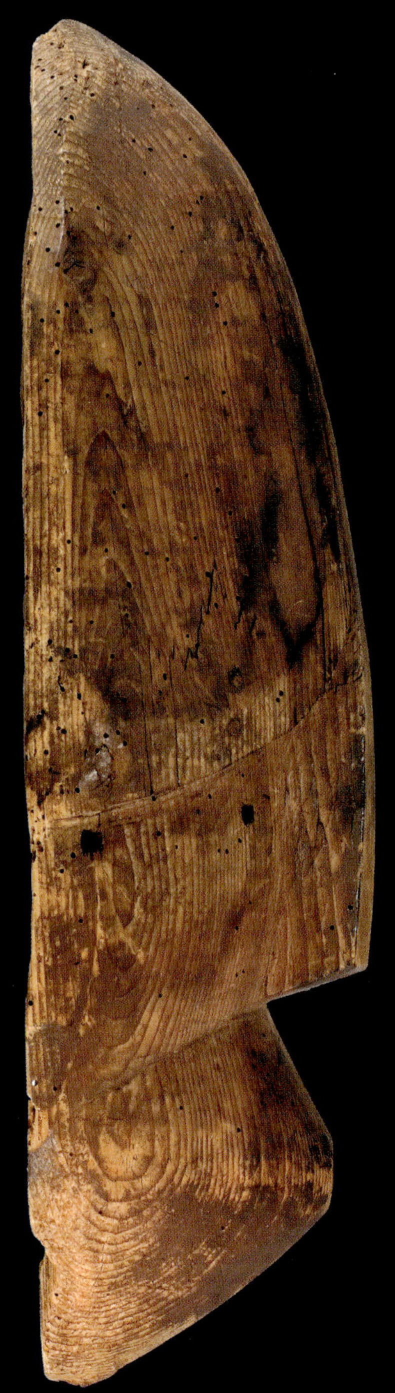

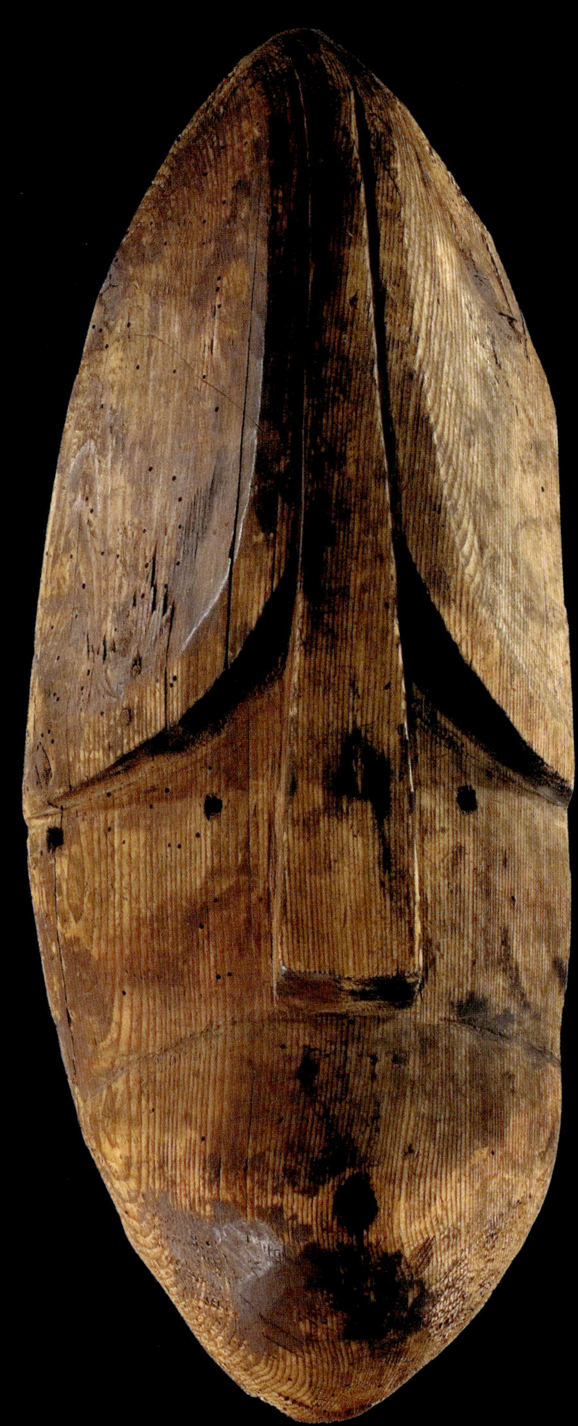

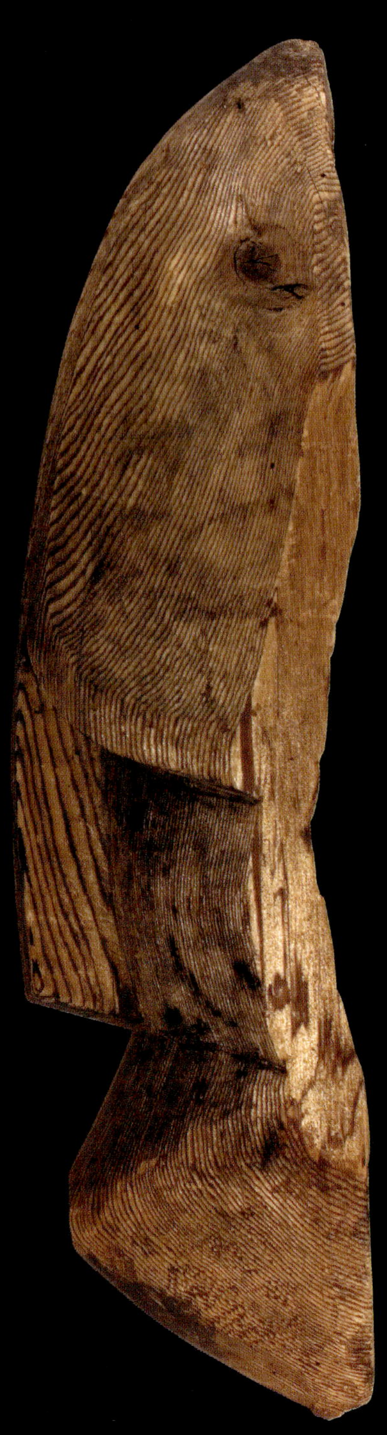

Alutiiq culture is being revived, last 10 years or so. People who go see the exhibit I think will go through the same thing. Emotions run really high. That stuff was made for a reason. The ritual purpose behind a lot of that stuff was just amazing.
— Alfred Naumoff

Tupasqaq "Surprised One"

H. 41 cm;
W. 15.5 cm;
D. 11 cm.

H. 16.14 in;
W. 6.10 in;
D. 4.33 in.

Spruce, remnants of paint

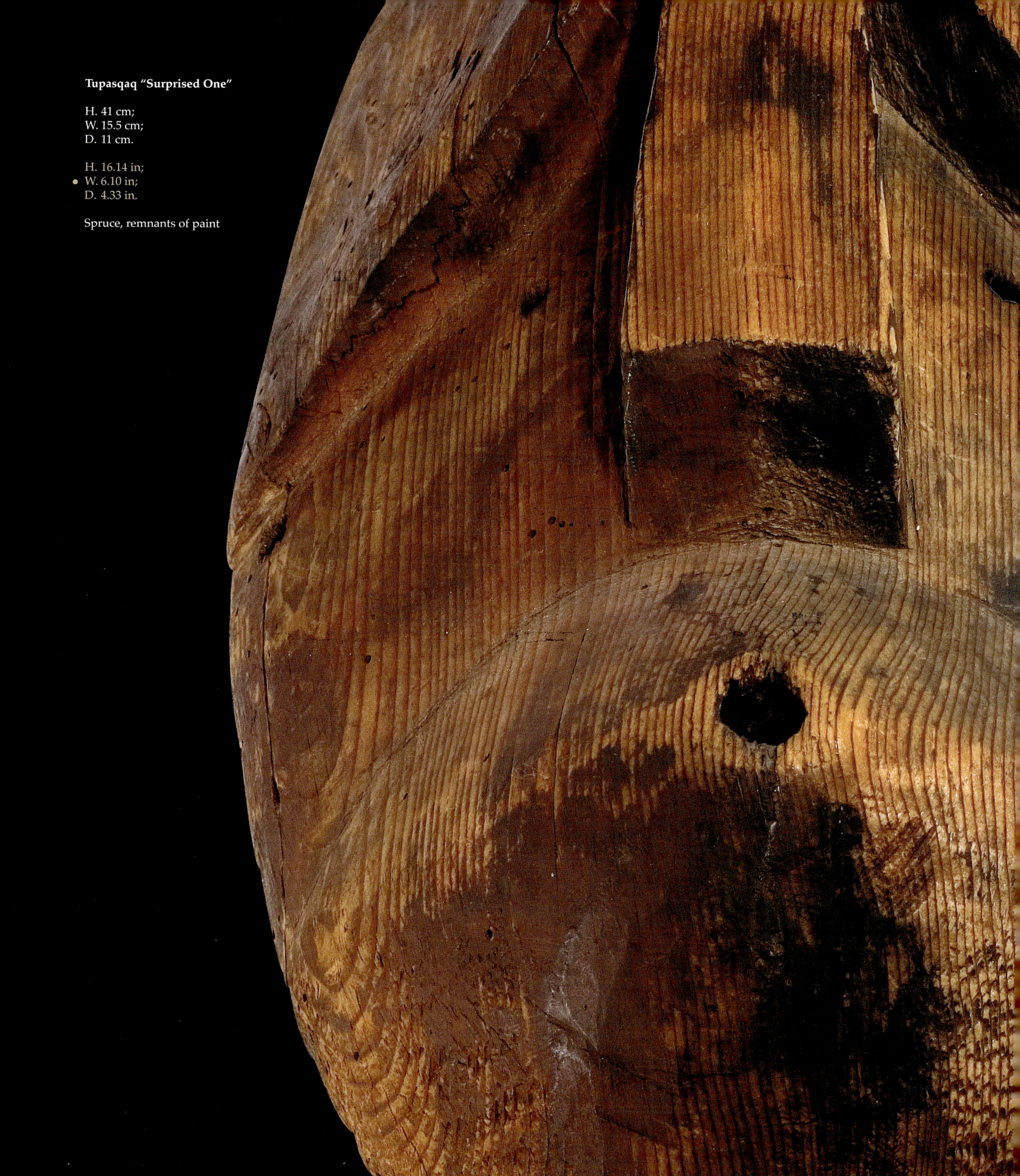

What shocked me was it wasn't just a mask collection, but beaded headdress from Kodiak and my mother's village of Afognak, bidarkas, wooden platters in the shape of halibut, wooden bowls in the shape of ducks, stone oil lamps, spears with the name inscribed Sezelnev. That was an old whaling famly of Afognak who Pinart certainly would have met. — **Helen Simeonoff**

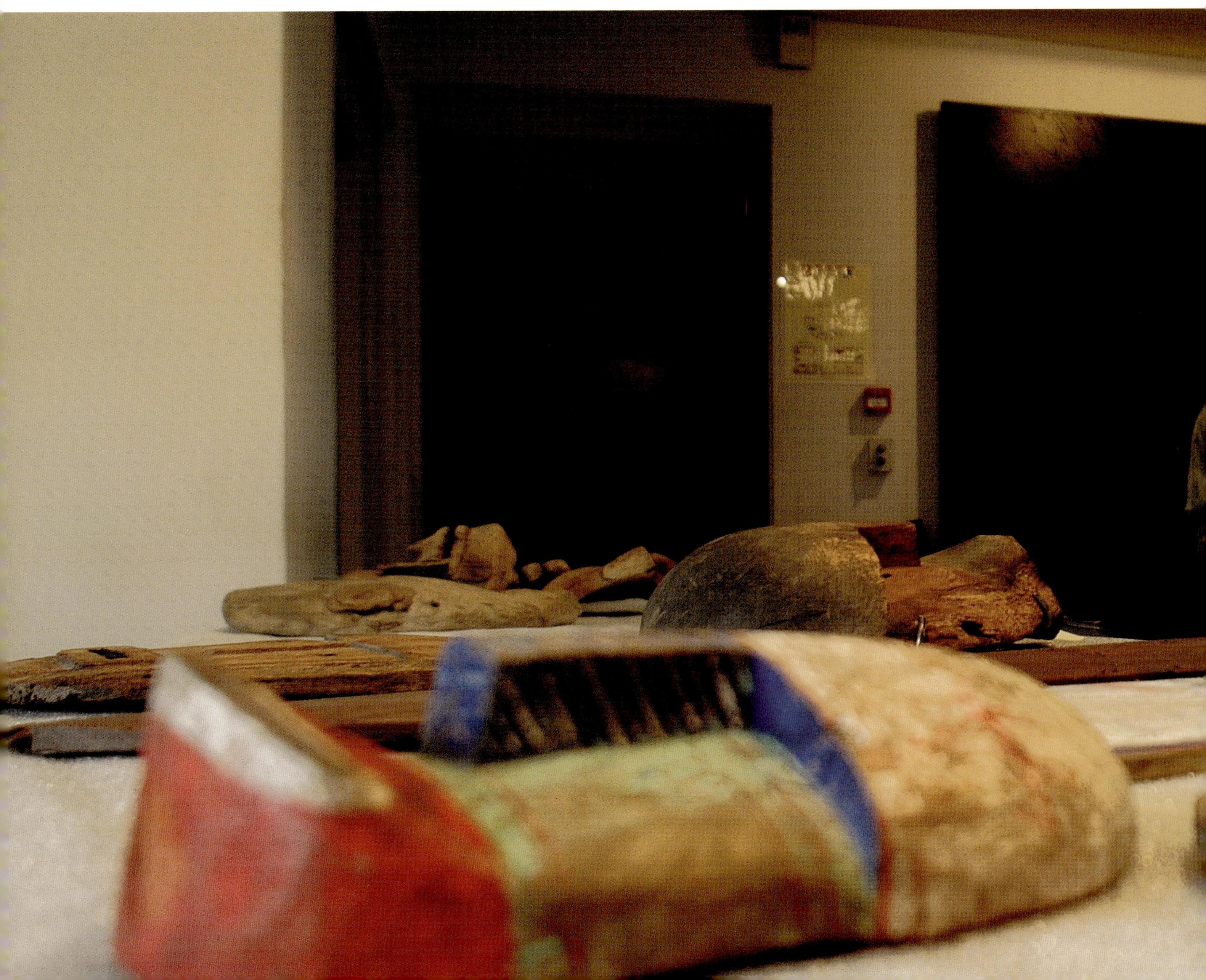

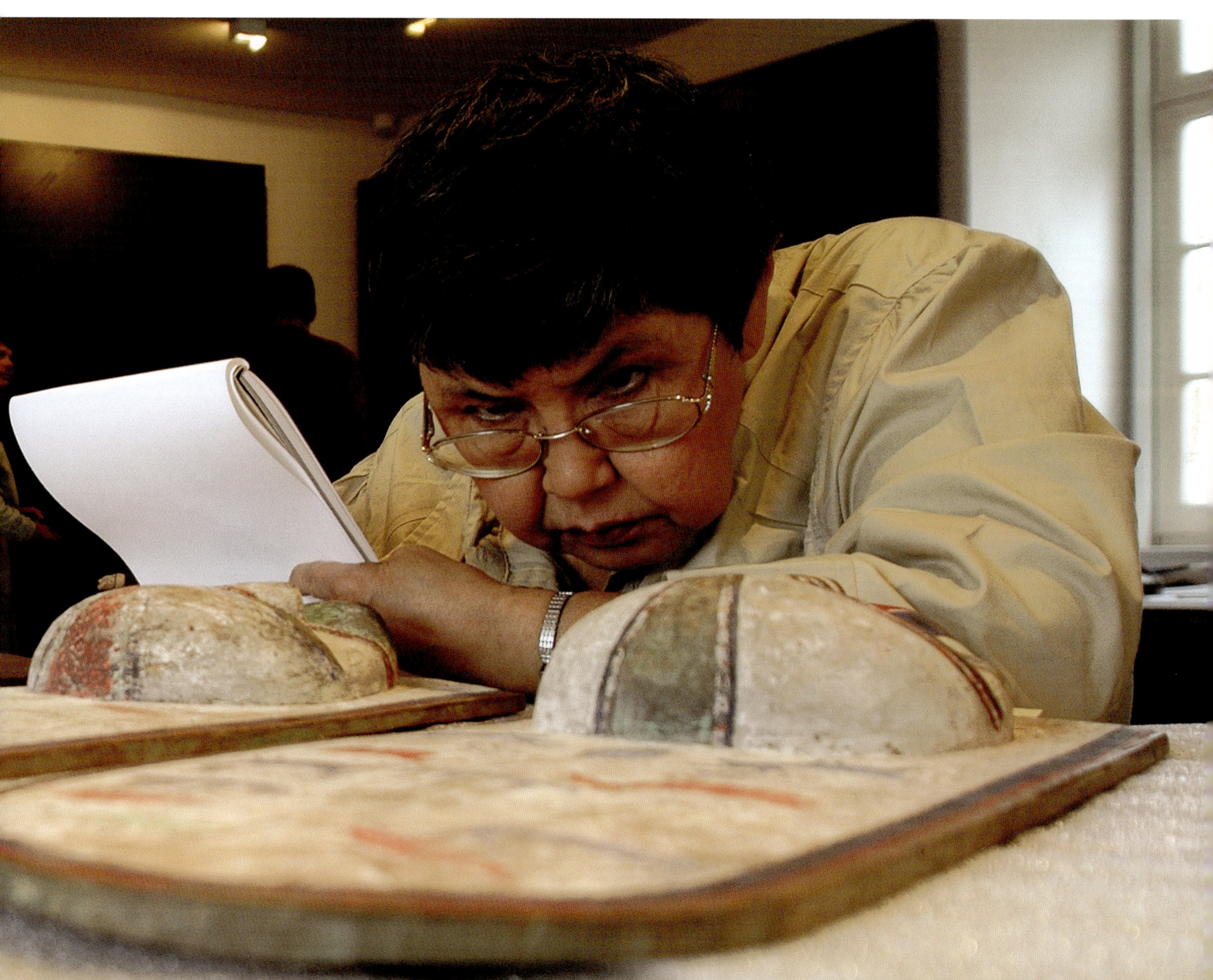

Cupuwasqaq
"Blowing One"

H. 31 cm;
W. 13 cm;
D. 9 cm.

H. 12.2 in;
W. 5.12 in;
D. 3.54 in.

Spruce, remnants of paint

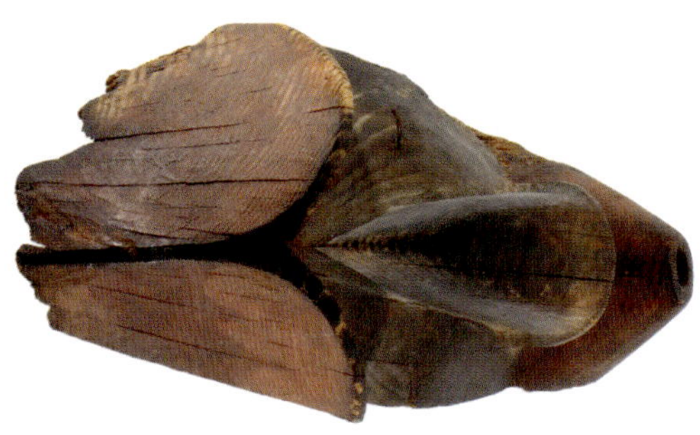

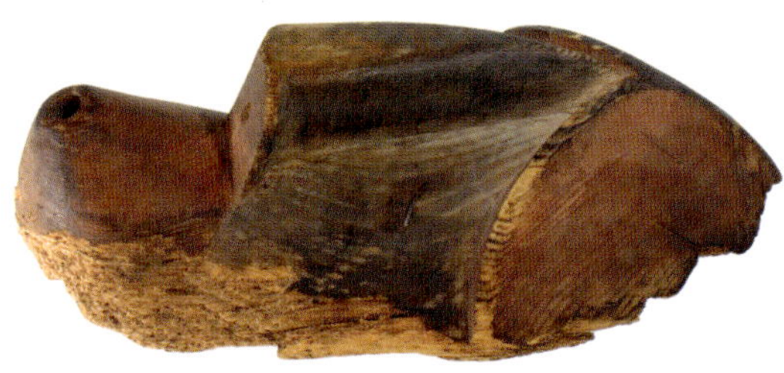

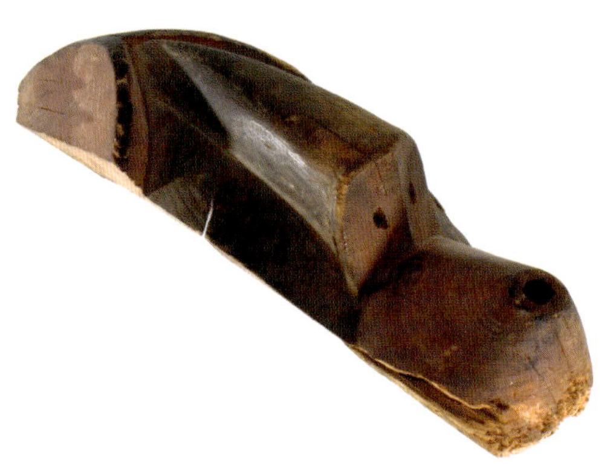

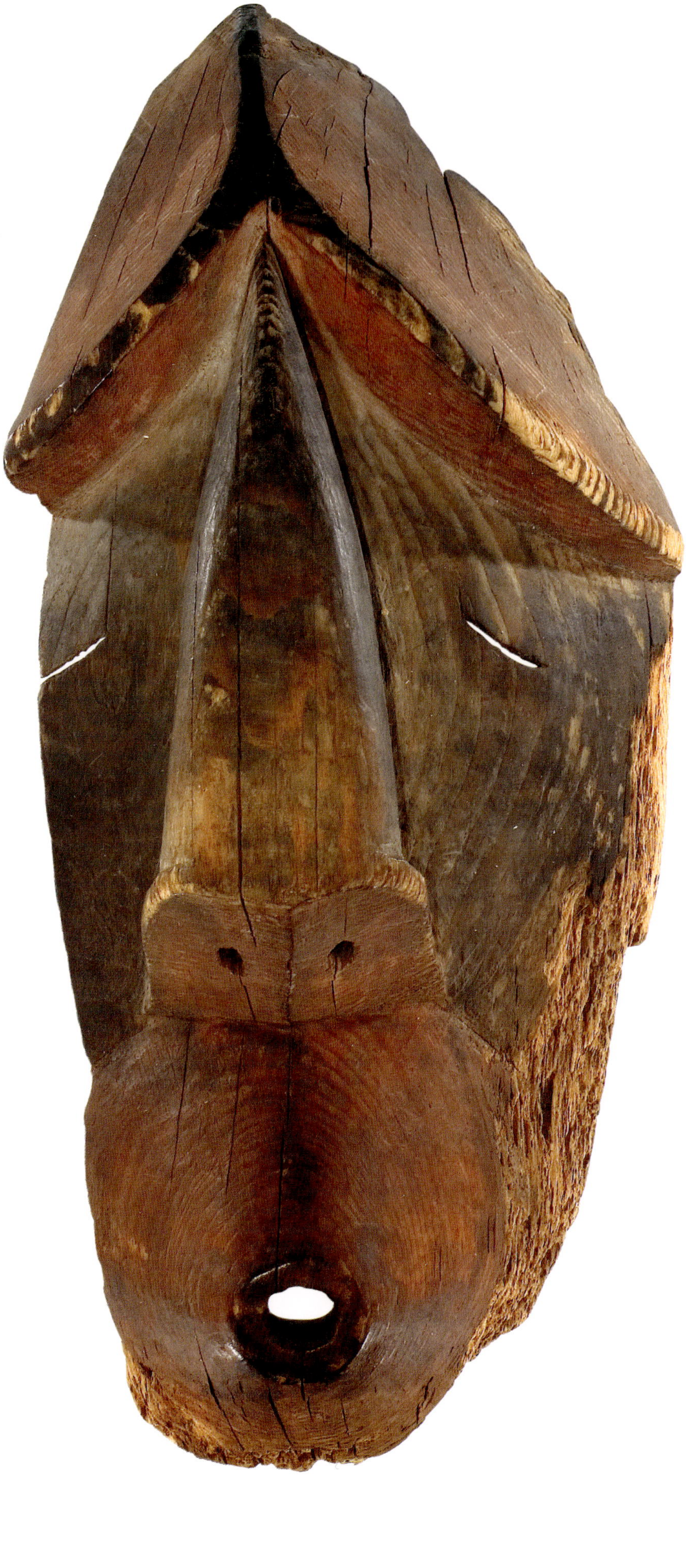

"In the early Russian sources, we find considerable information on the conduct of the festivals. Unfortunately, they do not provide any significant details on the uses and meanings of specific masks. Pinart, on the other hand, centered most of his descriptions around the mask and its meaning, providing information on the name of particular masks, the text of the songs associated with these masks, the dance in which the particular masks were used and sometimes, also, the story about their origins."

A few contemporary Alutiiq people knew of the Pinart collection, but Desson's doctoral thesis shed new light on it. Under the supervision and direction of Dr. Lydia Black, a noted anthropologist and Russian American historian at UAF, Desson studied the Pinart masks as the centerpiece of her thesis, "Masked Rituals of the Kodiak Archipelago."[3]

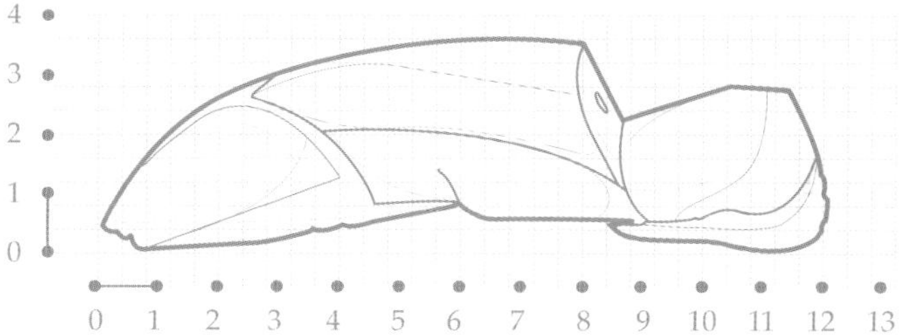

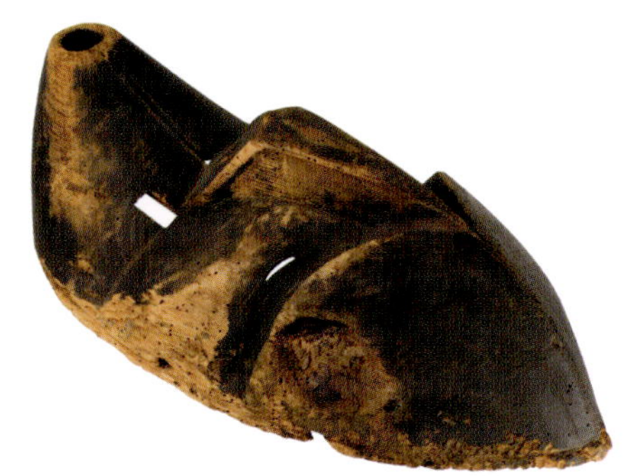

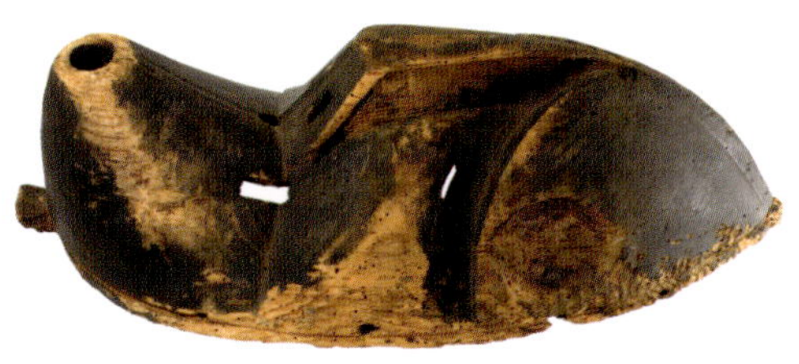

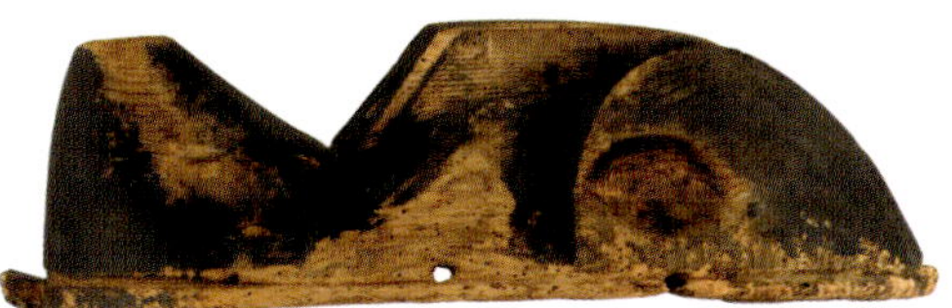

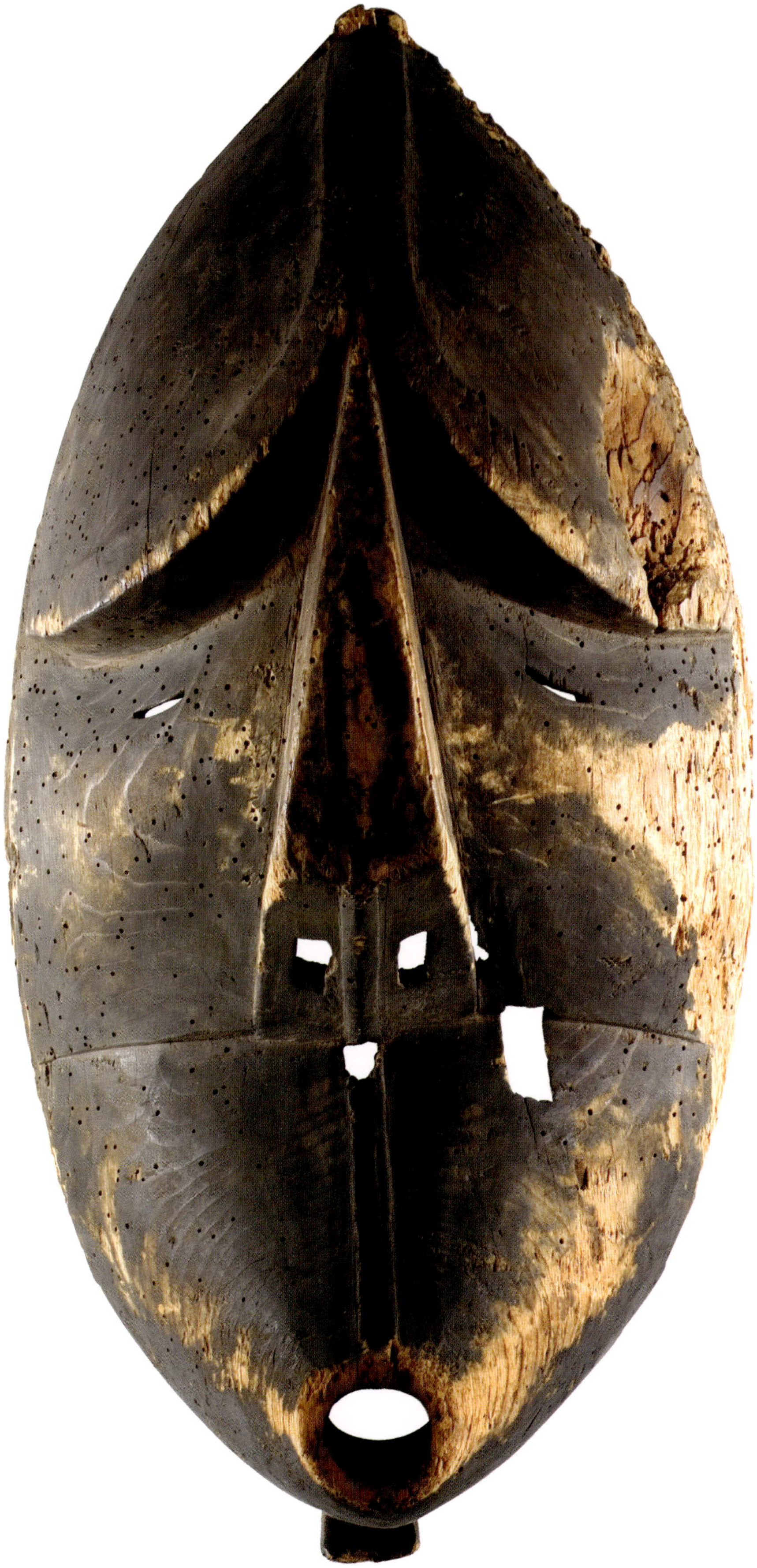

Kukumya'rngasaqaq
"Whistler"

H. 43 cm;
W. 20.5 cm;
D. 13 cm.

H. 16.93 in;
W. 8.07 in;
D. 5.12 in.

Spruce, remnants of paint

On August 20, 1994, Alutiiq artist Helen Simeonoff attended a lecture by Desson in Kodiak sponsored by the Kodiak Area Native Association (KANA). The subject of the slide show was Pinart's Alutiiq mask collection. Simeonoff was enthralled and frantically began to take notes.

She arranged to purchase a copy of the thesis when it was completed and told others about the collection. To Simeonoff it was important and exciting news, but no one seemed to share her fascination. She tried to raise funds for a trip to see the collection, but no one was interested. So, like Pinart, she used her own money to finance a trip. But while Pinart had family money, Simeonoff did not.

By April 2000, she had saved enough to make the trip. With advice and a letter of introduction from staff at the Anchorage Museum at Rasmuson Center, Simeonoff flew to France. *Continued on P. 28*

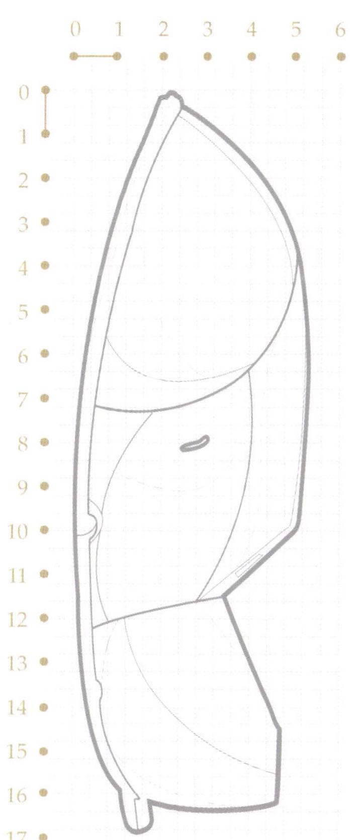

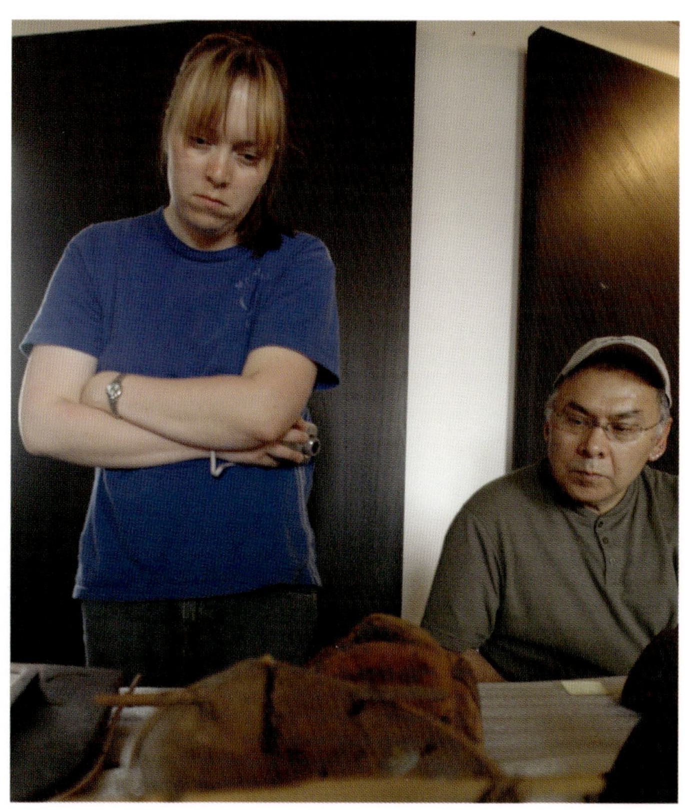

Lena Amason and Doug Inga

The pieces that most intrigued me were the ones that were shaped like boats, the ones that you could see where they had been painted and had attachments. You couldn't see that in a photograph.
— **Lena Amason**

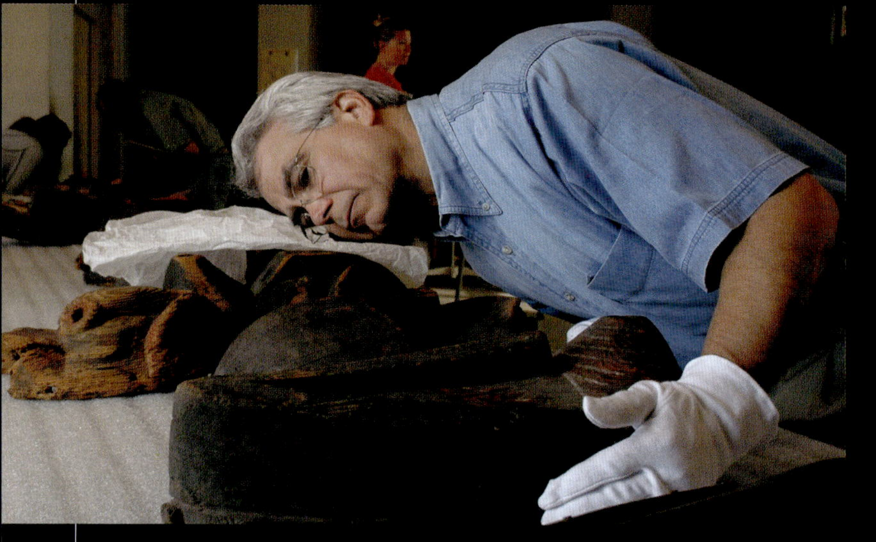

The size and shapes were so different from what I had expected from photographs. It's unfortunate that most photographs of masks are direct, face-on shots, with very few profiles or images that show the relief of the carvings. Some of the masks are six and seven inches deep — you can't begin to see that in a two-dimensional photo.

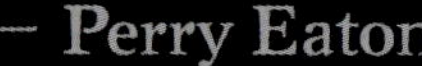

— Perry Eaton

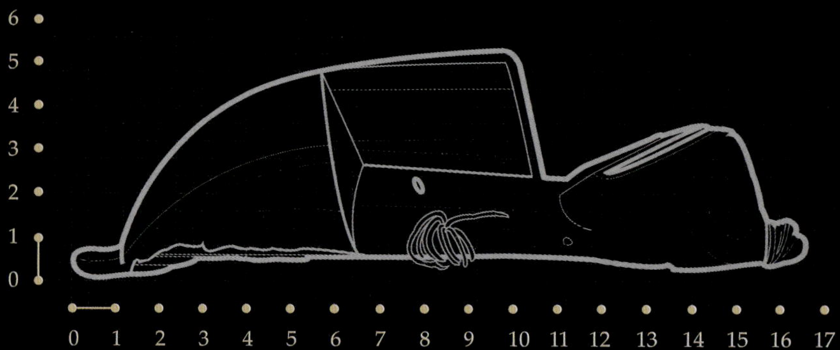

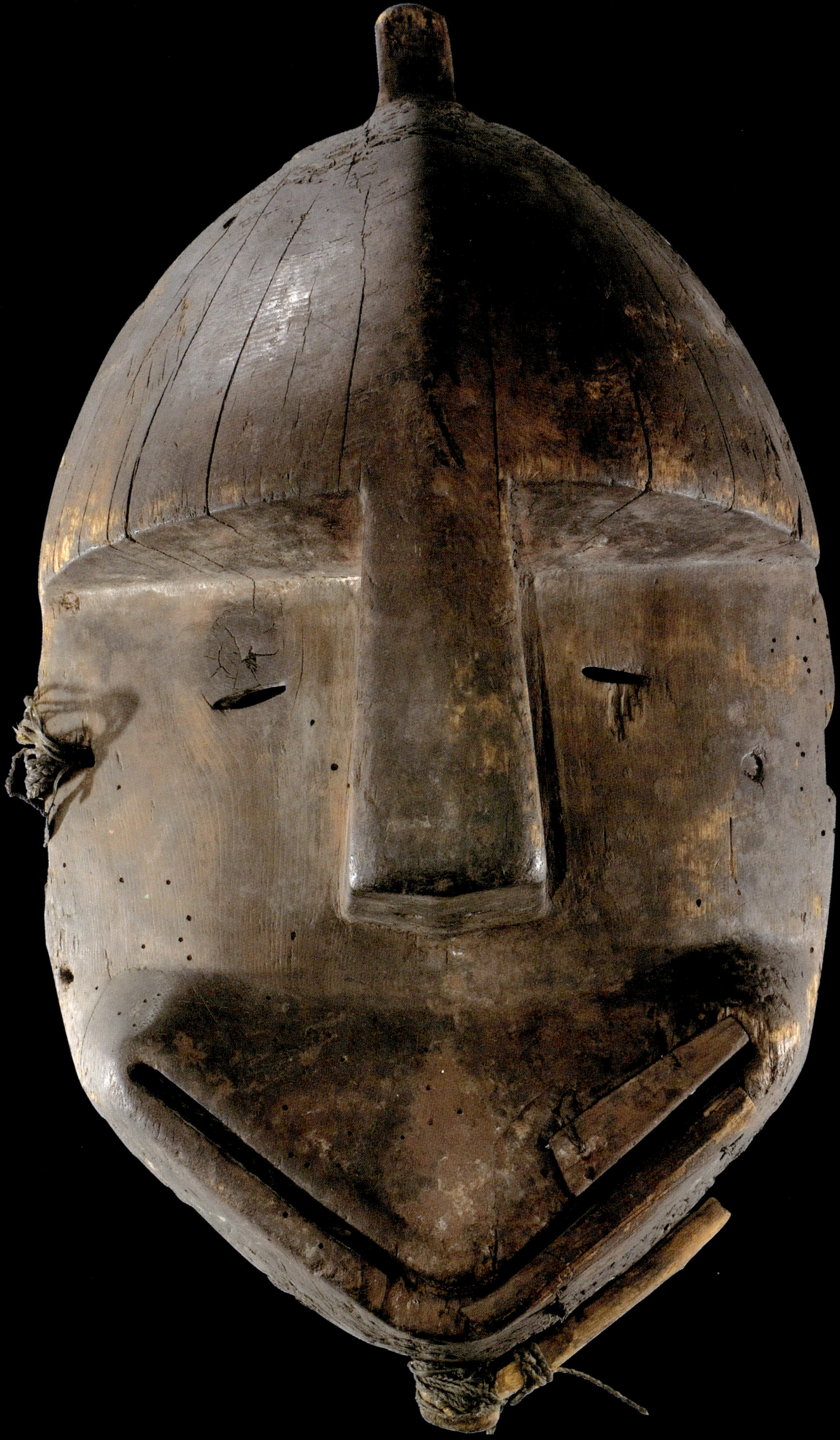

Nukallpiaq "Man"

H.42 cm;
W. 23 cm;
D. 13.5cm.

H. 16.54 in;
W. 9.06 in;
D. 5.31 in.

Spruce, remnants of
paint, tendons

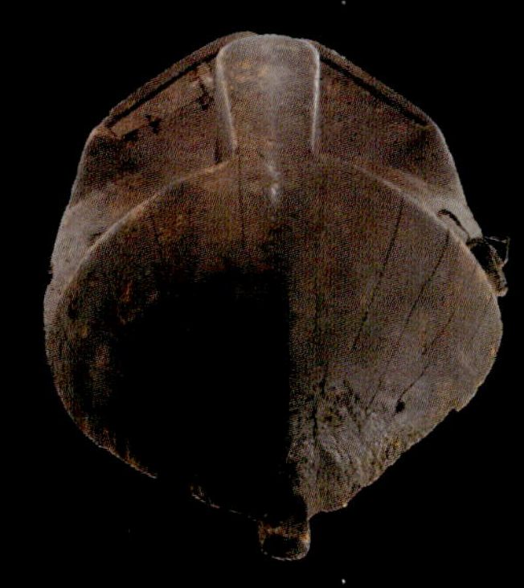

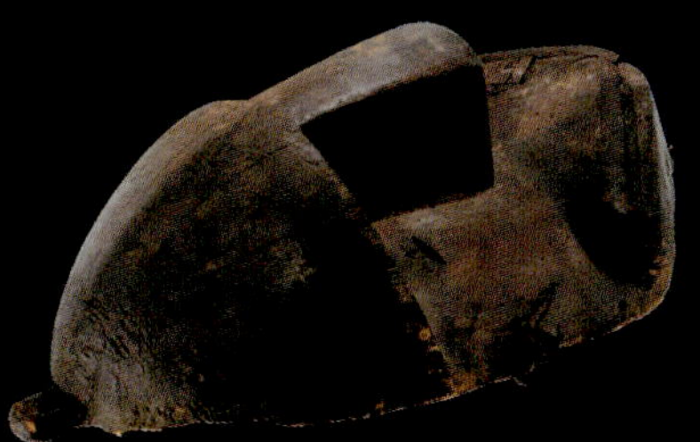

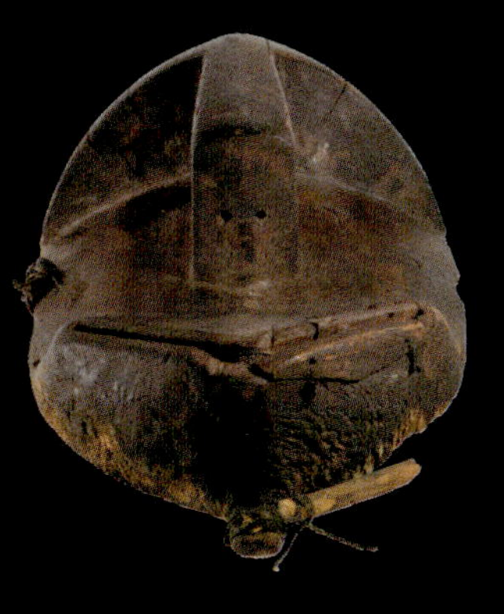

Nayurta "Watchman"

H. 44.5 cm;
W. 29 cm;
D. 12 cm.

H. 17.52 in;
W. 11.42 in;
D. 4.72 in.

Spruce, remnants of paint

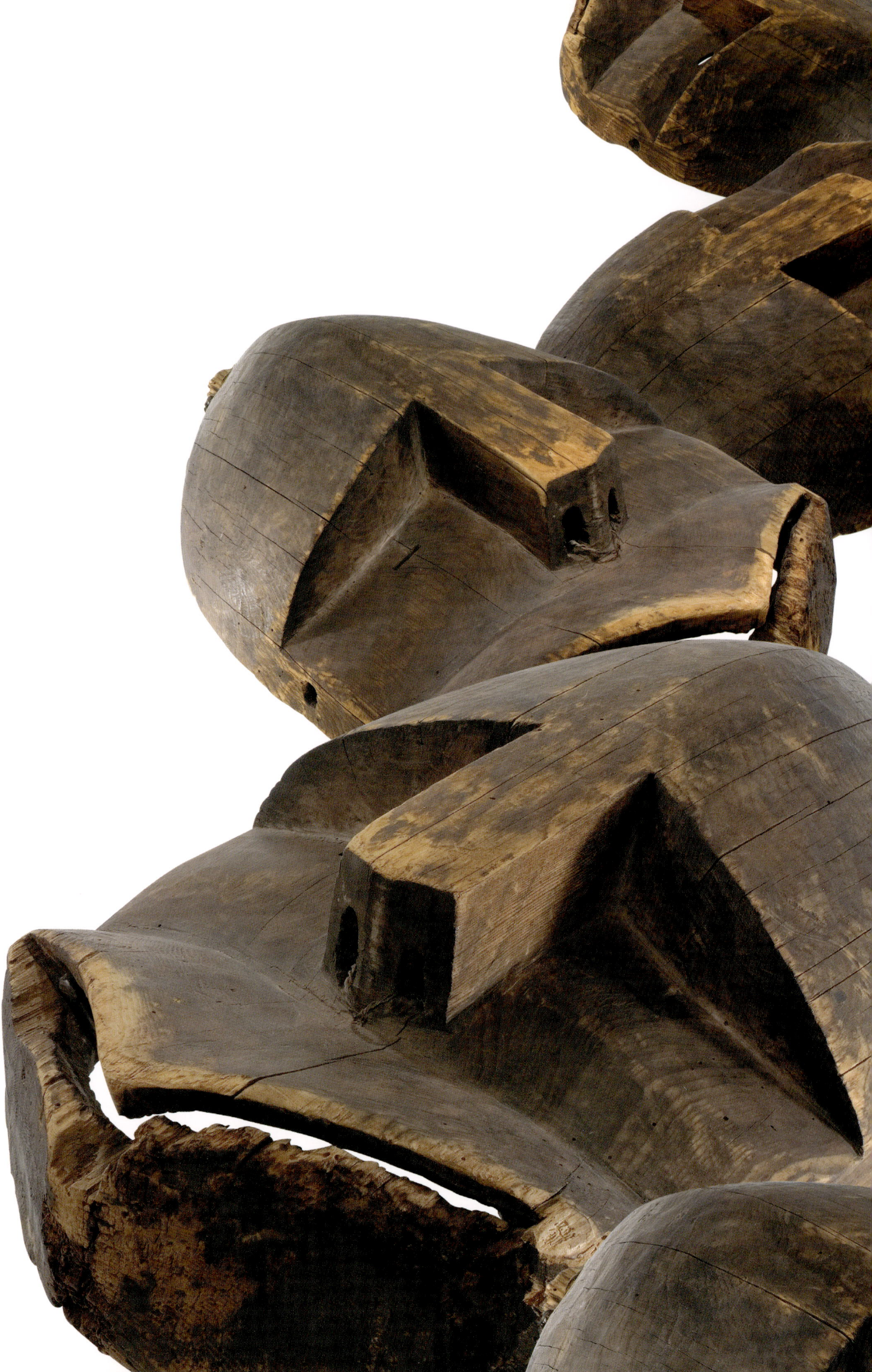

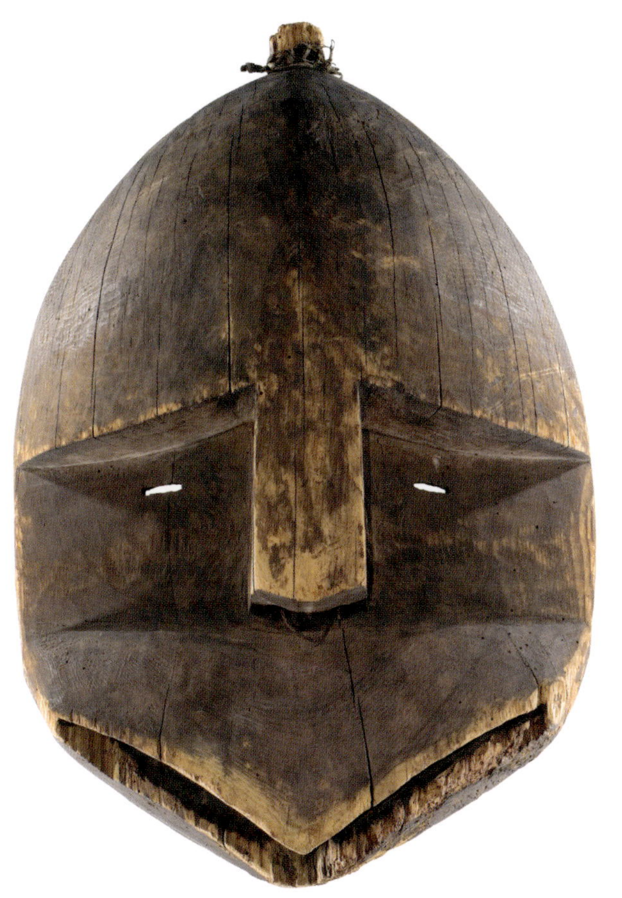

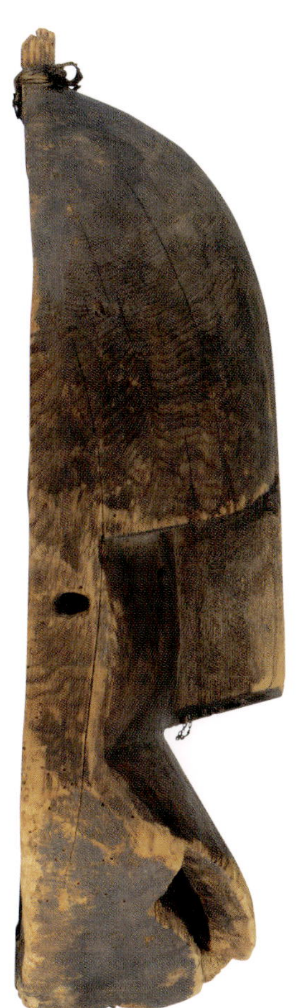

When we got to Boulogne,
I wasn't expecting that feeling I got. Like there was a presence there. It totally floored me. I was not ready for it. It sent chills up my spine. Something was there, I can't explain it. It felt like somebody or something was there, and it or they were happy we were there.

— **Gary Knagin**

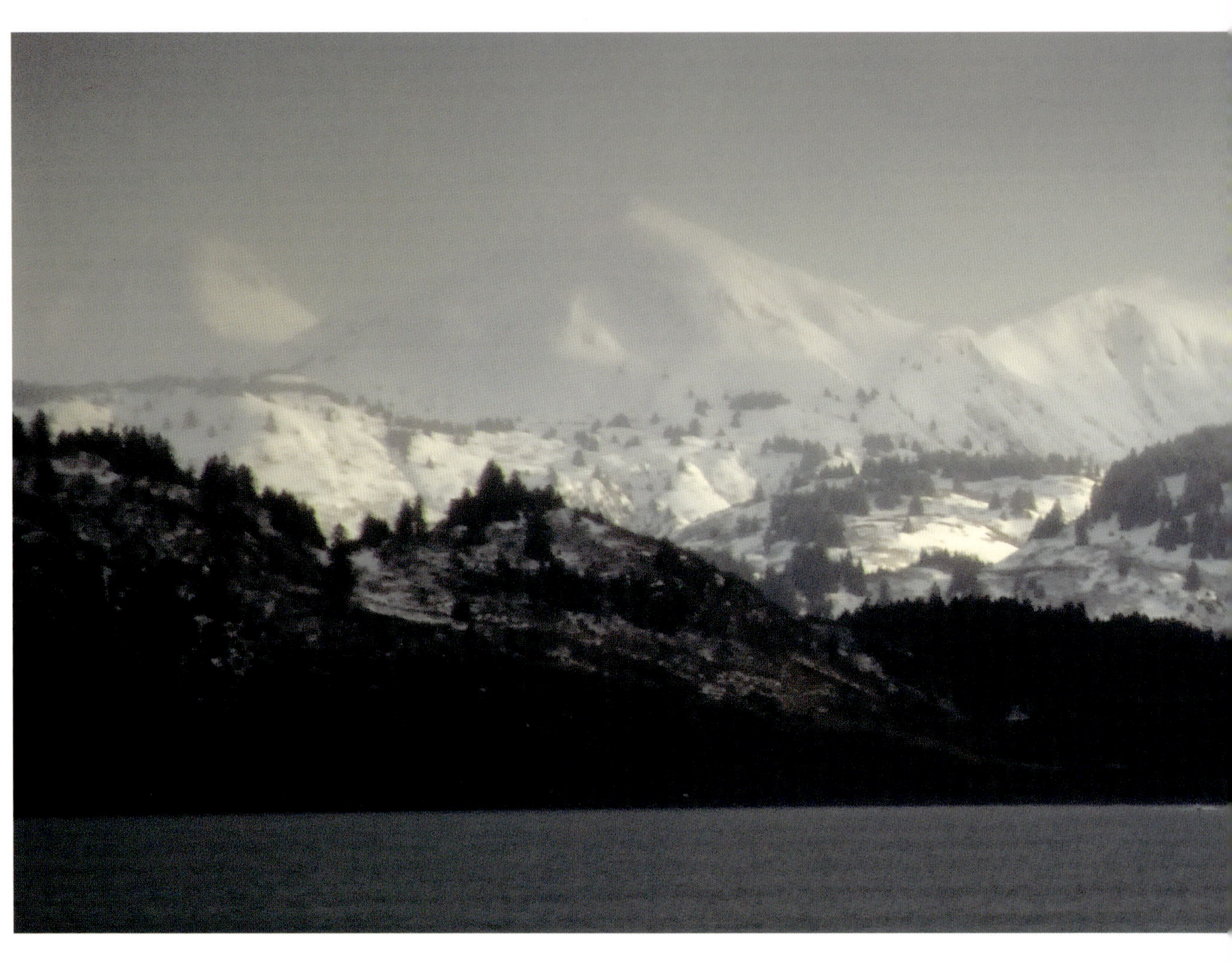

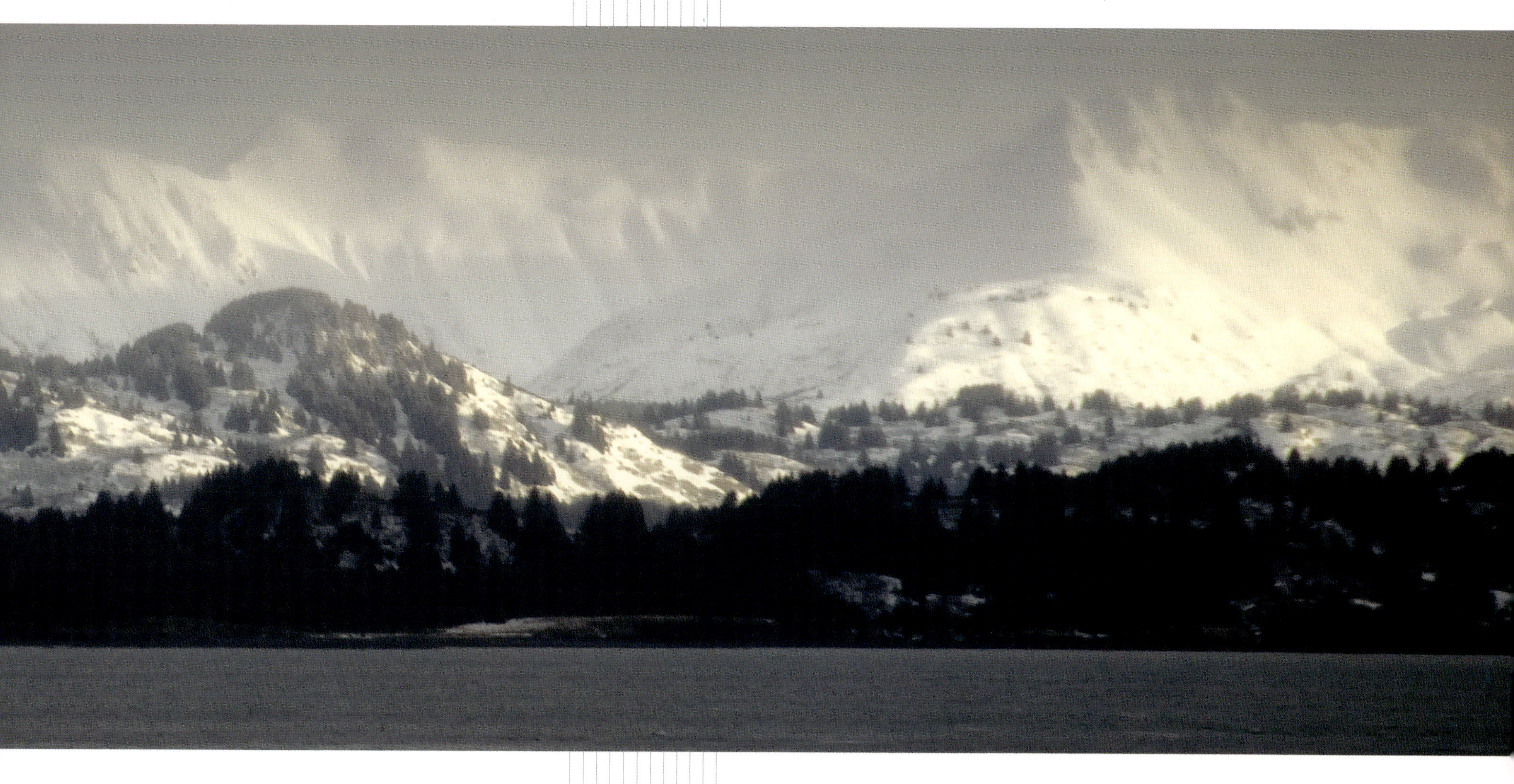

Where I go, you go, helper spirit.
You don't know where I will come from, the land or sea.
As I travel the universe, helper spirit, protect me.

— From a song collected by Alphonse Pinart in Eagle Harbor, March 1872 [4]

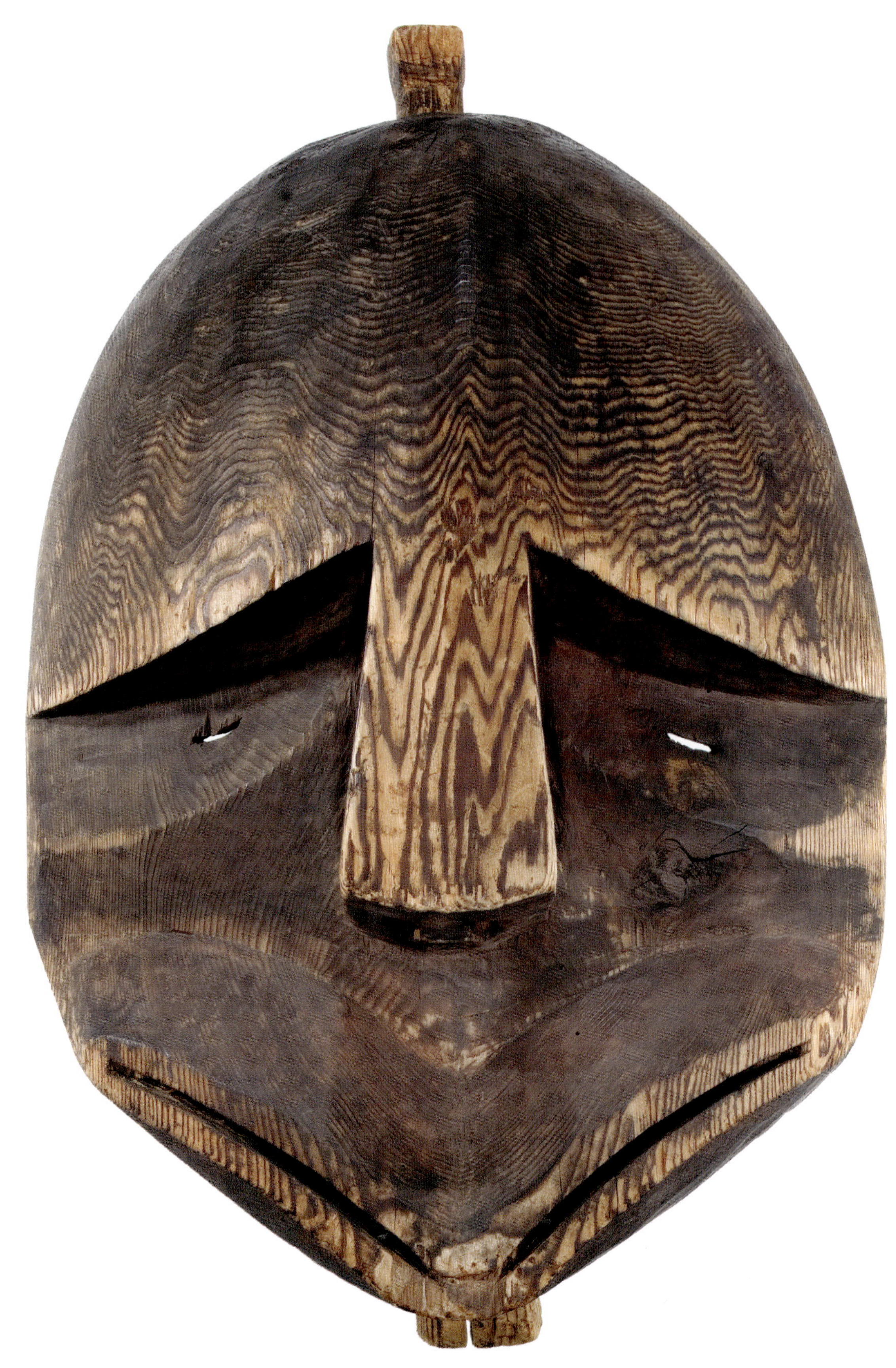

Englaryuumasqaq
"Grinning One"

H. 51 cm;
W. 32.5 cm;
D. 19 cm.

H. 20.08 in;
W. 12.8 in;
D. 7.48 in.

Douglas Fir, remnants of paint, plant fiber

Staying at a hotel across the street from the Château Musée, Simeonoff spent five days — sun-up to sundown, she says — photographing the exhibit. *What shocked me was it wasn't just a mask collection, but beaded headdresses from Kodiak and my mother's village of Afognak, bidarkas, wooden platters in the shape of halibut, wooden bowls in the shape of ducks, stone oil lamps, spears with the name Sezelnev inscribed – an old whaling family of Afognak who Pinart certainly would have met.*

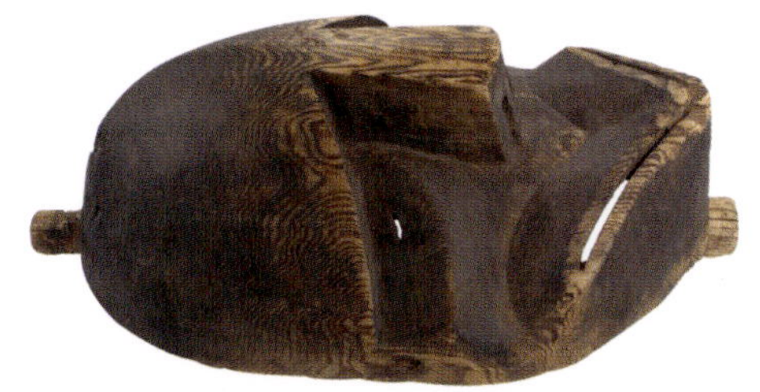

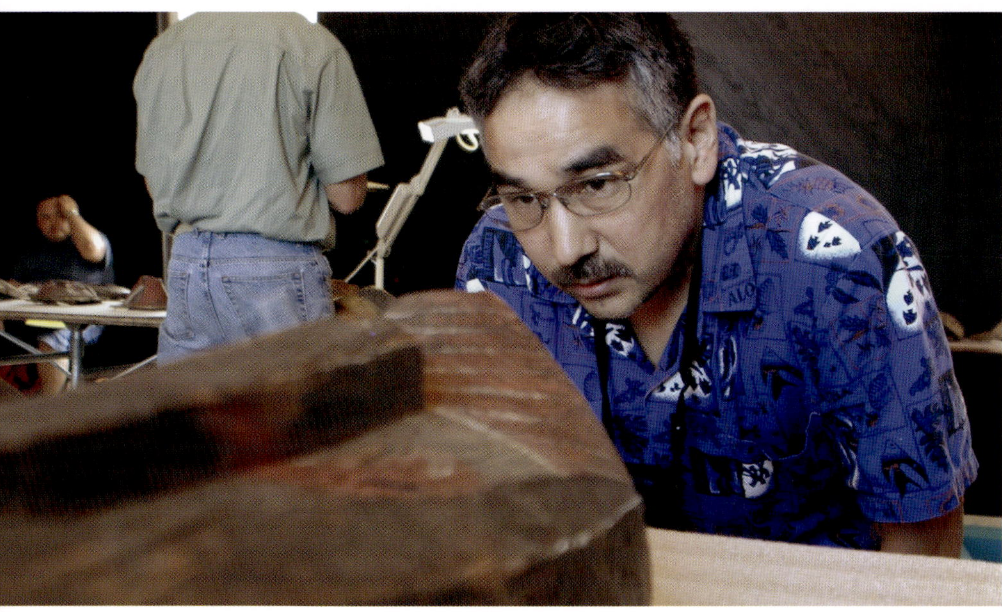

Alfred Naumoff

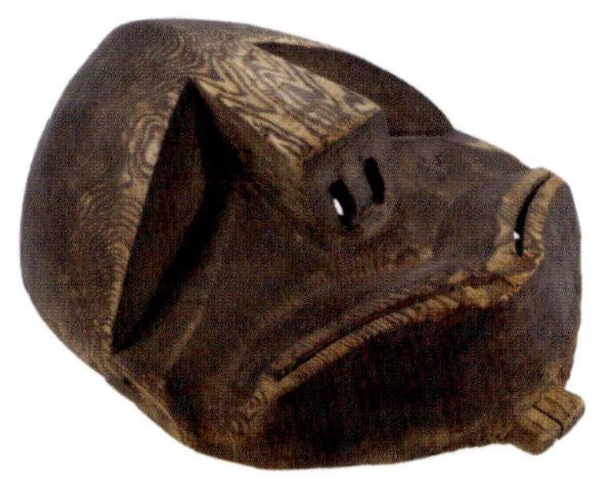

I wanted only to see the masks, bowls, platters, spears, bidarkas, stone oil lamps; I was hungry to feel reconnected with my 'vanished' culture. It was an overwhelming feeling to see my whole Sugpiaq culture unfold before my eyes.

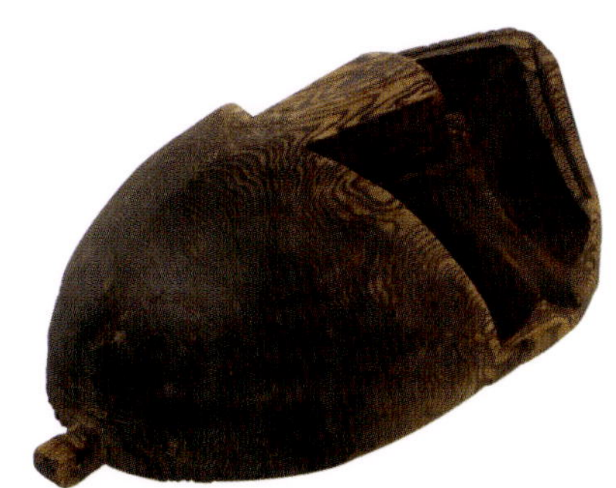

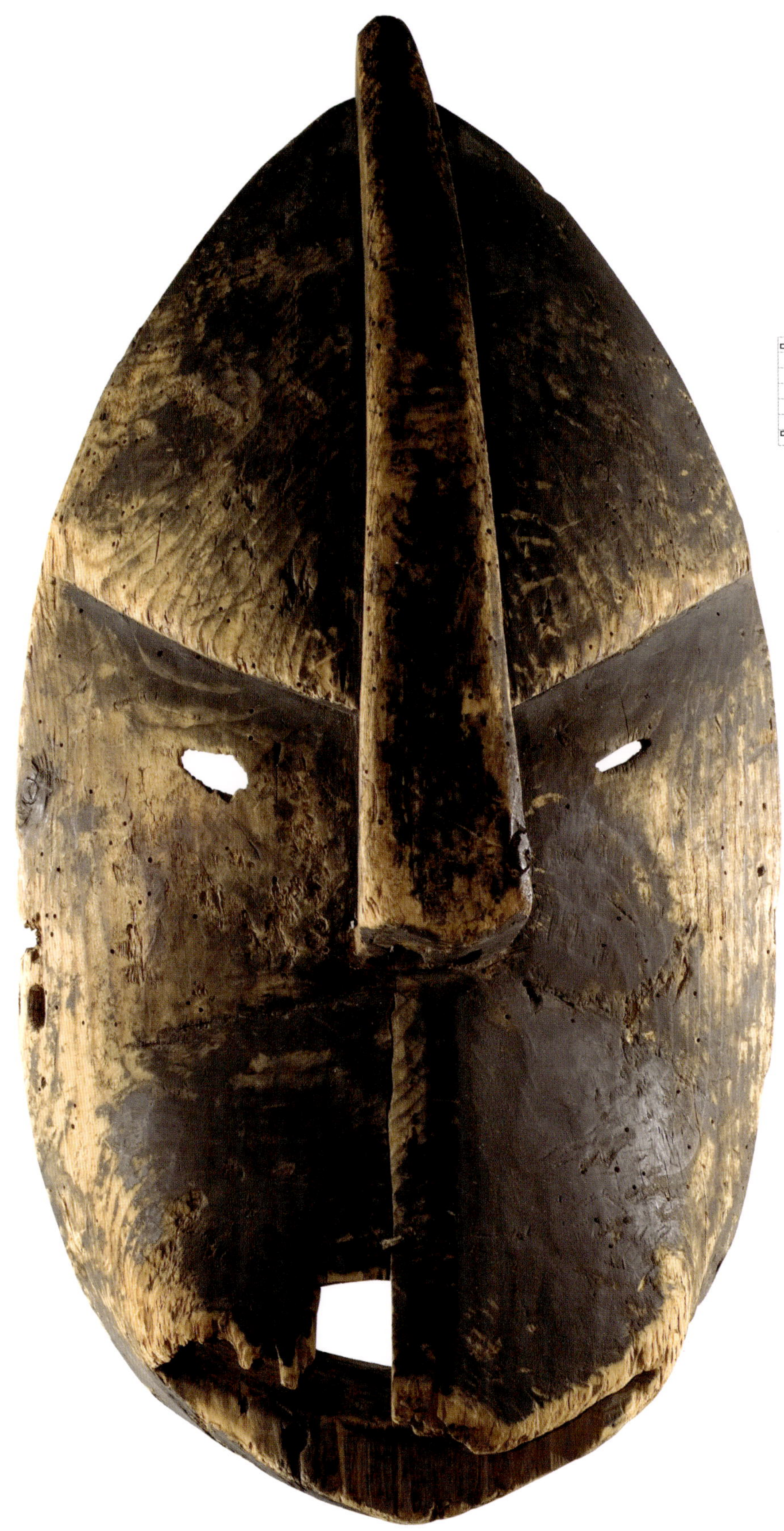

Nakllegnasqaq
"Pitiful One"

H. 43.9 cm;
W. 23.01 cm;
D. 15.01 cm.

H. 17.32 in;
W. 9.06 in;
D. 5.91 in.

Spruce, remnants of paint, baleen

Her last day in Boulogne-sur-Mer, Simeonoff sat quietly on a bench, meditating about the adventurous young explorer and linguist.

Thank you, Pinart, for caring about our culture and saving all these items for us. I am very grateful. Why did you do it? You spent your family fortune traveling to Alaska, all the hardships you must have suffered traveling in a small bidarka. And how in the world did you get a whole museum floor of items shipped back to France?

After she returned to Alaska, a mutual friend introduced Perry Eaton and Simeonoff. She told him of Pinart and showed him her photographs. Until then, Eaton's chosen artistic form was black and white photography. Like her, he was enchanted by the masks and had to see them for himself. Eaton traveled to Boulogne-sur-Mer later that year, marking his entry into mask-making in the Alutiiq tradition.

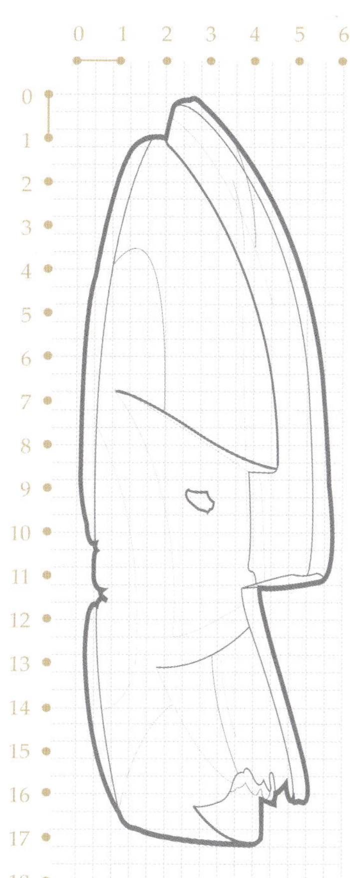
0 1 2 3 4 5 6
0 1 2 3 4 5 6 7 8 9 10 11 12 13 14 15 16 17 18

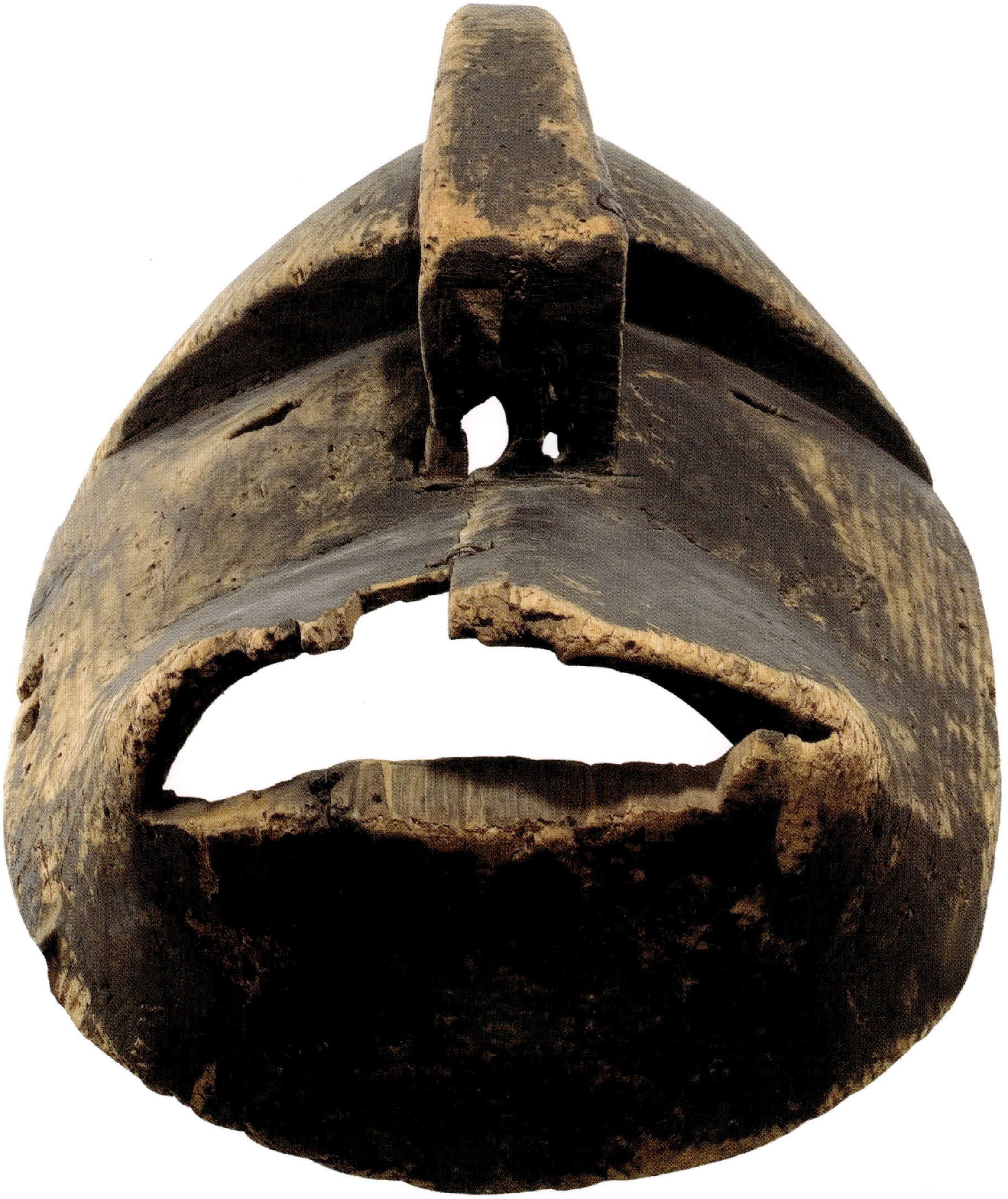

Re-emergence Of Cultural Identity

The Russian occupation of the Kodiak Archipelago was first and foremost a commercial enterprise, and the domination and assimilation of the Alutiiq people furthered the Russian cause. In the Kodiak area, intermarriage was common. Russian culture and religion were powerful and dominant forces to those who chose a more Russian lifestyle. Russian influence through the church remained strong even after the United States purchased Alaska in 1867.

> I went with a very analytical mindset, with a focus on studying the masks' design, proportions, and color schemes . . . I was surprised to find that when it came time to see the masks for the first time I was literally overcome with emotion.— **Will Anderson**

As the middle-aged and elders tell it in "Looking Both Ways,[5]" a publication on Alutiiq heritage and identity, before the Alaska Native Claims Settlement Act (ANCSA) of 1971, many people in the Kodiak area did not acknowledge their Alutiiq heritage. Some actively "passed" as white or called themselves Russian.

That began to change when the land settlement in 1971 required that people register as shareholders in the new corporations. ANCSA was a monumental settlement of aboriginal land claims to all of Alaska. In exchange for the natives' agreeing to extinguish those claims, the federal and state governments agreed to a settlement in which land and money were divided among regional and village corporations. To qualify as a shareholder in the native corporations, one had to be one-quarter native.

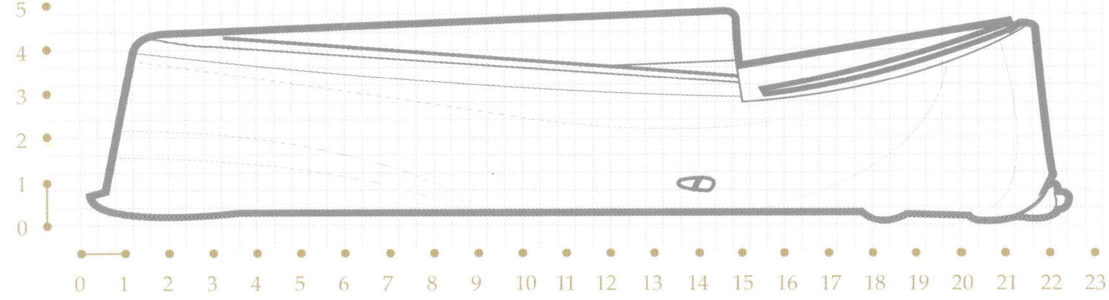

Igyuyrtulik
"Searcher"

H. 57 cm;
W. 22.5 cm;
D. 12.5 cm.

H. 22.44 in;
W. 8.86 in;
D. 4.92 in.

Spruce, paint

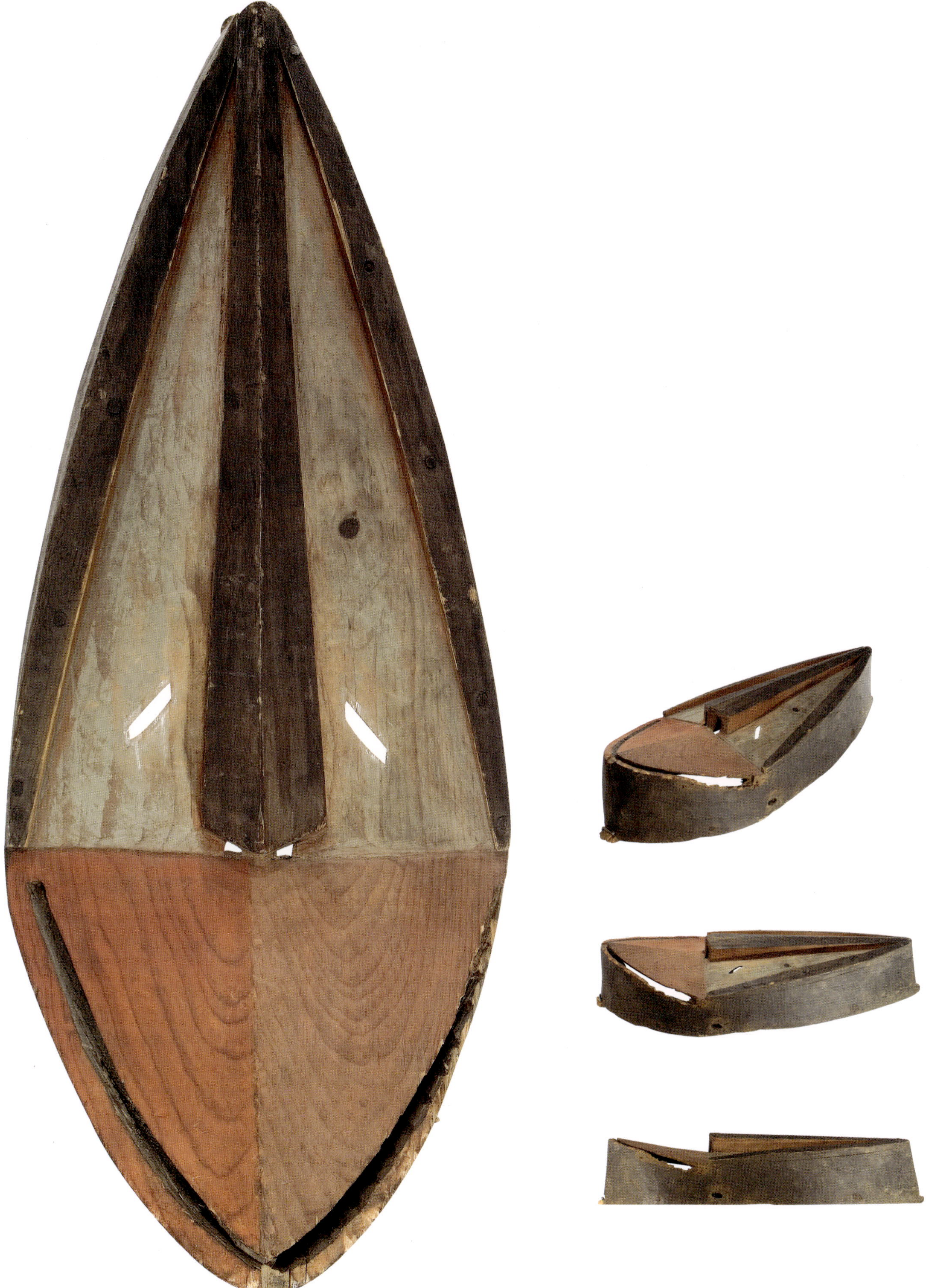

Lurtusqaq
"Wide One"

H. 54 cm;
W. 44 cm;
D. 16 cm.

H. 21.26 in;
W. 17.32 in;
D. 6.3 in.

Spruce, remnants of paint, tendons, iron

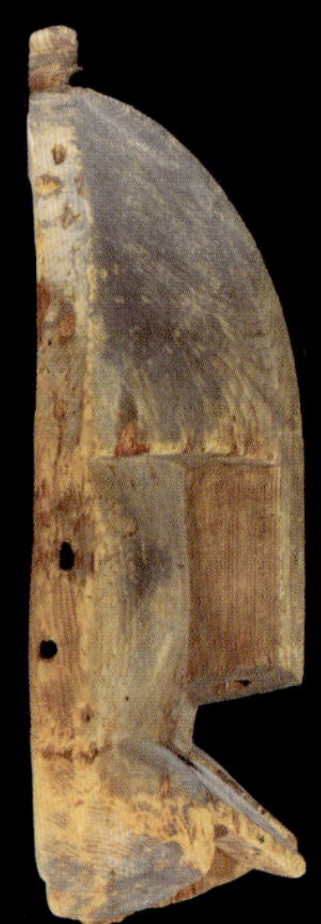

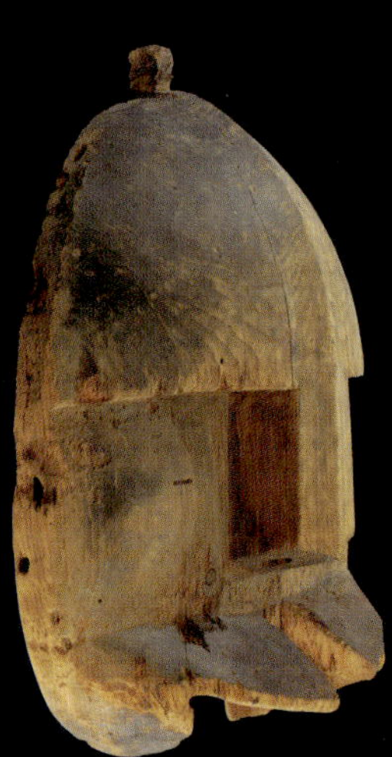

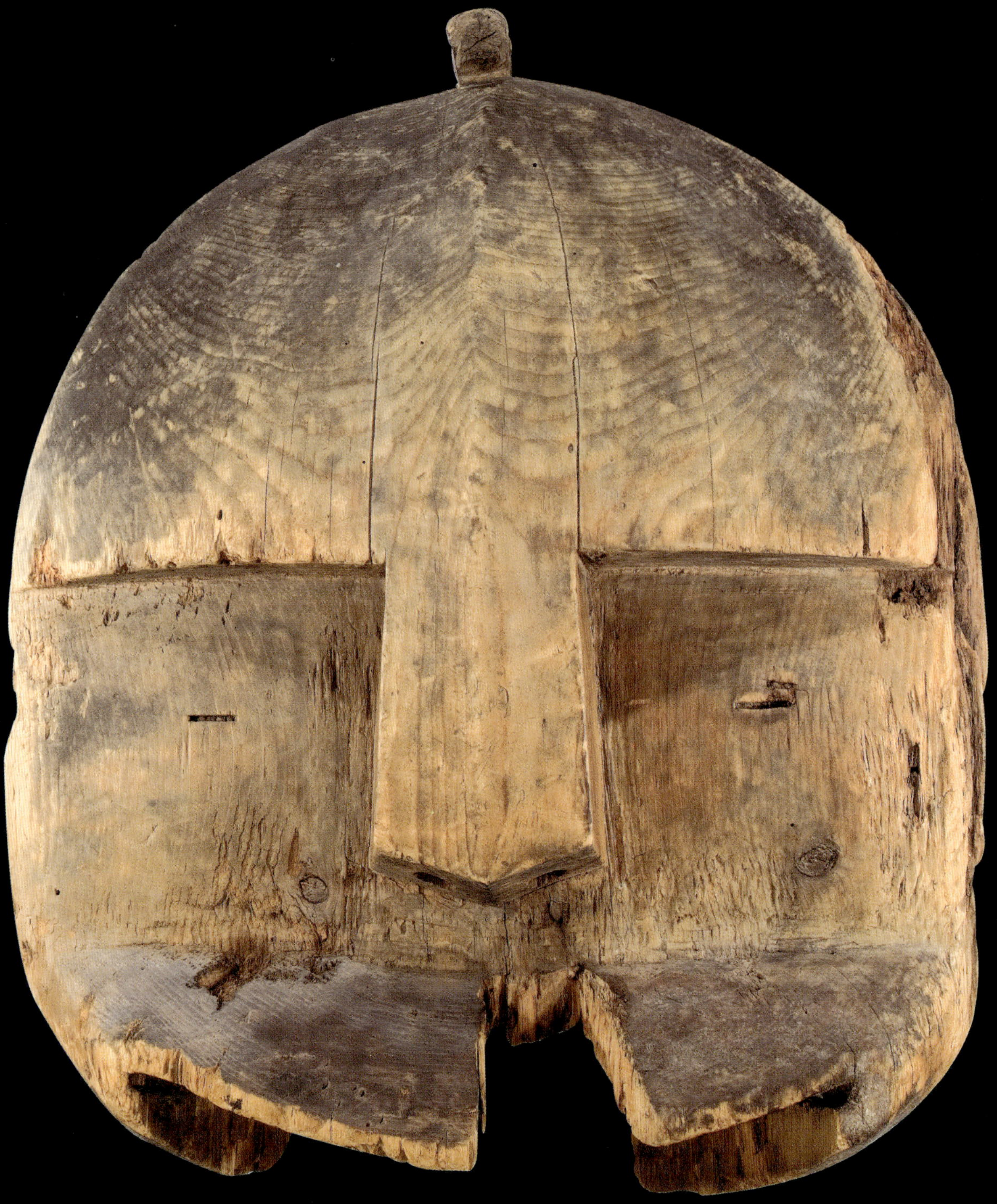

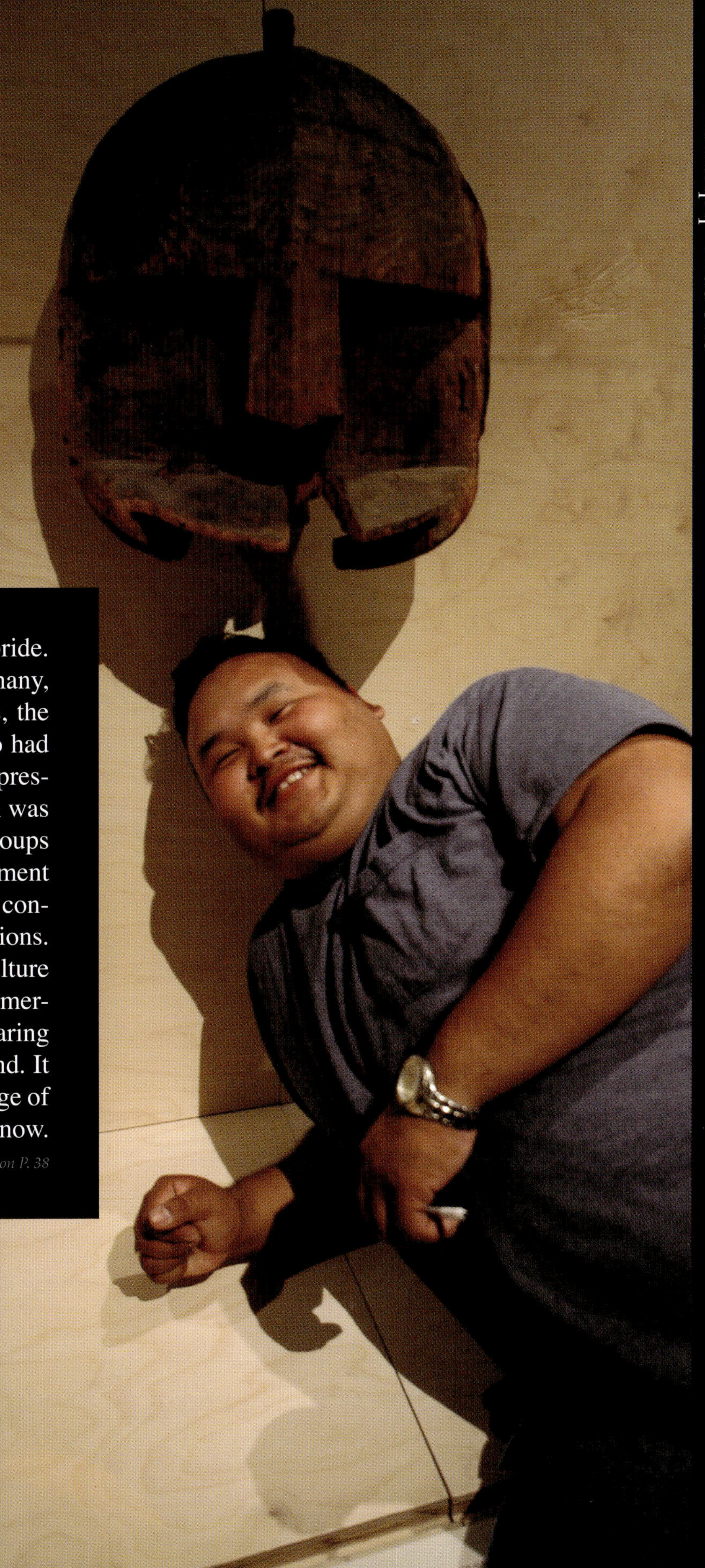

One's native heritage became a source of pride. But what did it mean exactly? For many, the old ways – the language, the rituals, the beliefs and traditions – seemed lost to those who had chosen to identify themselves as Russian. The suppression of traditional beliefs and knowledge of them was by no means universal among the various native groups across Alaska. In regions where Western encroachment had been more recent or less extensive natives continued to pass on their old ways to new generations.

But in the Kodiak area, where traditional culture had been profoundly dominated for so long the re-emergence of cultural identity has been a flowering of sharing and rediscovery for all the people across the island. It has been a reawakening – the expanding knowledge of who the Alutiiq people were enriches who they are now.

Continued on P. 38

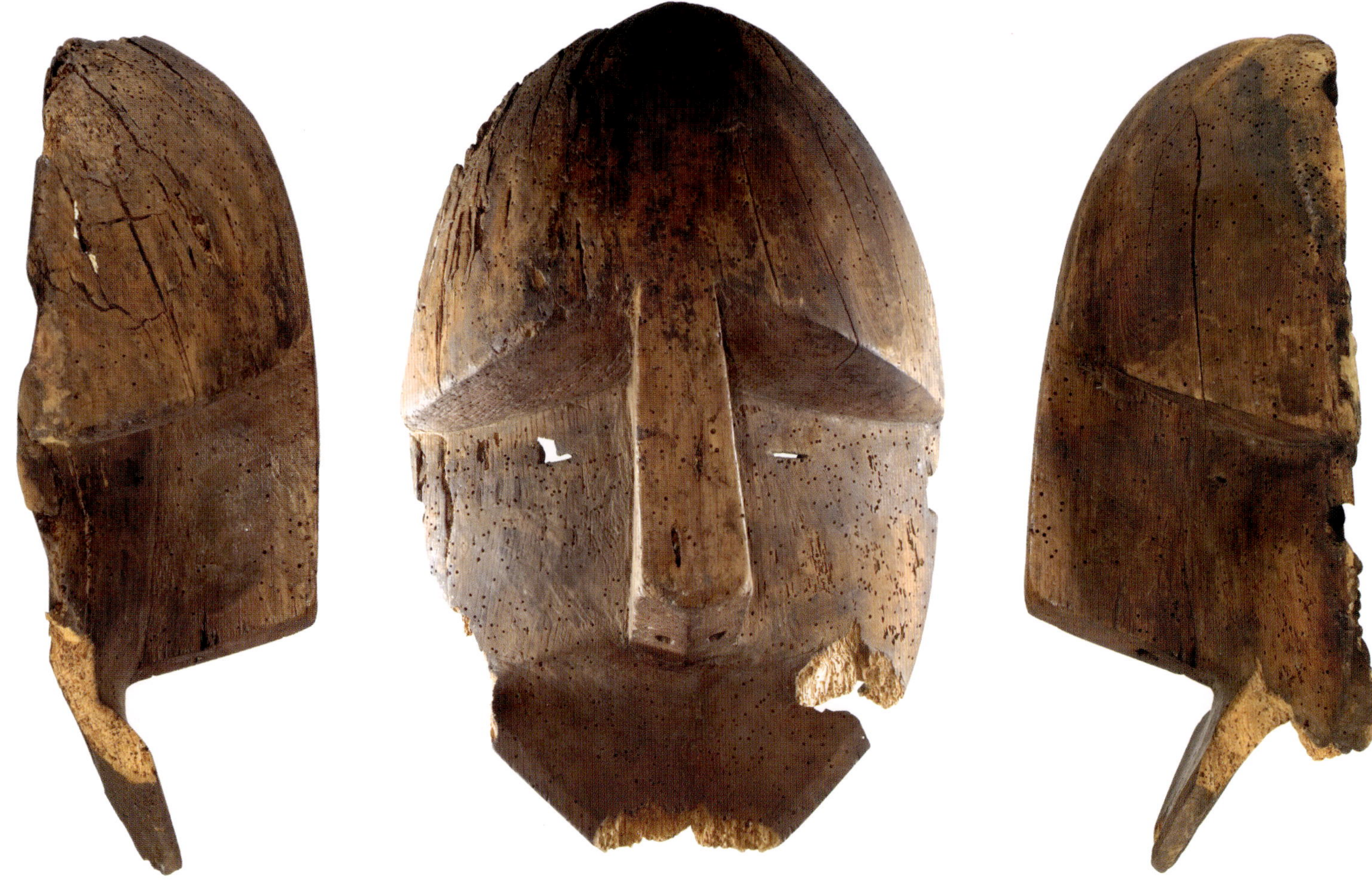

These masks were made for festivals and had songs and stories tied to them that we can never fully understand. We will never hear the melodies or the way the songs were sung, what they really mean.
— Lena Amason

Qup'arngasqamek Qanlek
"Broken Mouth"

H. 54 cm;
W. 29.5 cm;
D. 10.5 cm.

H. 21.25 in;
W. 11.6 in;
D. 4.13 in.

Spruce

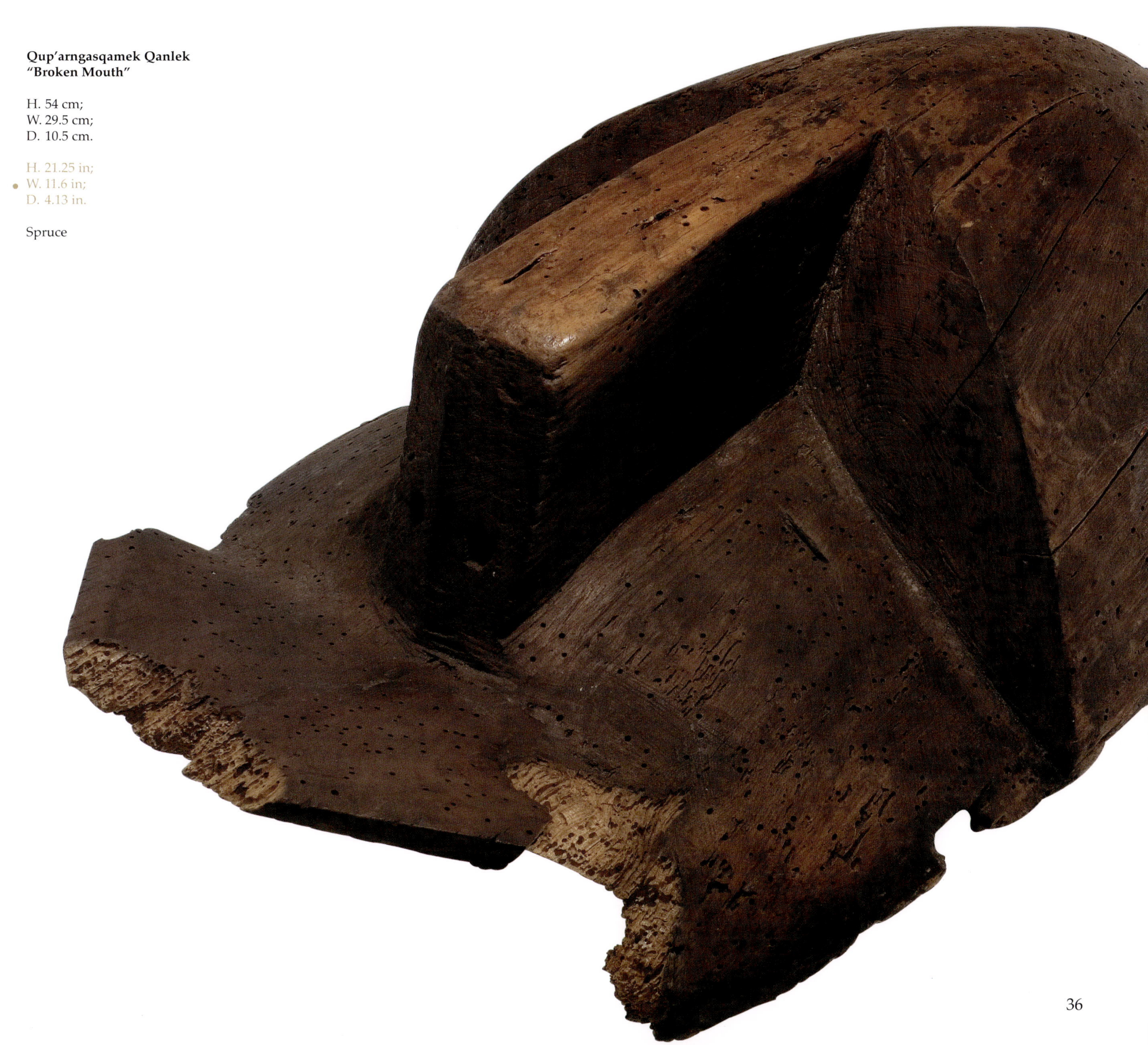

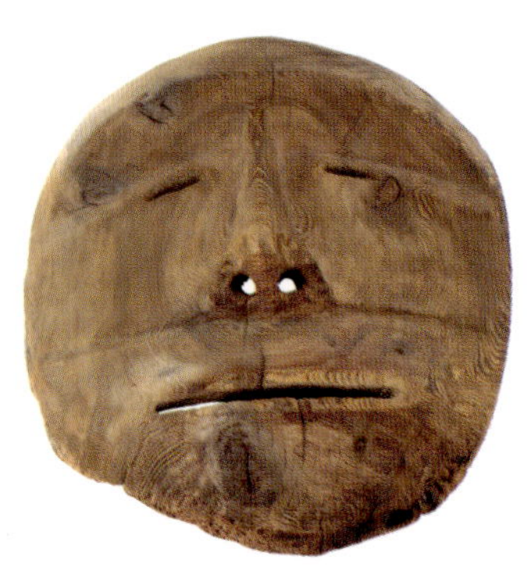

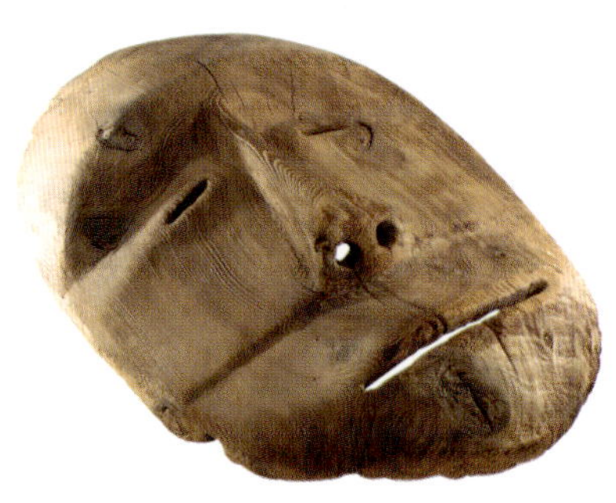

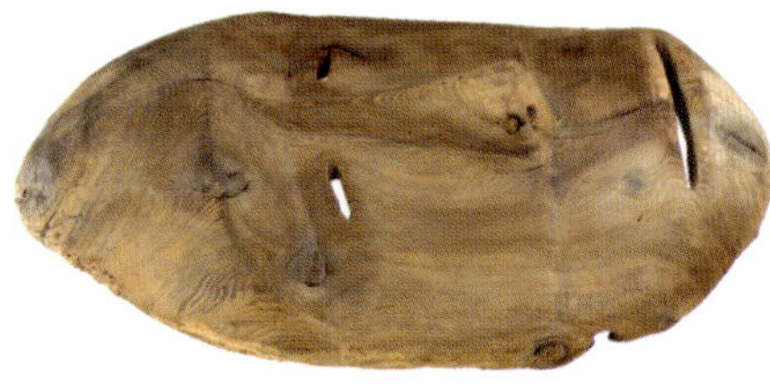

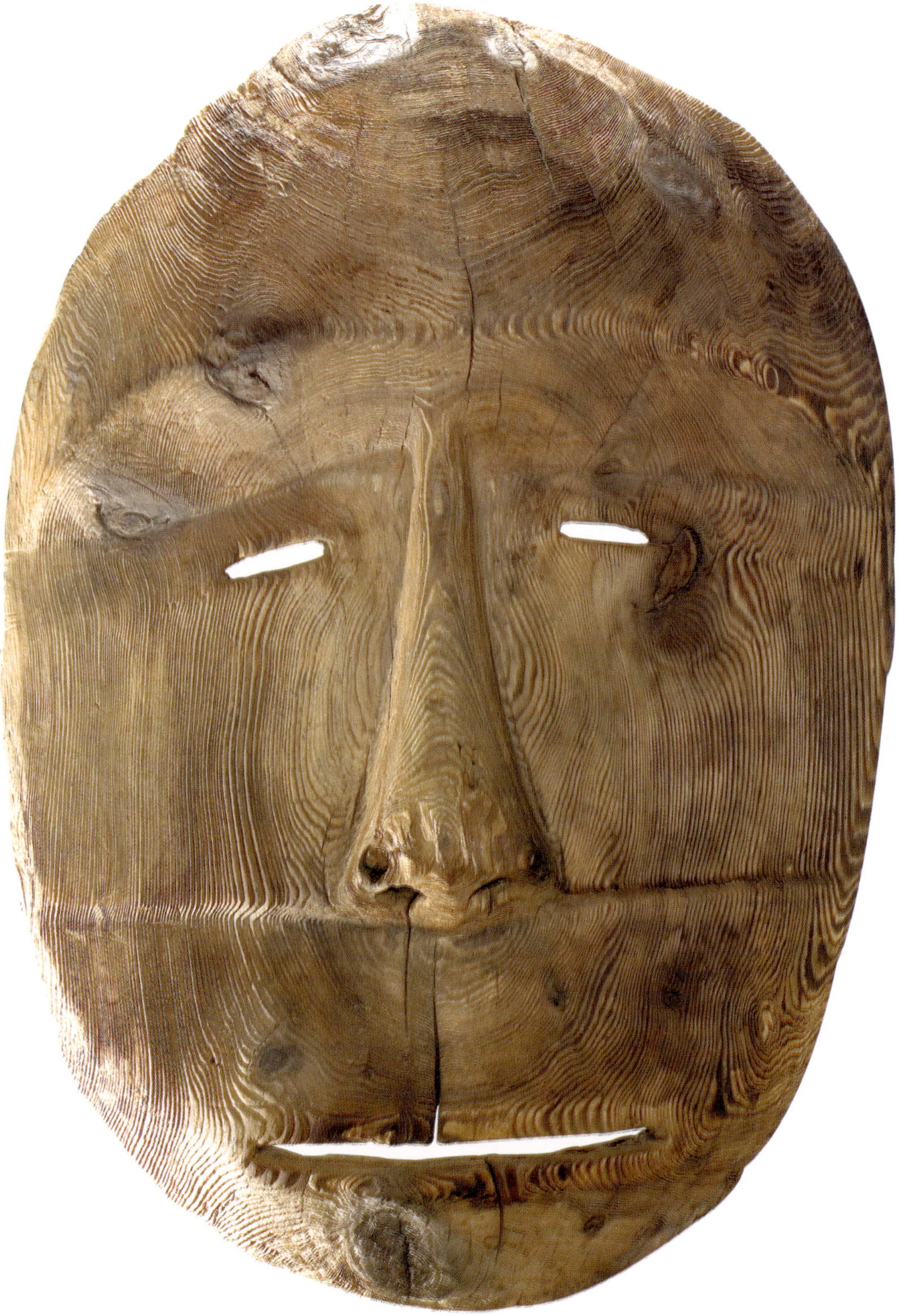

Putumasqaq
"Pouting One"

H. 38 cm;
W. 25.5 cm;
D. 8 cm.

H. 14.96 in;
W. 10.04 in;
D. 3.15 in.

Spruce, remnants of paint

Had Alphonse Pinart not collected the Alutiiq masks, along with other artifacts, they likely would have been lost altogether. Because he took them back to France, the collection survived. Boulogne-sur-Mer was ravaged during World War II; most of the town was destroyed. Museum staff and city officials moved all of the museum's collections four times for safekeeping. Continued on P. 44

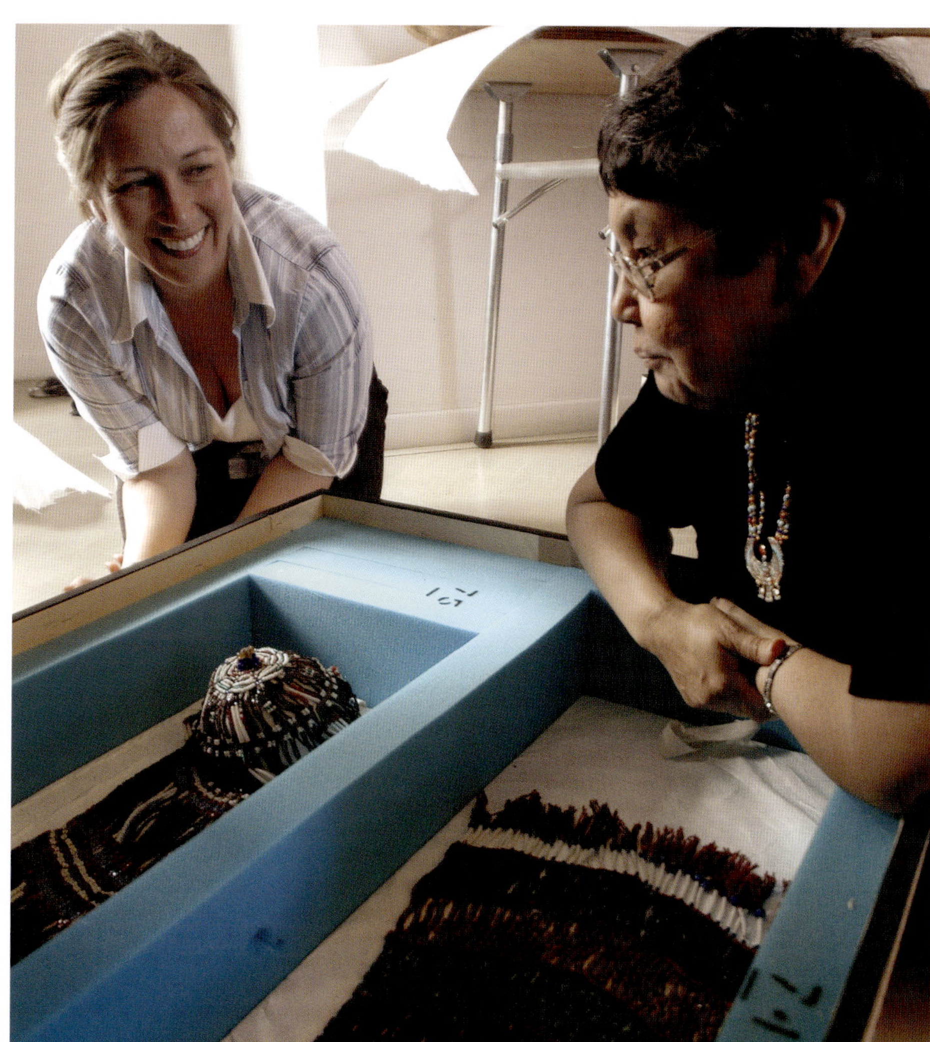

Coral Chernoff and Helen Simeonoff admire headdresses

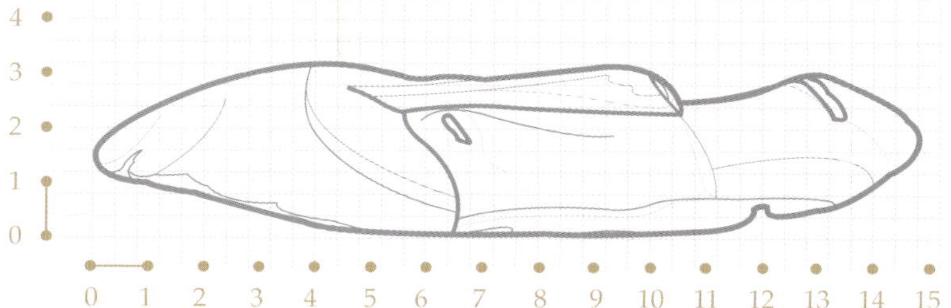

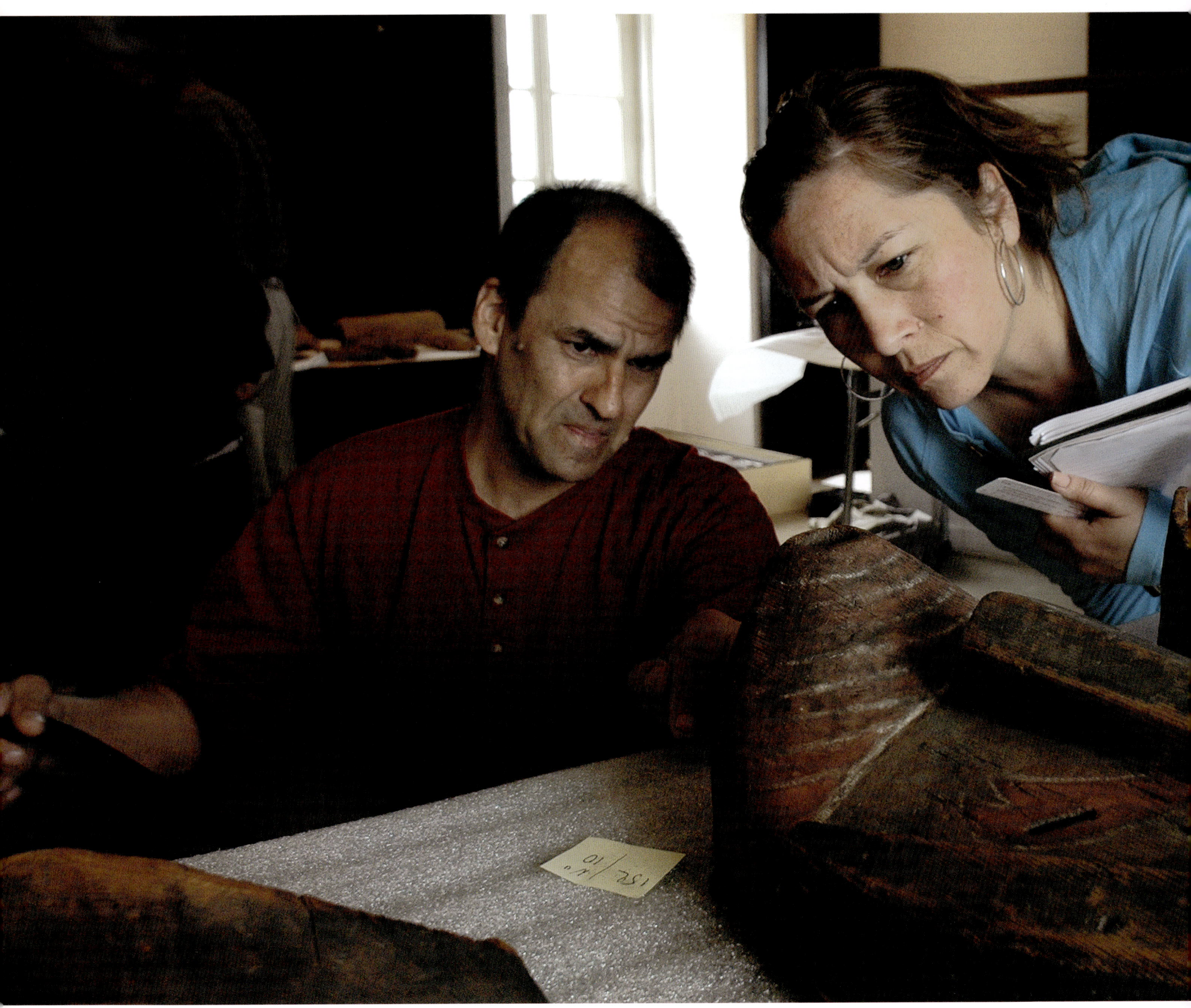

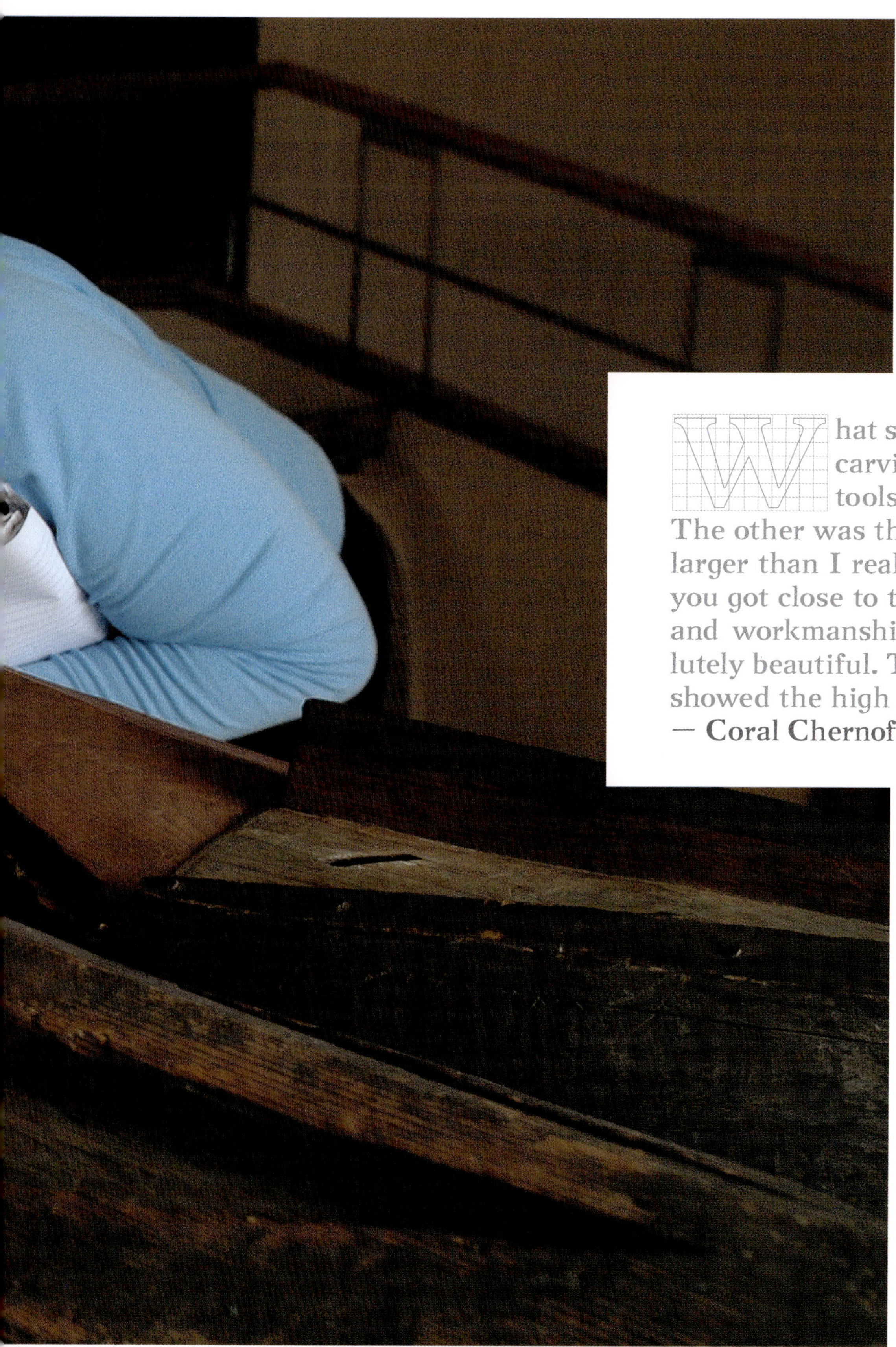

What struck me most was the mastery of the art, the carvings themselves, knowing they had primitive tools, and they still made these beautiful masks. The other was the sheer size of the masks — they were much larger than I realized. The size was amazing, and then when you got close to them, the mastery in the carvings, the details and workmanship put into each mask. They were so absolutely beautiful. The Alutiiq pieces I had seen until then never showed the high level of artistry. It still leaves me speechless.
— **Coral Chernoff**

Gary Knagin and Coral Chernoff

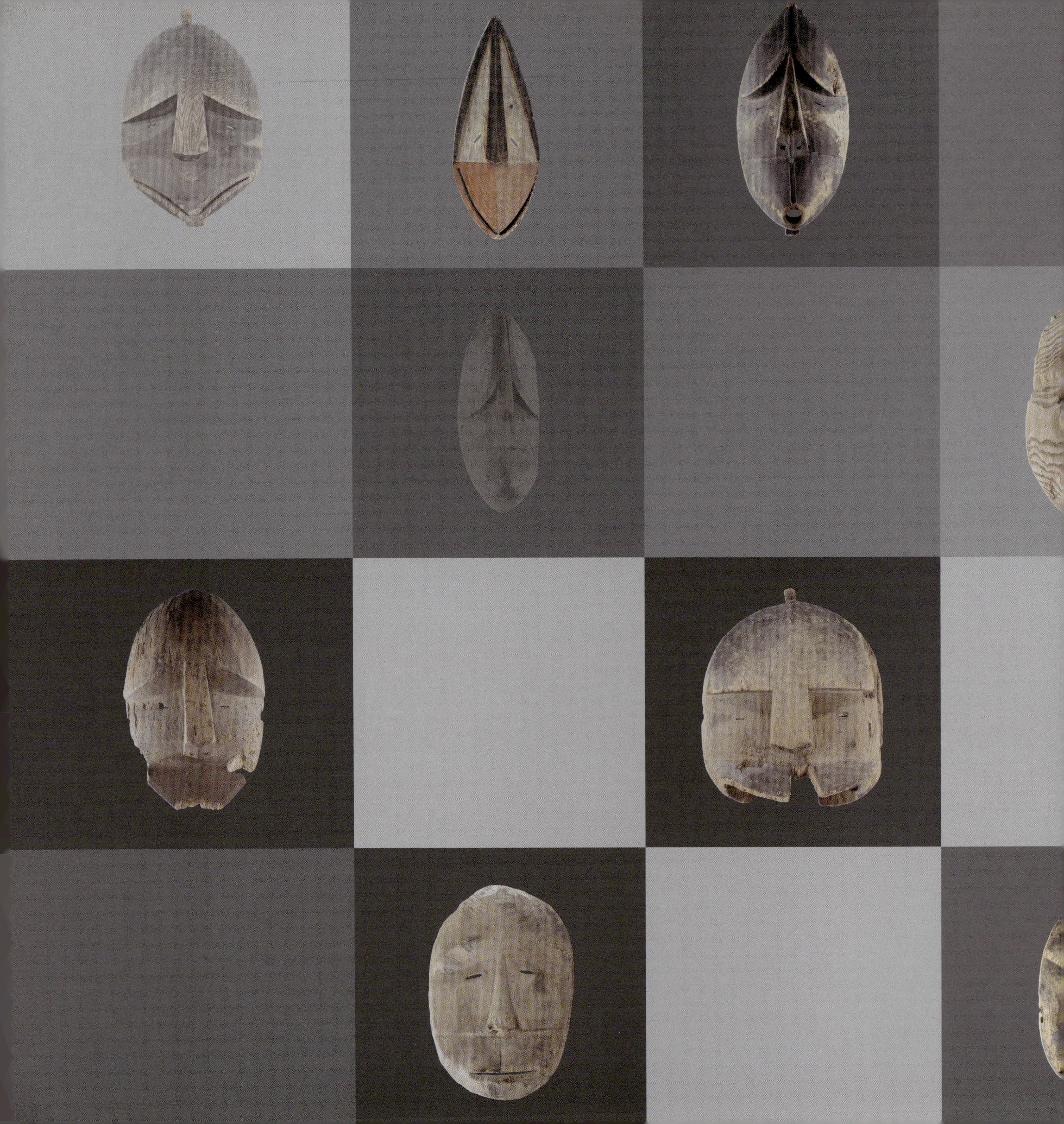

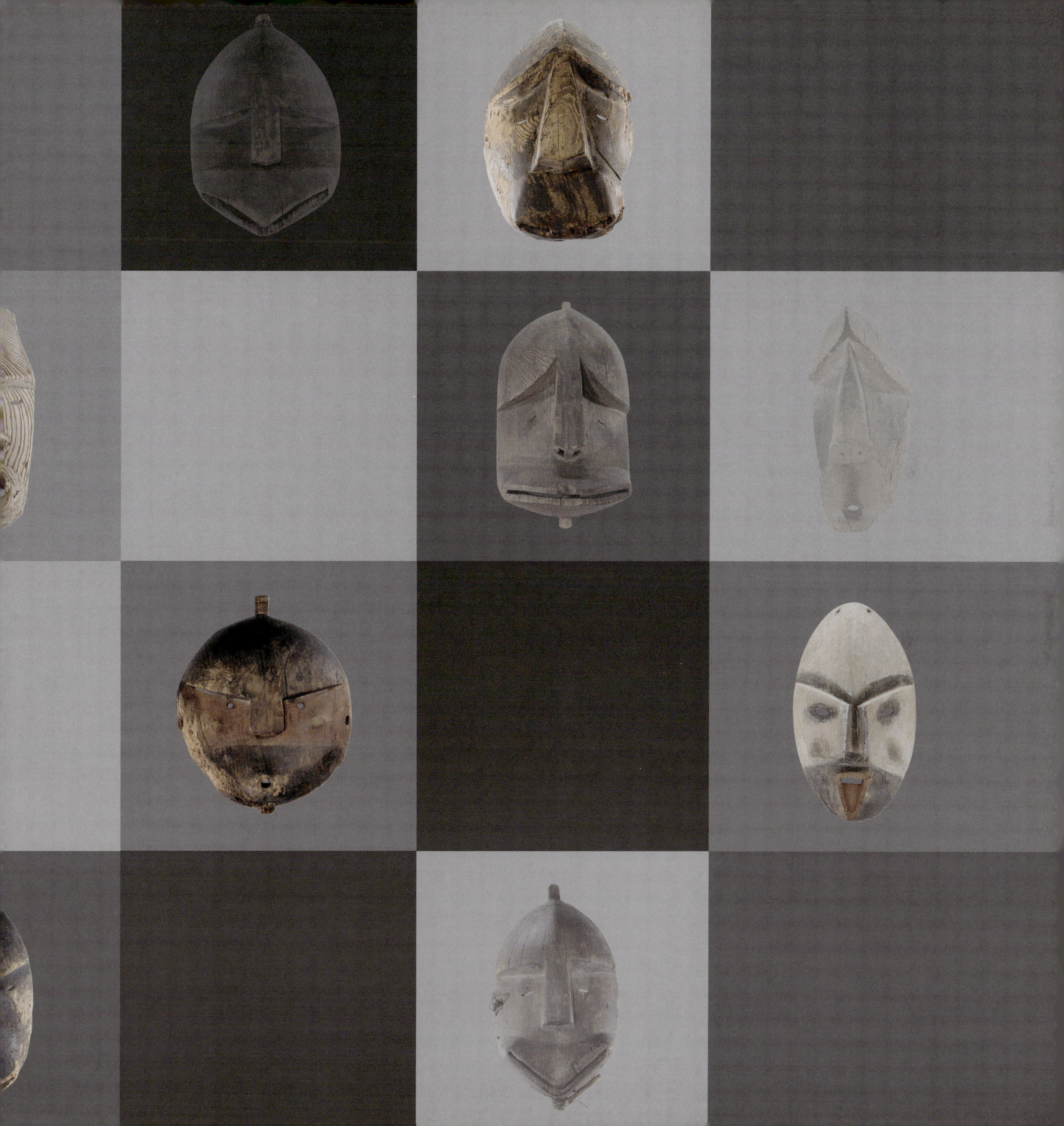

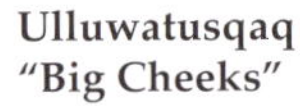

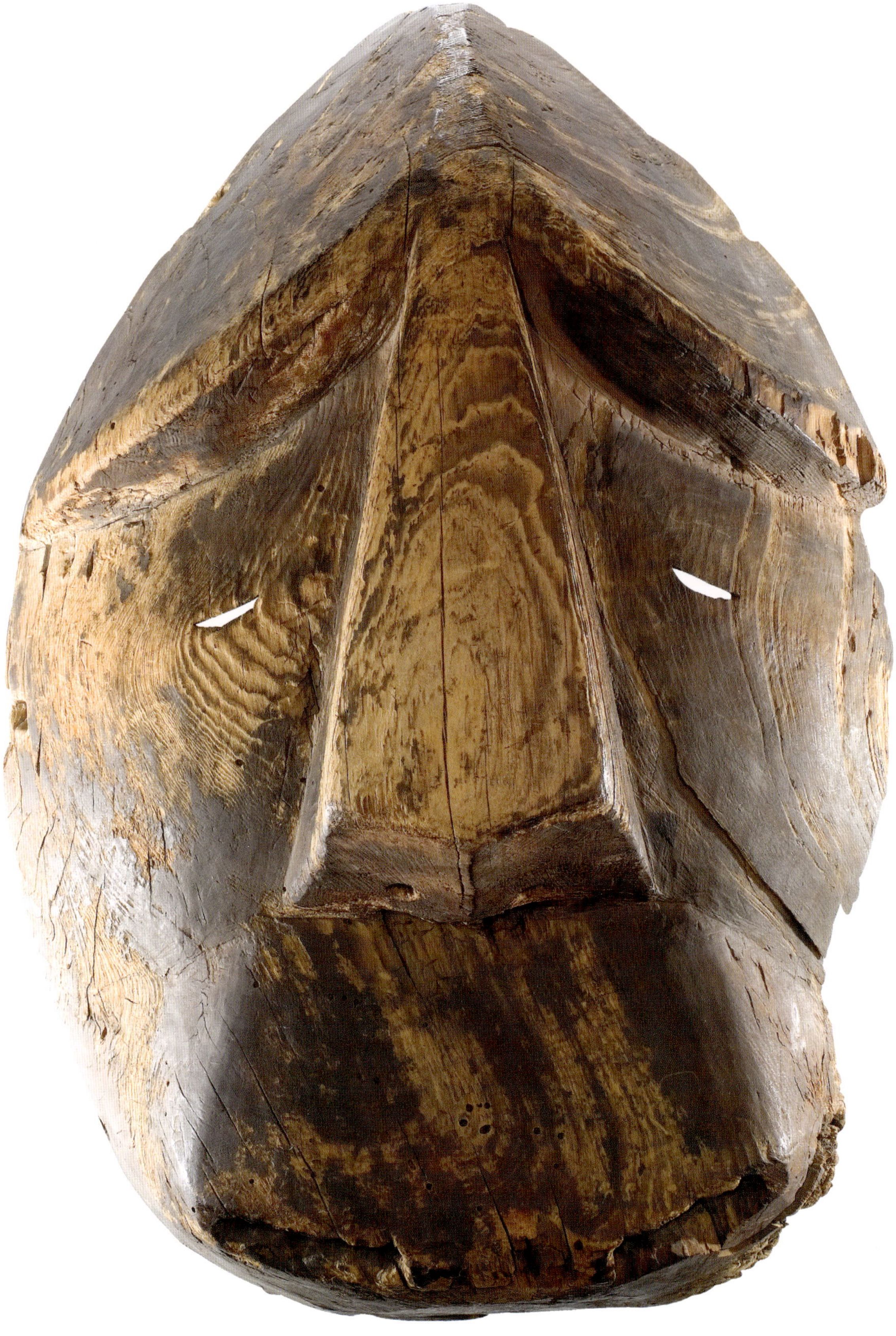

Ulluwatusqaq
"Big Cheeks"

H. 36 cm;
W. 25 cm;
D. 14 cm.

H. 14.17 in;
W. 9.84 in;
D. 5.15 in.

Spruce, remnants of paint

Perry Eaton was about 14 when he first heard about masks. It was 1958, he was in Kodiak fishing with his father, Hank, but the fishing was terrible. As Eaton relates it:

Charlie Christofferson was saying he'd heard that in an effort to improve the fishing, "them guys in Karluk had done an Aleut dance that week." "Wow, I didn't think they did that anymore," Hank responded. "Yes," Charlie said. "They paint their faces with soot and jump around to drumming. You know, in the old days they used to wear masks and everything." At this point, an elderly woman, Mrs. Heitman, joins the conversation. "That mask stuff all ended, and they took all the masks away," she said. "They are all gone, there are none left on Kodiak. They took them all away."

Eaton now believes that Mrs. Heitman had heard stories from her father about Pinart collecting the masks. The implication was not that Pinart had stolen the masks, but that he had done a good thing by taking them away.

Continued on P. 48

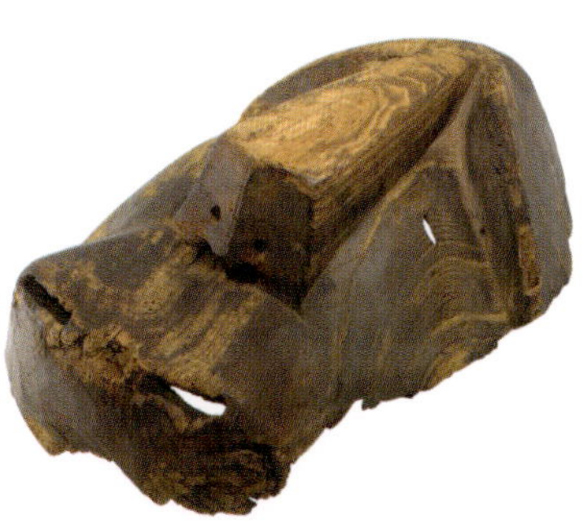

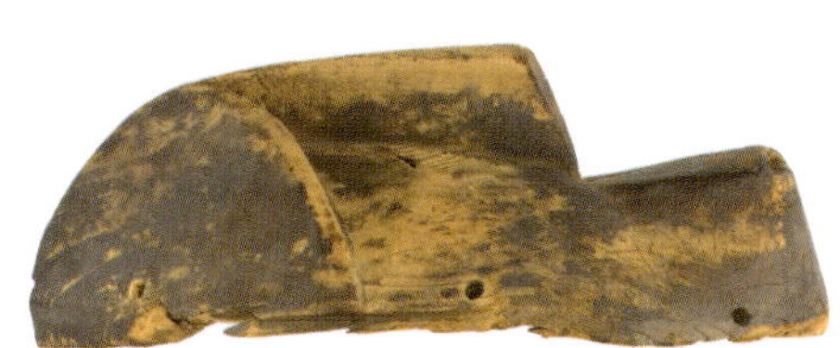

Giinasinaq
"Big Face"

H. 60 cm;
W. 33 cm;
D. 20 cm.

H. 23.62 in;
W. 12.99 in;
D. 7.87 in.

Spruce, remnants of paint, leather

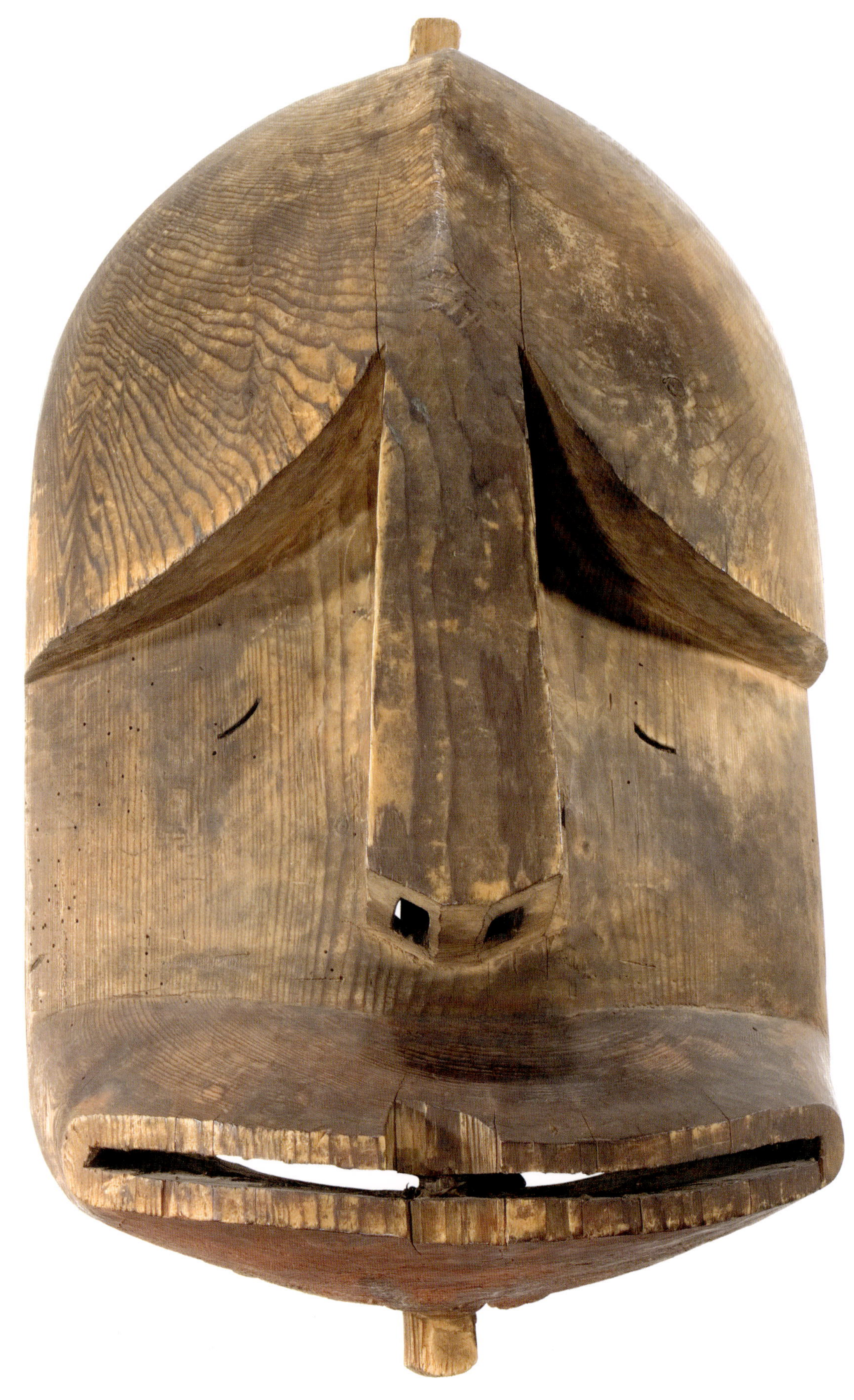

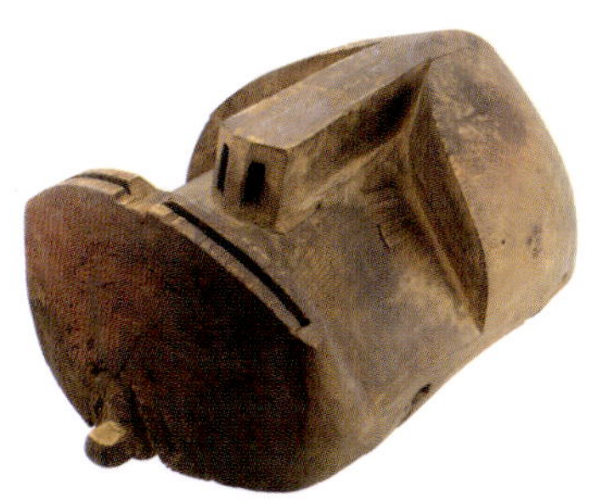

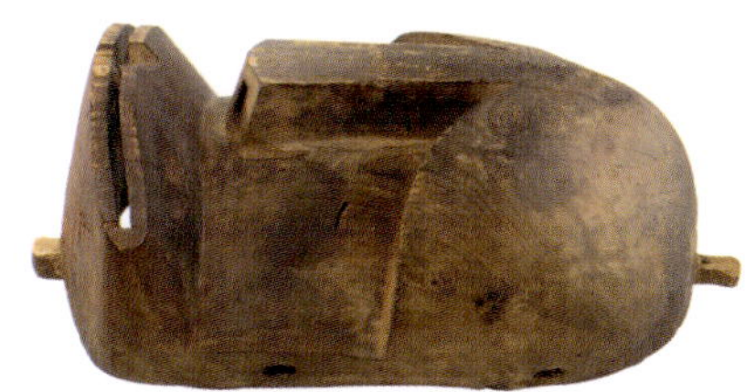

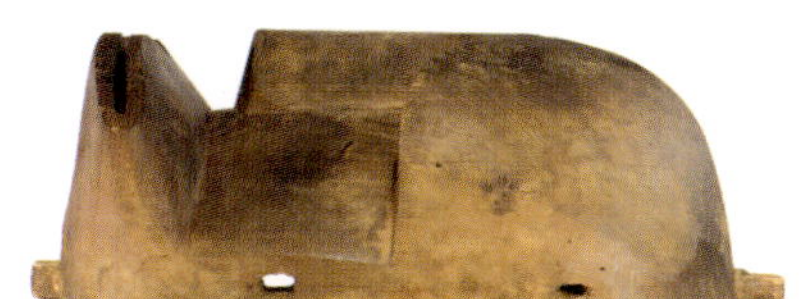

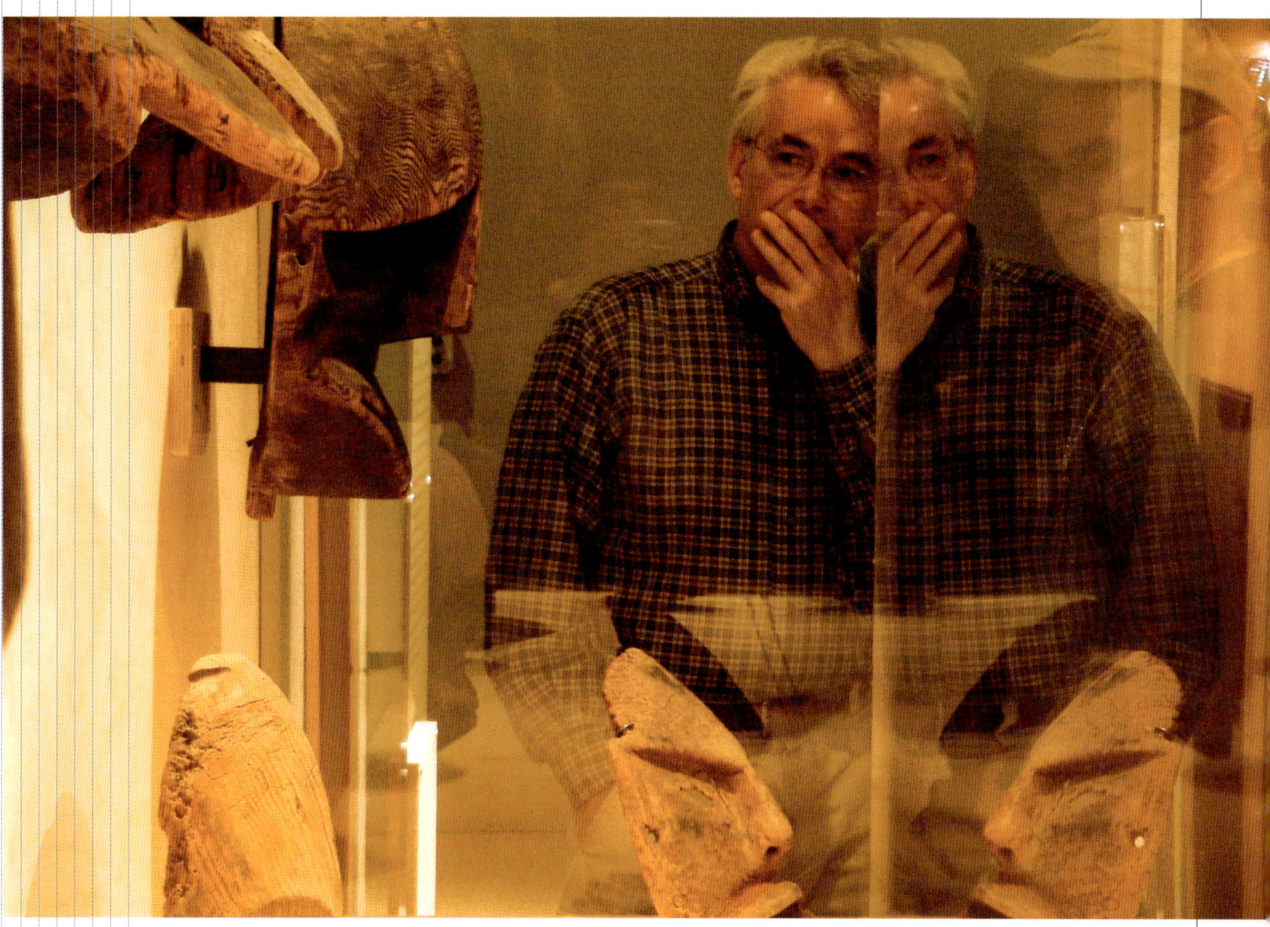

Perry Eaton

The masks have a life unto themselves. When you are in their presence, you are linked to the lands' people in ways that can't be explained in words. To me, the most valuable thing about this collection is that it shows us the shape and form — the attributes that define a Sugpiaq mask. No other single collection has this kind of substance.

— **Perry Eaton**

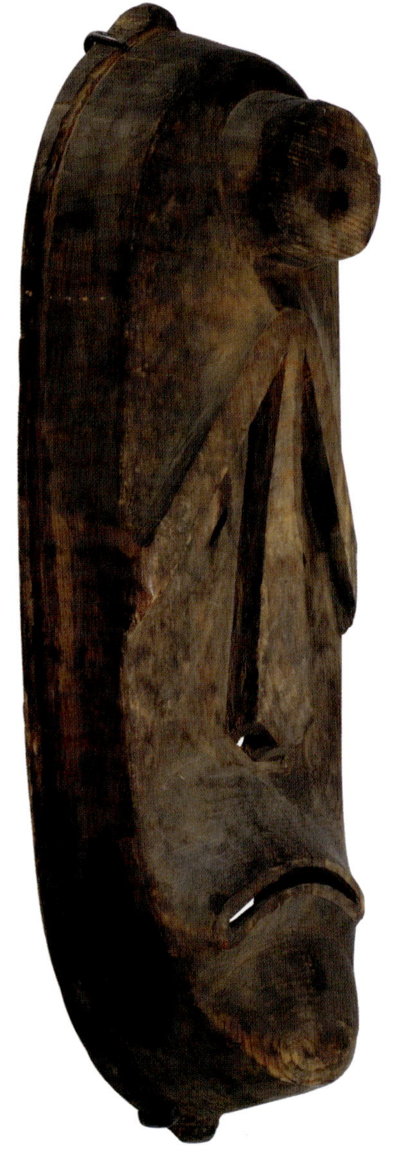

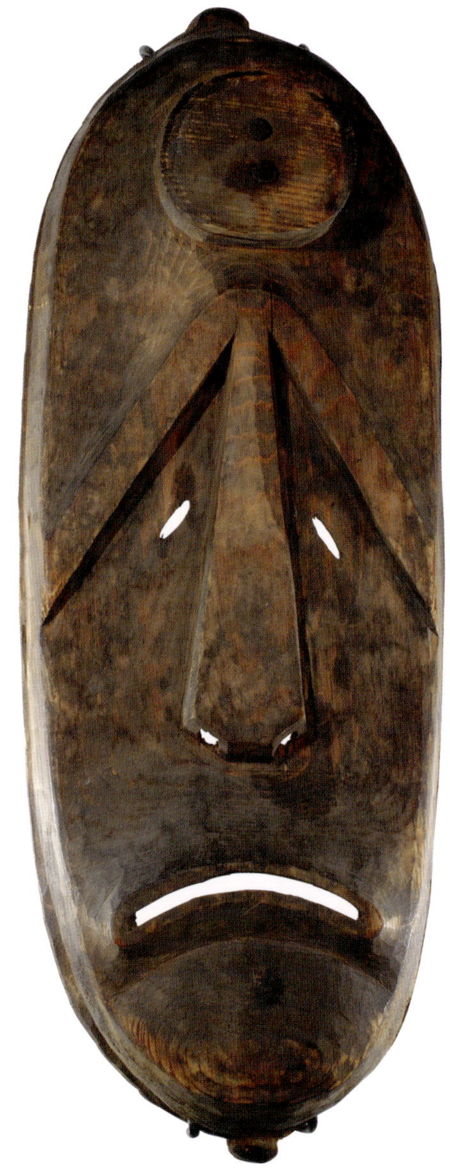

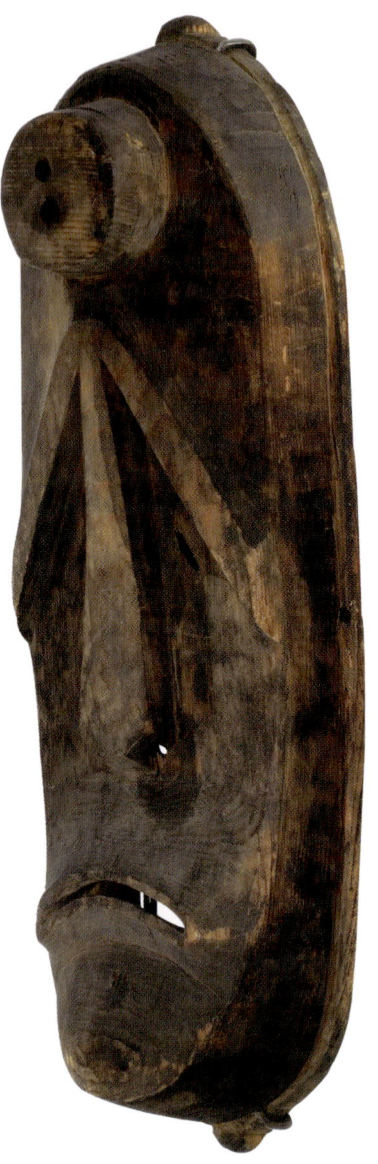

Angun Qiaculngusqaq
"Old Man Who Wants to Cry"

H. 49 cm;
W. 18 cm;
D. 10 cm.

H. 19.29 in;
W. 7.09 in;
D. 3.94 in.

Spruce, remnants of paint

In traditional Alutiiq culture, everything in nature had a spirit that could take different forms. Masks represented spirits; they were alive. Masks were used for a variety of purposes – to teach proper behavior, to recall mythical events, to remind the living of the departed, to reaffirm traditions and to reaffirm identity with a particular group.

Masks were essential to the practice of rituals, and rituals were part of everyday life. There were public masked rituals and private rituals. Since most masks were destroyed after use, masks still in existence were those collected by Europeans and Russians in the 19th century. [6]

Traditionally, Sugpiaq people believed that a mask held two spirits, one of the person or spirit being honored and one of the mask itself. The mask shared a story and represented part of it as a prop for a dance or play. It allowed the wearer and the observer to transcend time and space to experience another world.[7]

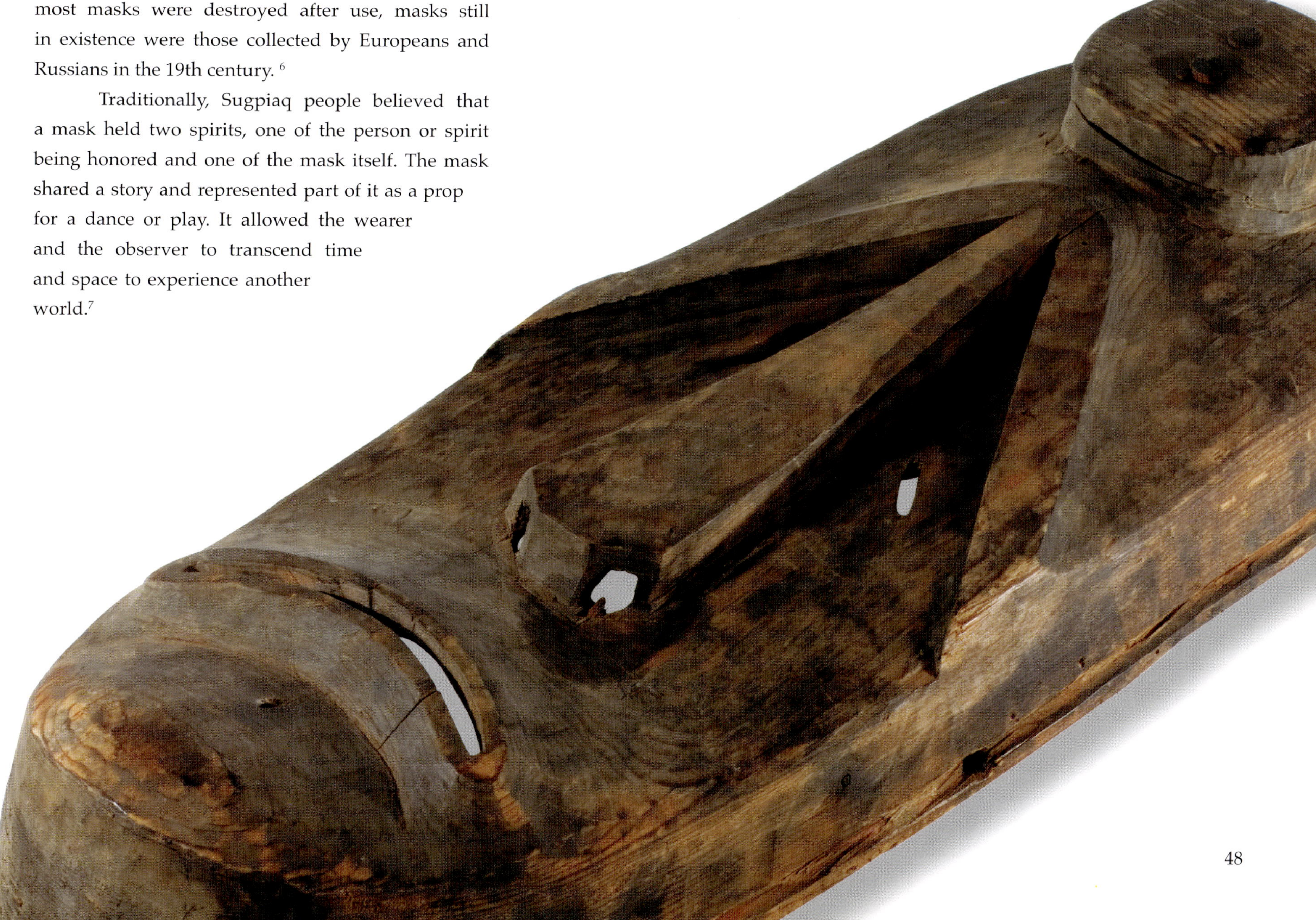

Alutiiq Pursuit Of A Kodiak Exhibition

The Pinart collection at the Château Musée appears to have attracted little attention, apart from a handful of anthropologists, between 1875 and 2000. Indeed, the Château Musée did not mount its first exhibition of Pinart pieces until 2002. Later the same year, the exhibition was taken to the Musée de l'Homme in Paris, marking the first time any part of the collection had left Boulogne.

In 2001, Sven Haakanson Jr. took the first of many trips in his quest to bring at least some of the masks to Kodiak from France. Haakanson knew of the Pinart collection from his student days at the University of Alaska Fairbanks in the late 1980s. Dr. Black had told him about the masks, which she knew from her own work on Alaska native history and culture in the Russian era. Haakanson had also seen a Desson presentation.

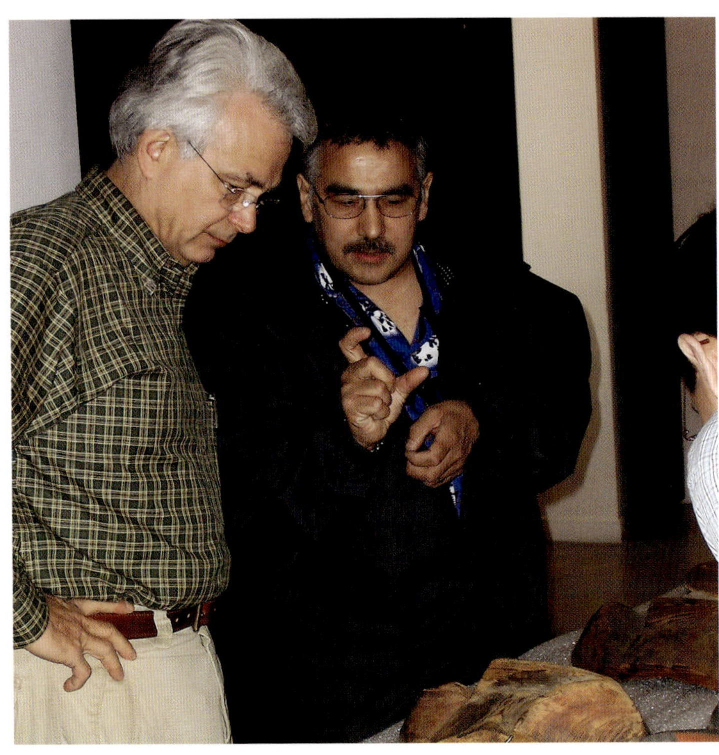

Perry Eaton and Alfred Naumoff

The design of all the masks was quite different. Distinct shapes. I did notice some similarities with Yup'ik and Chugach masks.
— Alfred Naumoff

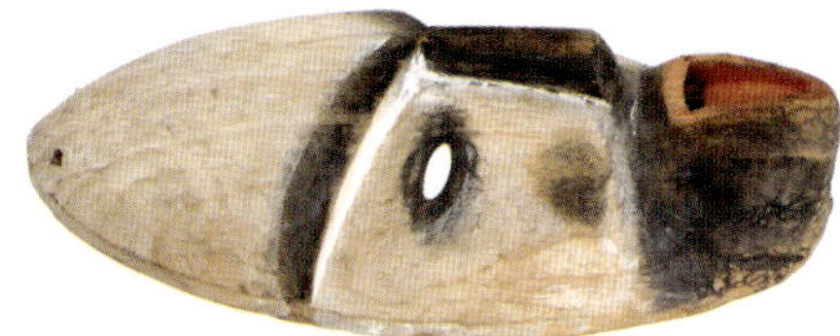

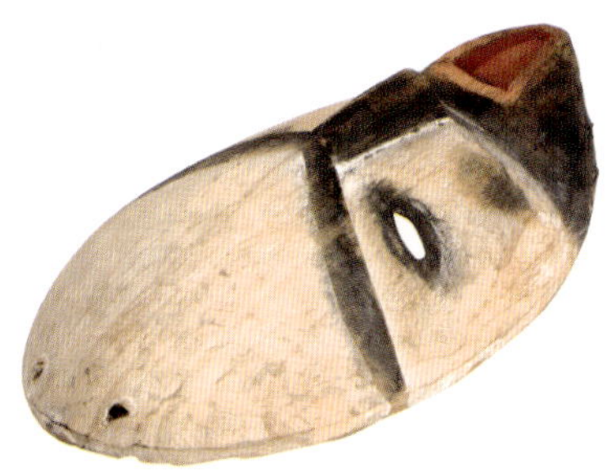

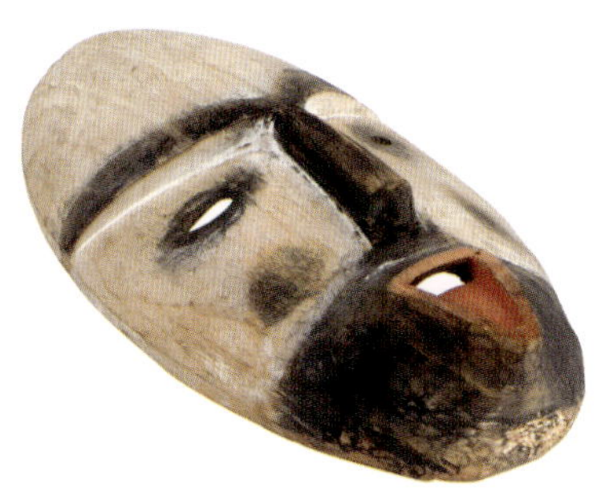

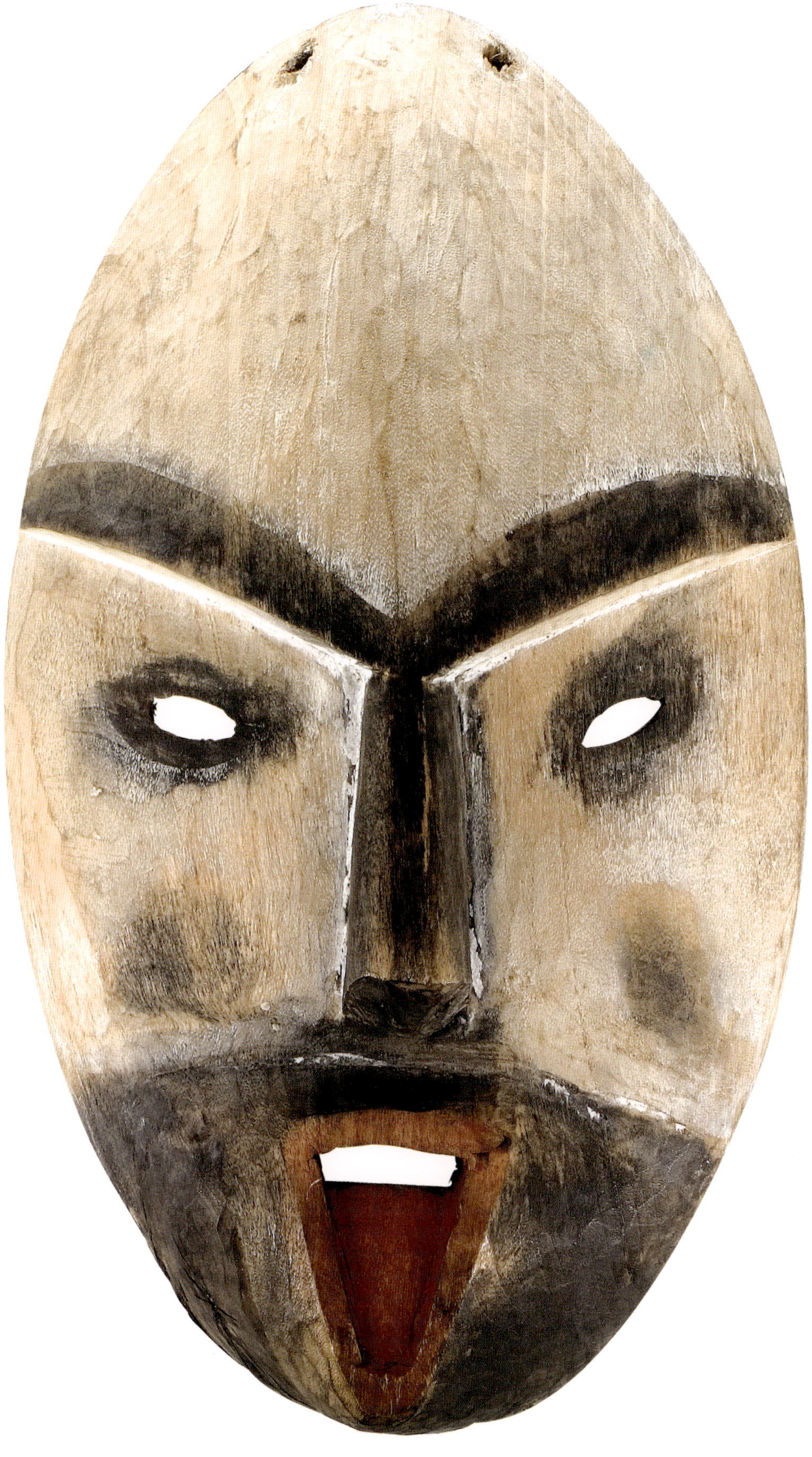

Angun
"Old Man"

H. 12 cm;
W. 12 cm;
D. 5.5 cm.

H. 4.72 in;
W. 4.72 in;
D. 2.17 in.

Cotton, paint

Payulik
"Bringer of Food"

H. 20 cm;
W. 14.4 cm;
D. 3 cm.

H. 8.07 in;
W. 5.71 in;
D. 1.18 in.

Cotton Wood, paint, seal leather

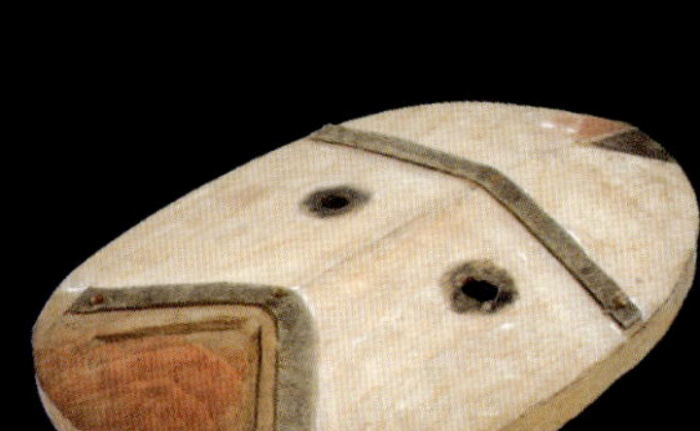

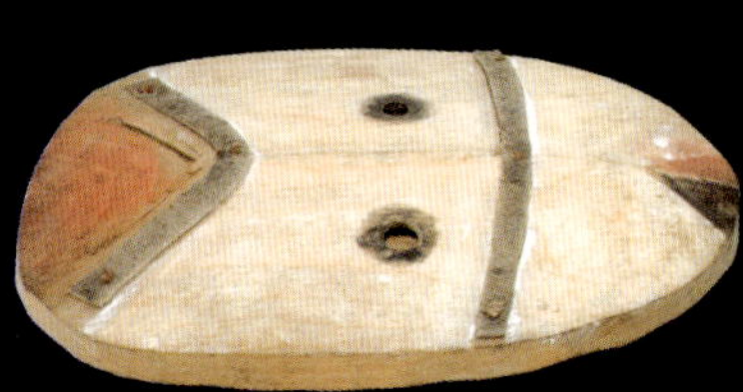

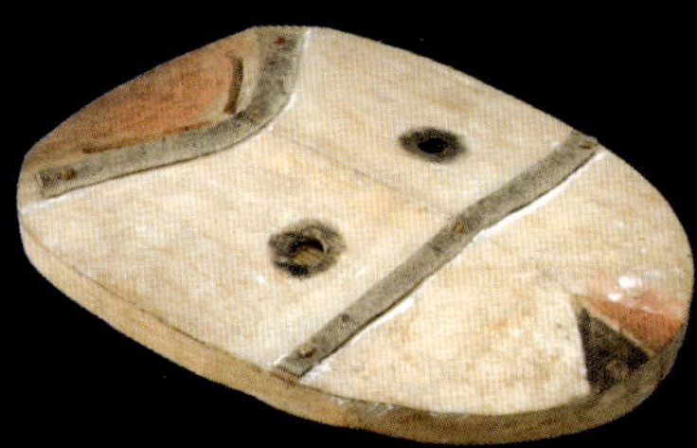

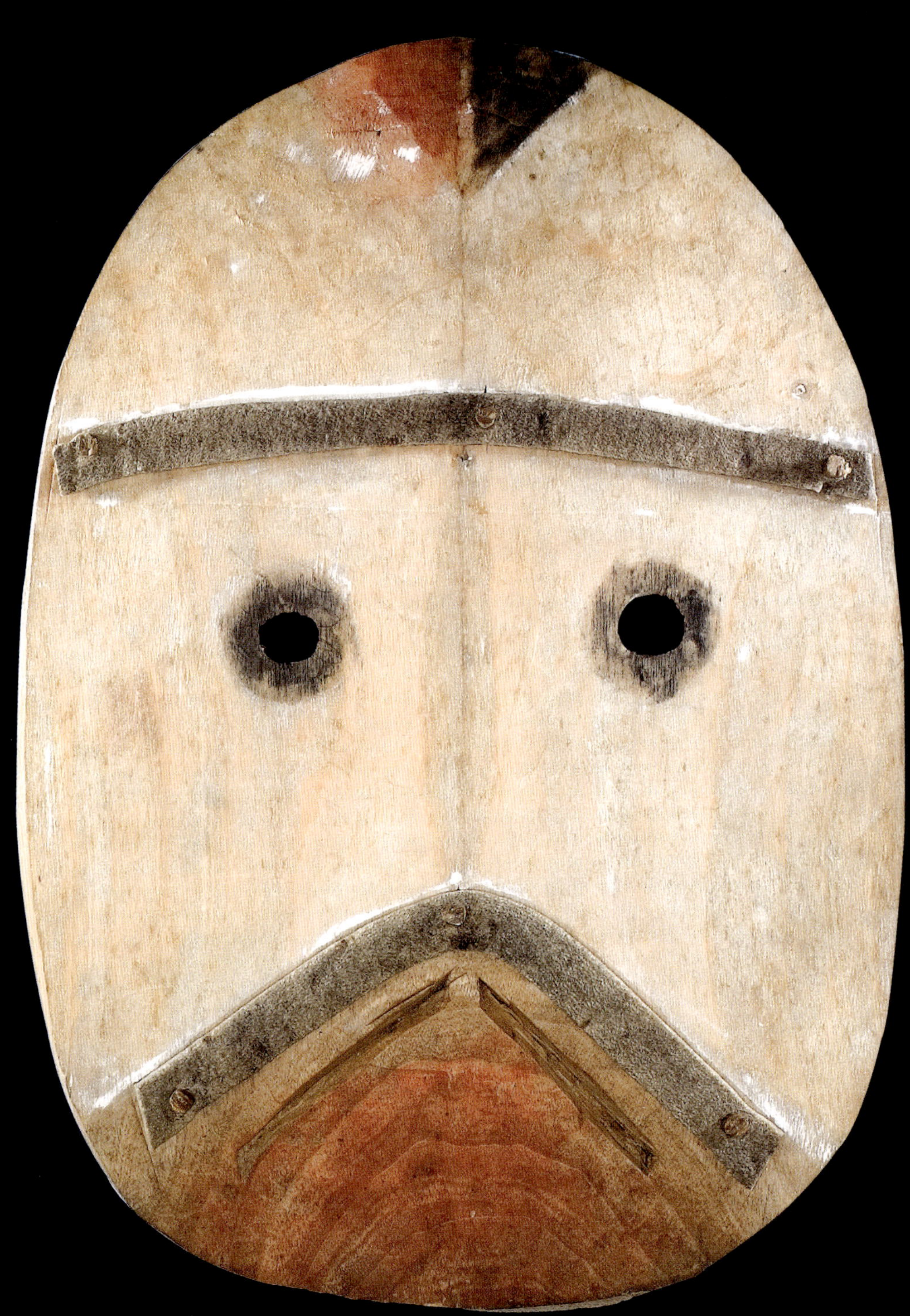

As executive director of the Alutiiq Museum and Archaeological Repository, Haakanson had the academic credentials to work with museum officials in their language. And while financial support has never come easy, Haakanson knew where to go and how to ask for assistance. There was a succession of trips to France by Haakanson, Eaton and others.

In 2002, Haakanson wrote an article for the Musée du Quai Branley catalogue and collaborated on its first-ever exhibition based on the Pinart masks. The exhibition was titled Kodiak, Alaska.

In celebration of this first national showing of the masks, the Alutiiq Museum developed Islanders, a special exhibition for the Château Musée. This exhibition included a contemporary photographic portrait of the Alutiiq people and a dance group led by Sperry Ash. In honor of the event, Eaton presented the Château Musée with a special mask he had made, and Ash presented two traditional Alutiiq dolls.

Continued on P. 58

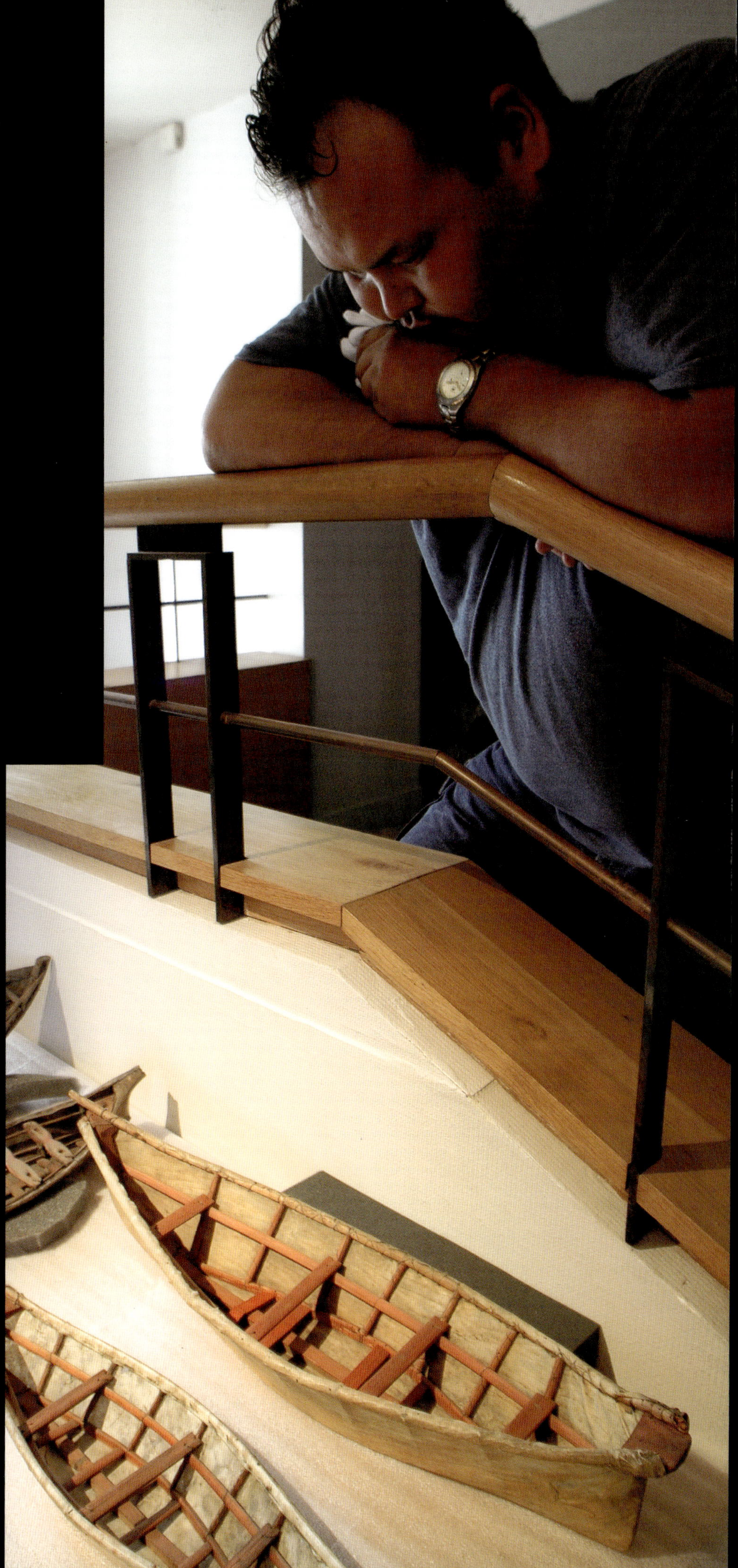

Speridon Simeonoff

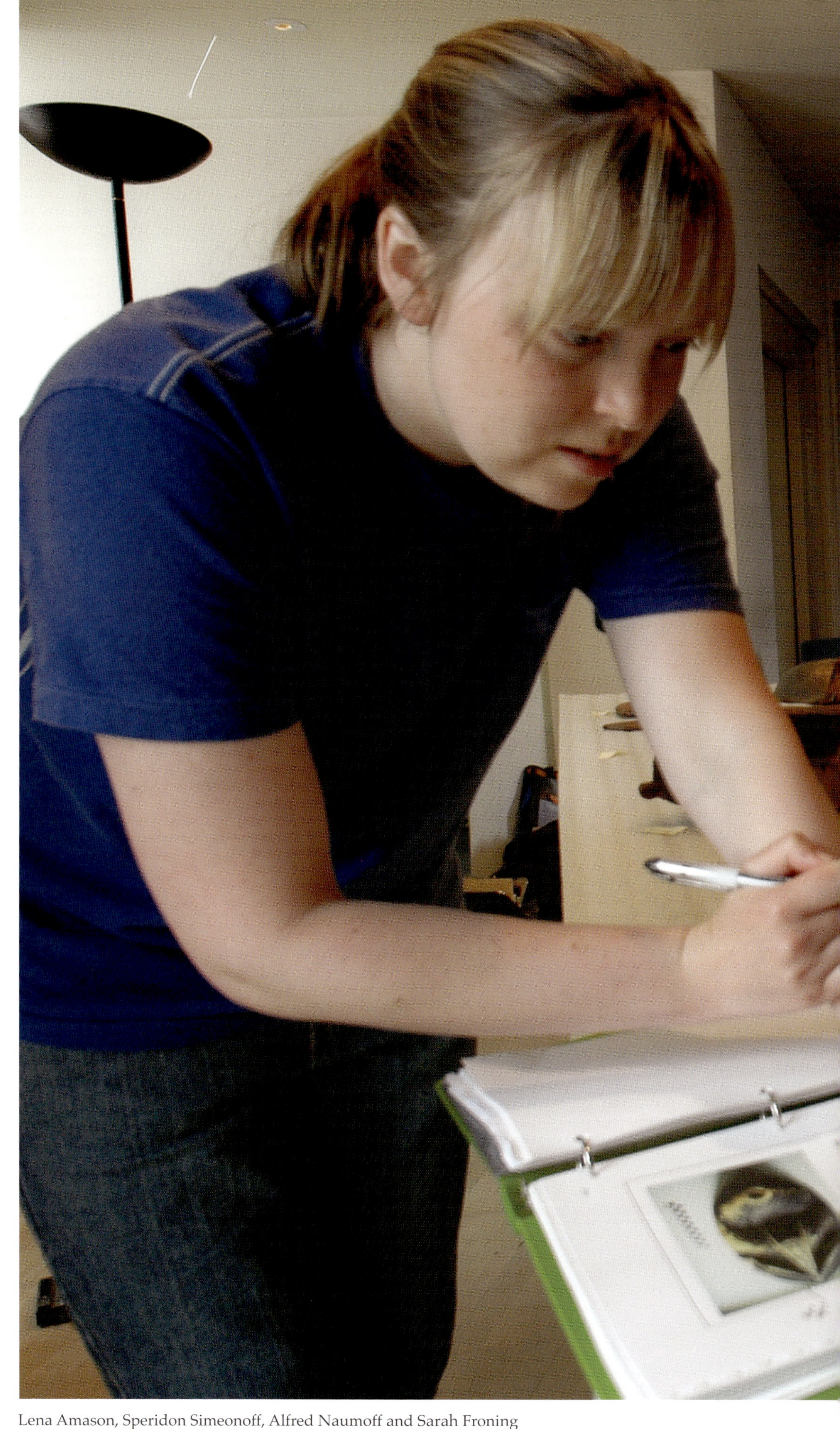

Lena Amason, Speridon Simeonoff, Alfred Naumoff and Sarah Froning

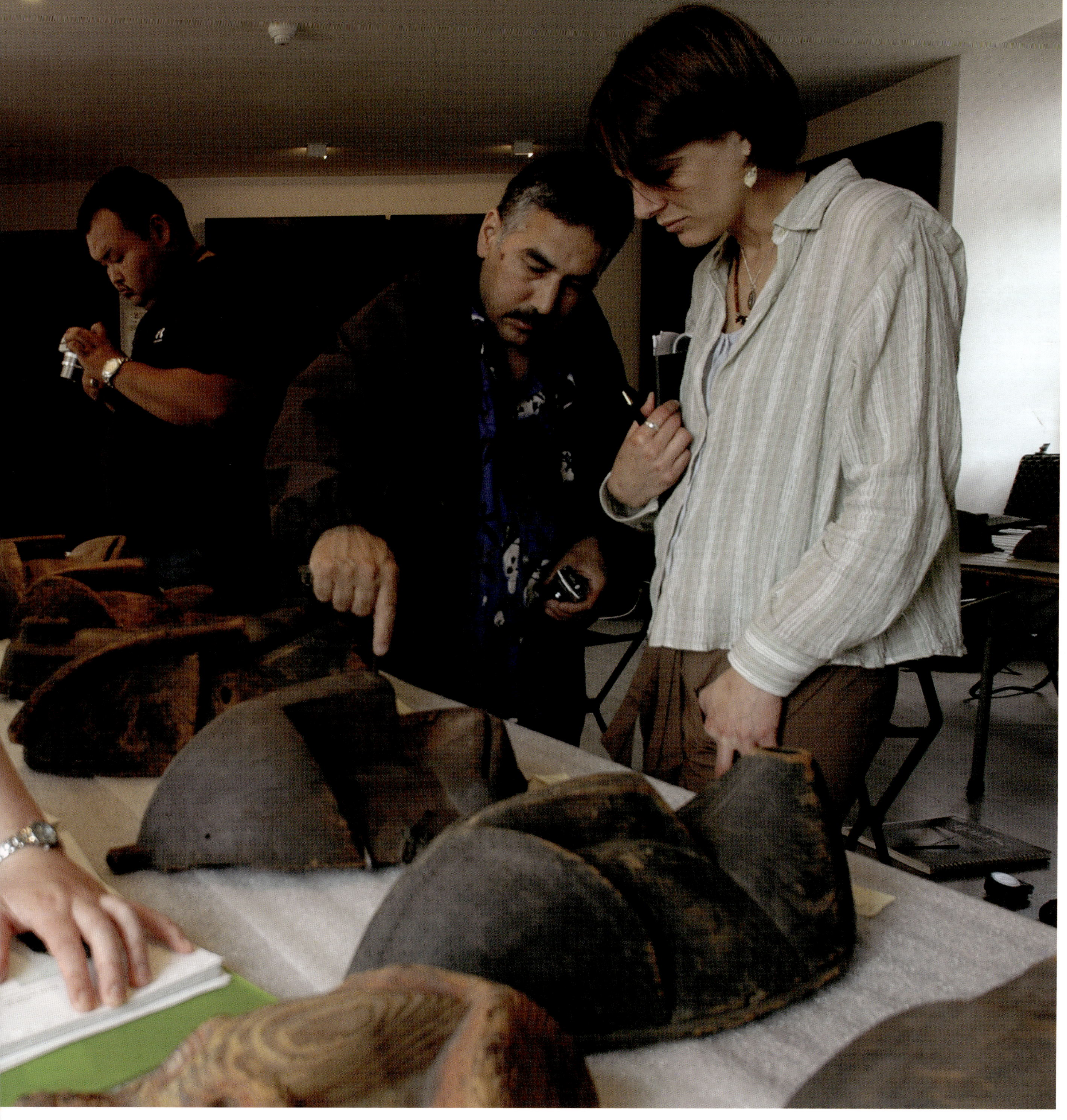

Nakirnalik
"Snub-Nosed One"

H. 30.5 cm;
W. 20 cm;
D. 10.5 cm.

H. 12.01 in;
W. 7.87 in;
D. 4.13 in.

Spruce, paint, tendons

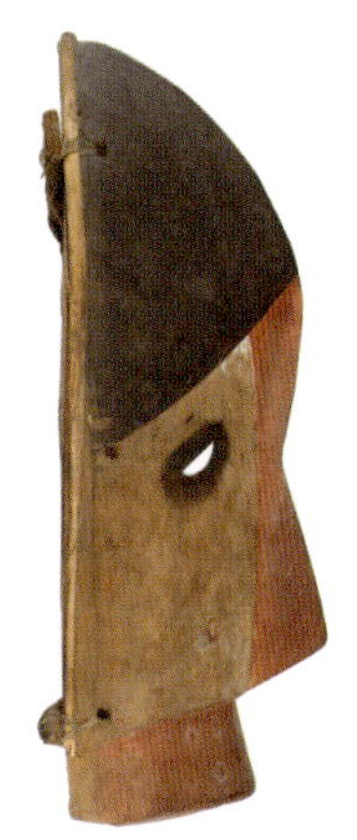

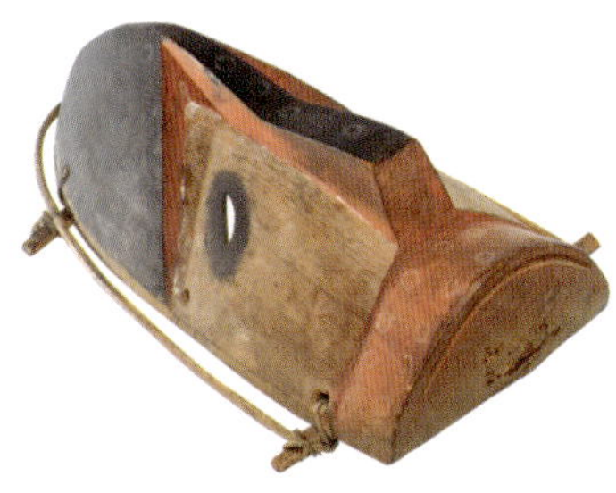

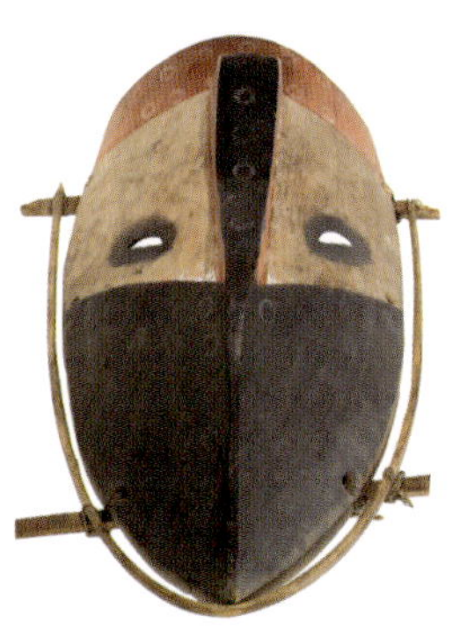

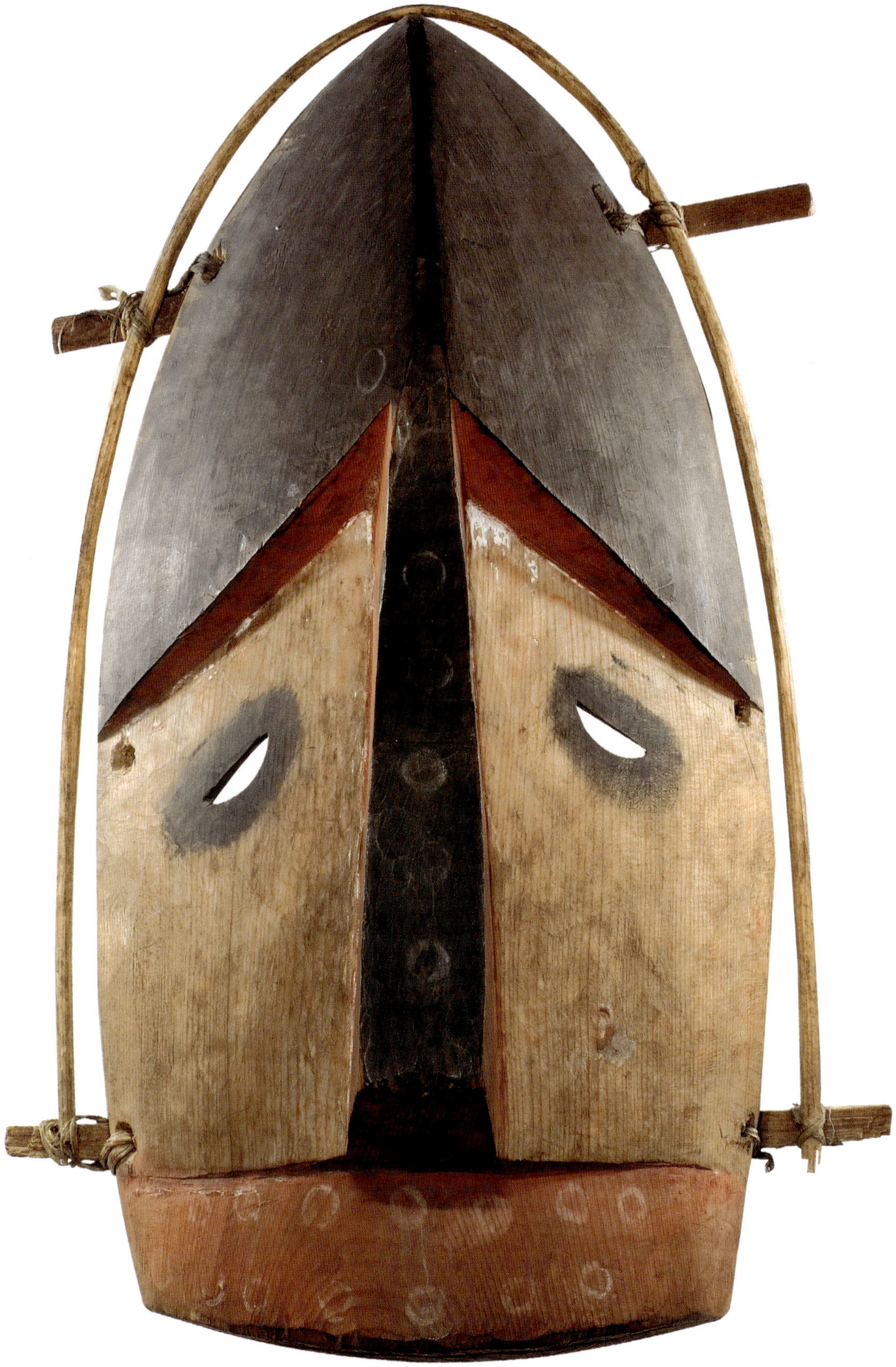

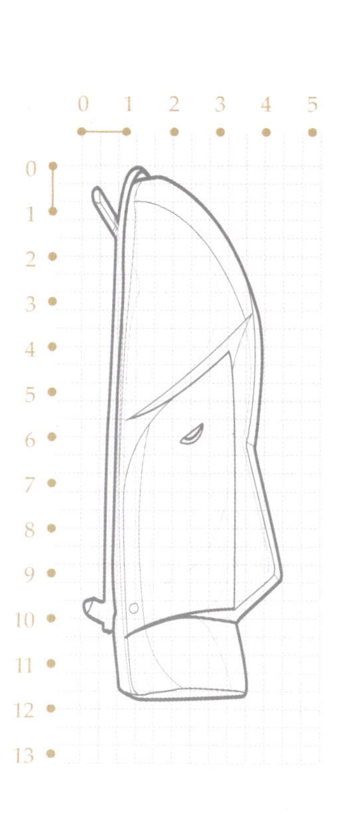
0 1 2 3 4 5
0 1 2 3 4 5 6 7 8 9 10 11 12 13

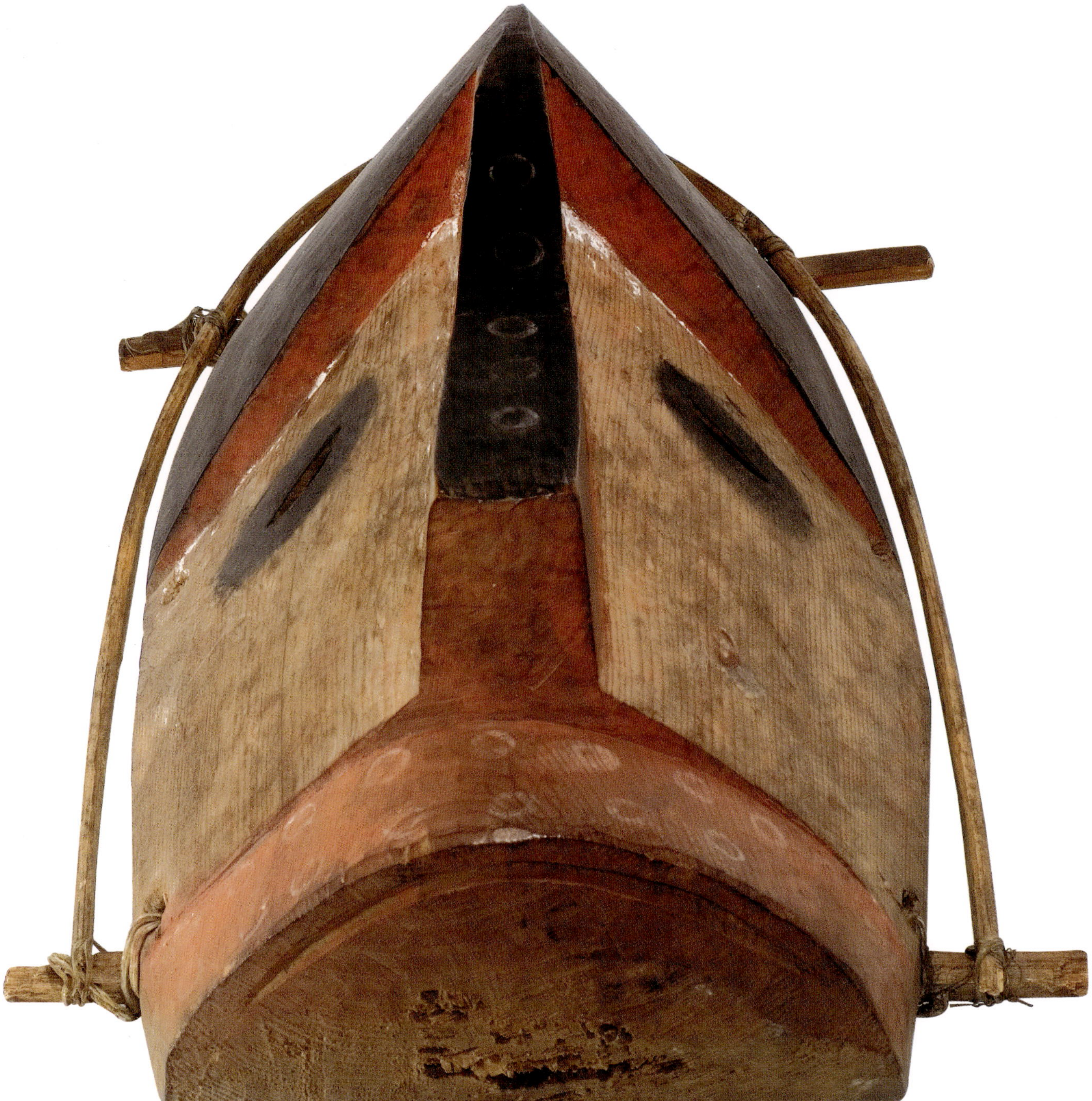

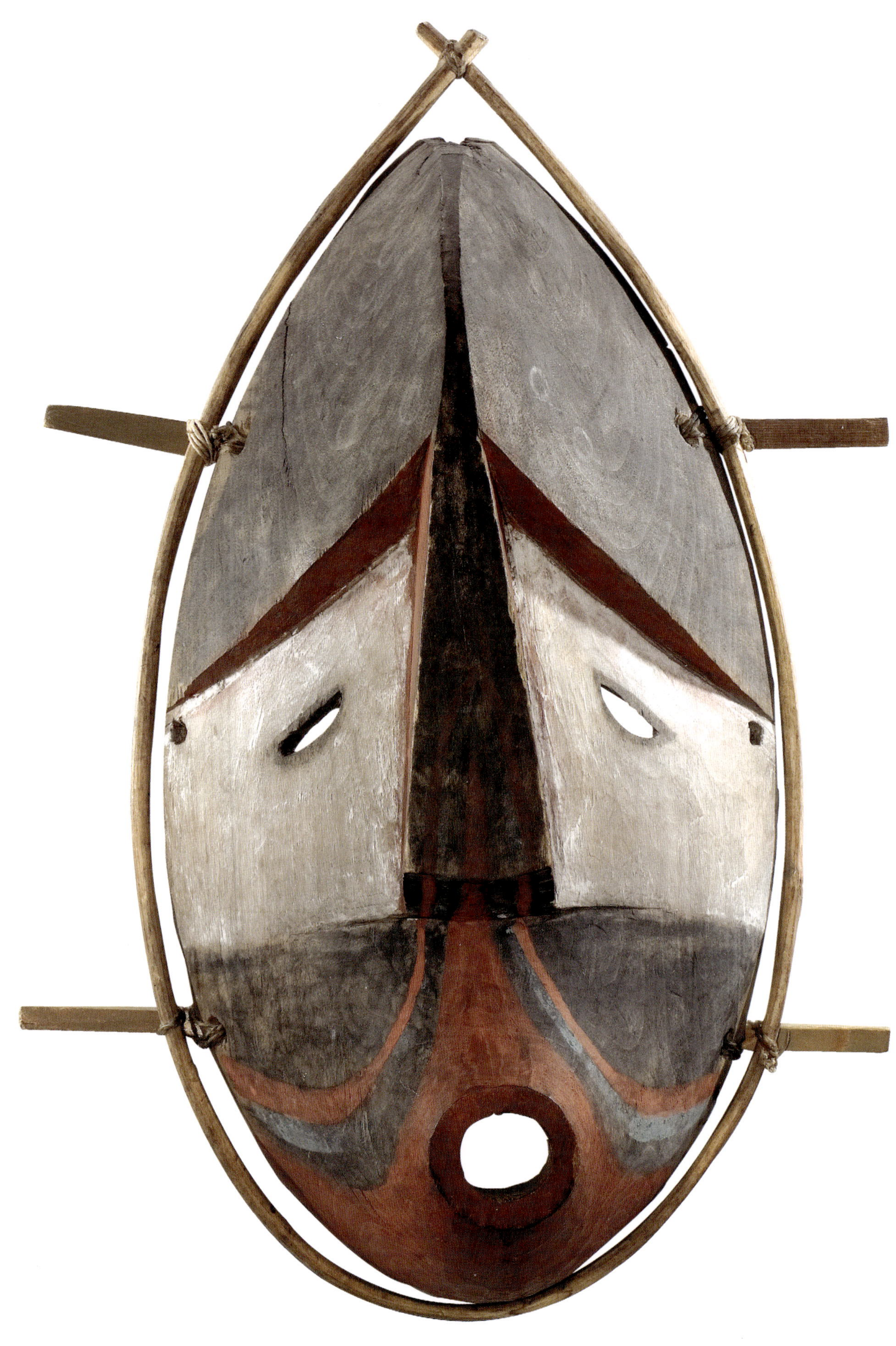

Chumliiq
"First One"

H. 32 cm;
W. 21 cm;
D. 10 cm.

H. 12.6 in;
W. 8.27 in;
D. 3.94 in.

Cotton, paint, tendons

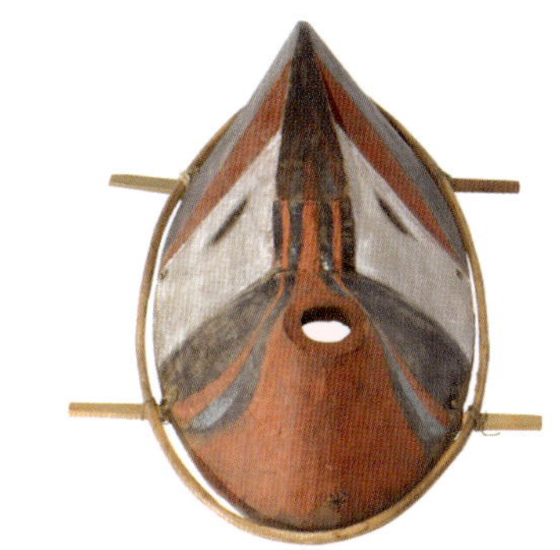

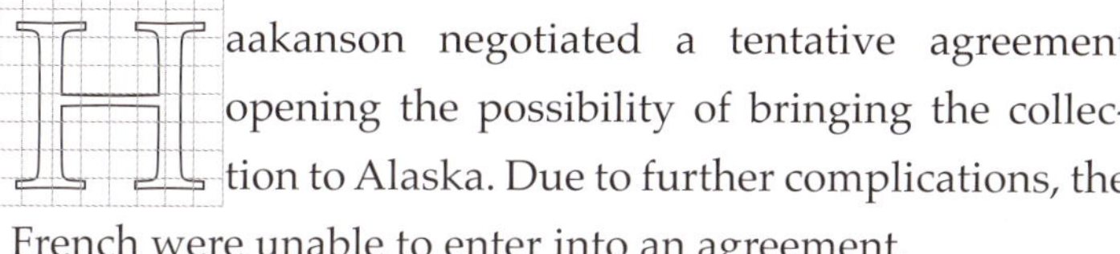

Haakanson negotiated a tentative agreement opening the possibility of bringing the collection to Alaska. Due to further complications, the French were unable to enter into an agreement.

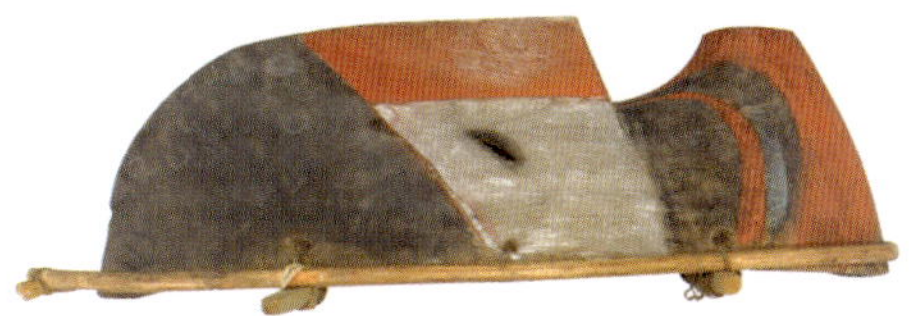

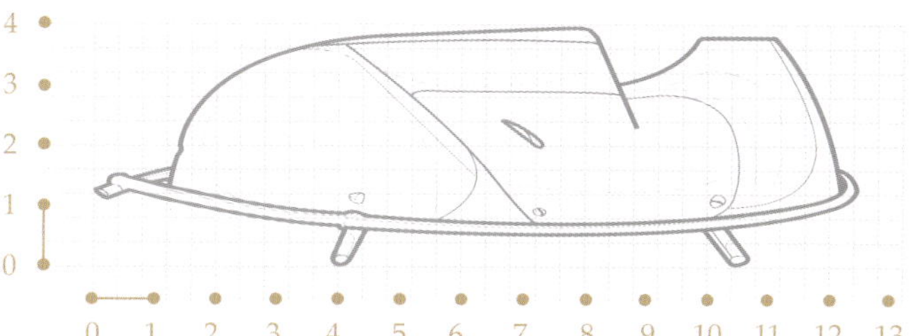

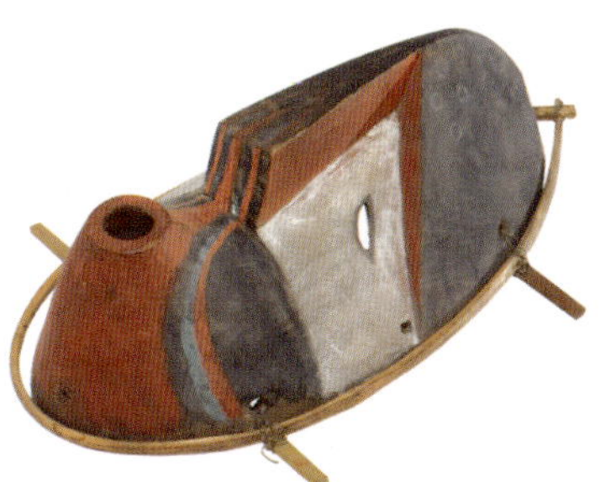

In 2004, Haakanson traveled to Belgium to present the work of the Alutiiq Museum at a conference on Native American collections in Europe. During his talk, he mentioned his desire to bring some of the Pinart masks to Kodiak. In the audience was an American student, Sarah Froning, who offered to help him negotiate the French system. Froning had written her dissertation on museums in France, spoke fluent French and understood the political landscape of French museums and their collections.

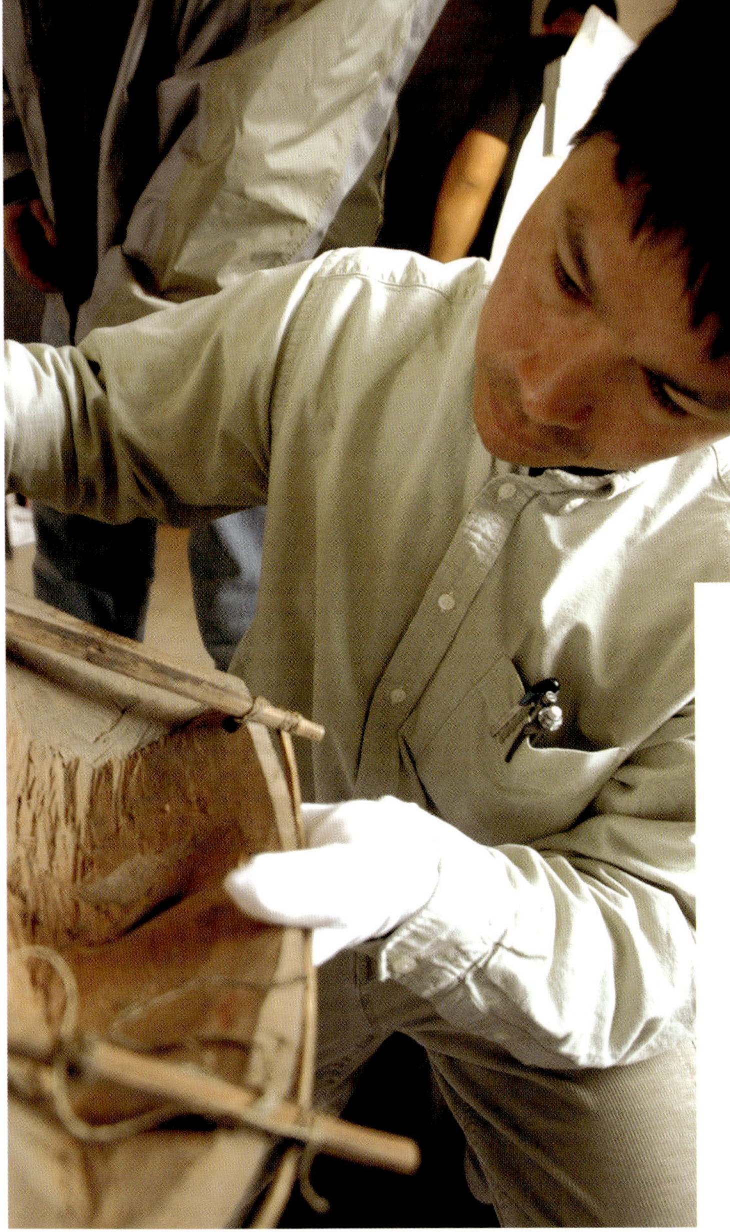
Sven Haakanson Jr.

When the Château Musée hired a new director in 2004, Haakanson and Froning approached her about taking part of the collection to Kodiak. The director agreed to consider sending just one mask; Haakanson declined. One mask would not be worth the effort. When that director was replaced by director and curator Anne-Claire Laronde in 2005, the talks grew more promising.

That same year, the Alutiiq Museum received an economic development grant from a federal agency, the Institute of Museums and Library Services. During a carving workshop, Haakanson, Simeonoff and Eaton came up with the idea to take Alutiiq artists on a pilgrimage to Boulogne-sur-Mer to learn from the masks. The hope was that seeing the collection for themselves would encourage the artists to follow the traditional forms of Alutiiq masks. But it was just as important that those who went give something in return. Haakanson worked out a contract asking each participating artist to carve and donate a danceable mask for the Alutiiq Museum's permanent collection and spend a week in one of the villages to teach mask-carving as part of the museum's annual arts outreach program.

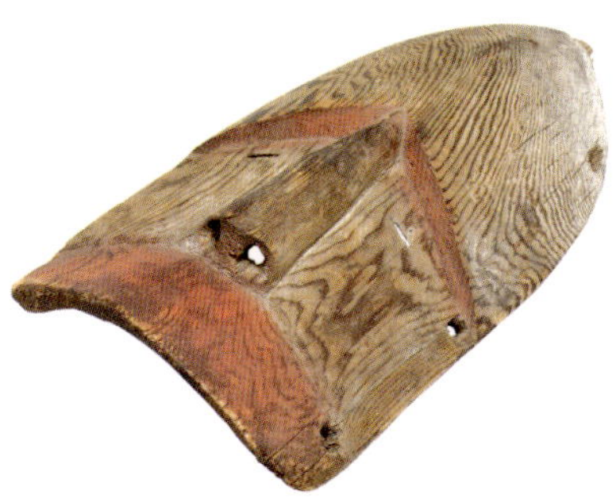

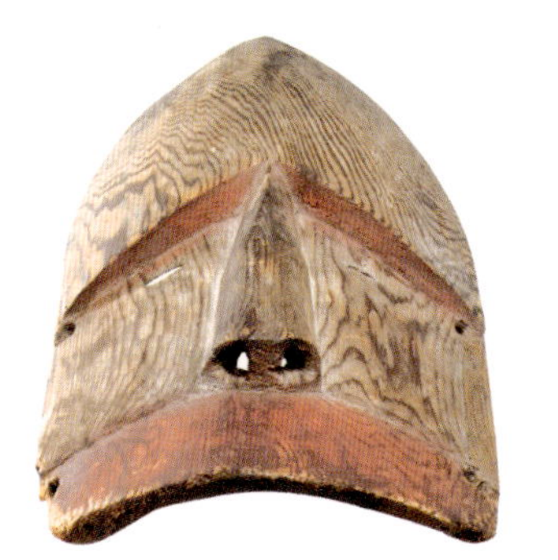

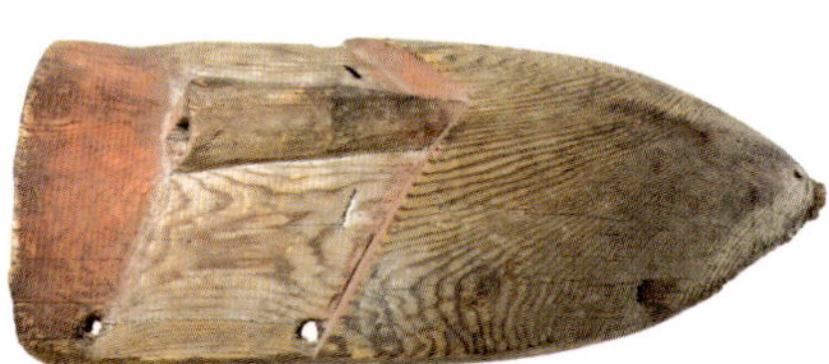

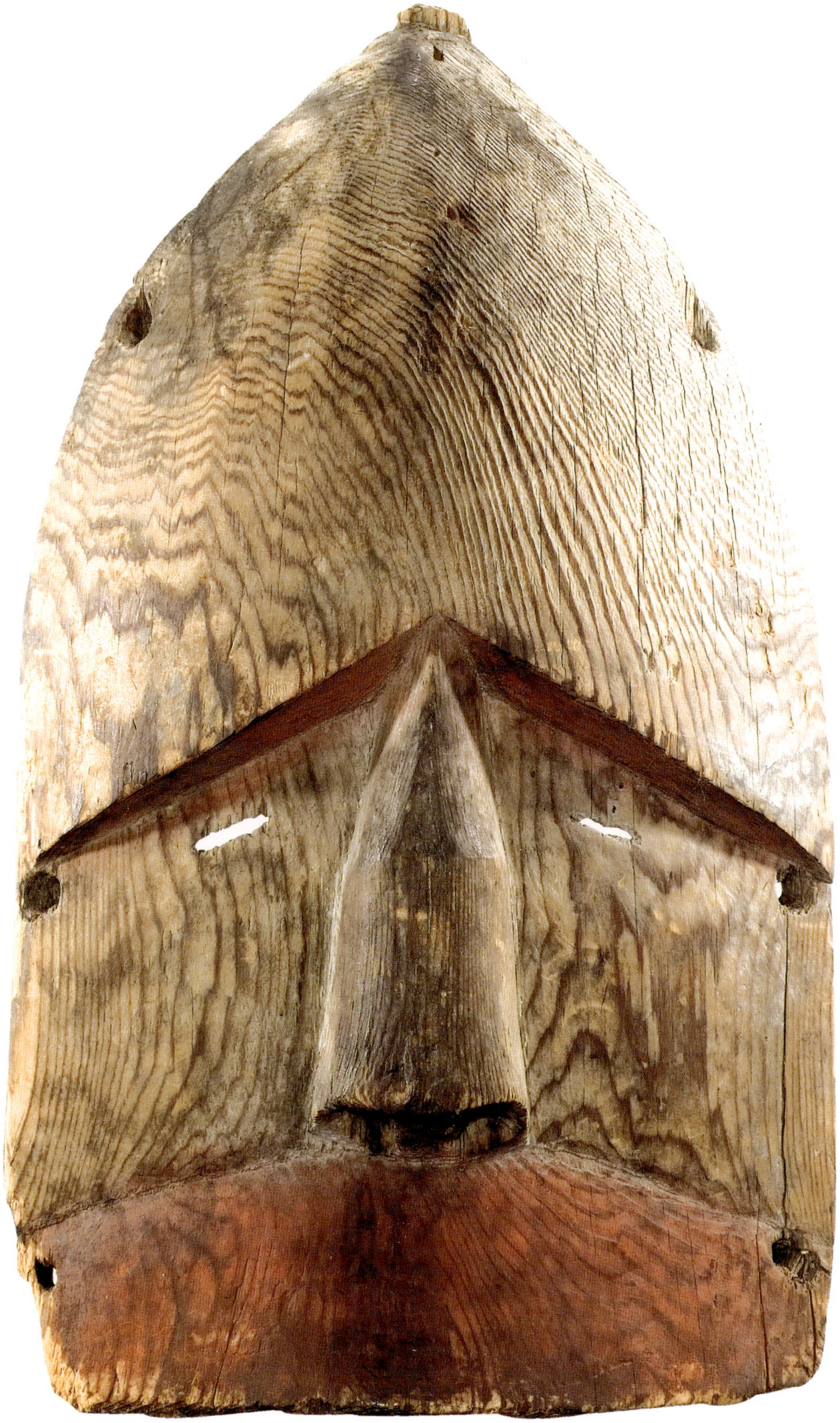

Qanri'lgnuq "Mouthless One"

H. 26 cm;
W. 15 cm;
D. 5 cm.

H. 10.24 in;
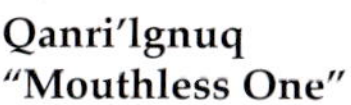
W. 5.91 in;
D. 1.97 in.

Douglas Fir, paint

Kuyauq
"Big-Nosed One or Thankful Person"

H. 36 cm;
W. 25 cm;
D. 6 cm.

H. 14.17 in;
W. 9.84 in;
D. 2.36 in.

Spruce, paint, tendons

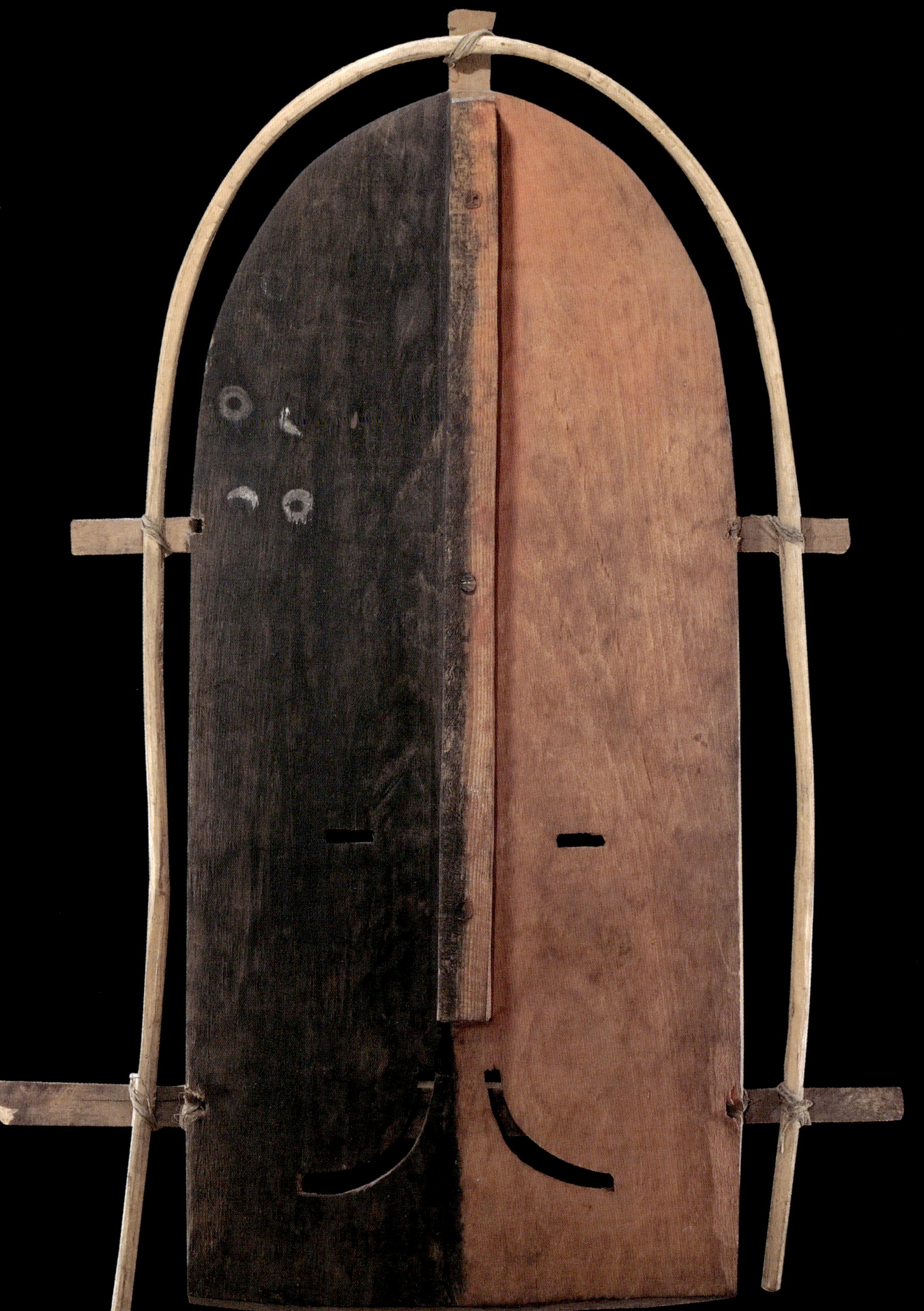

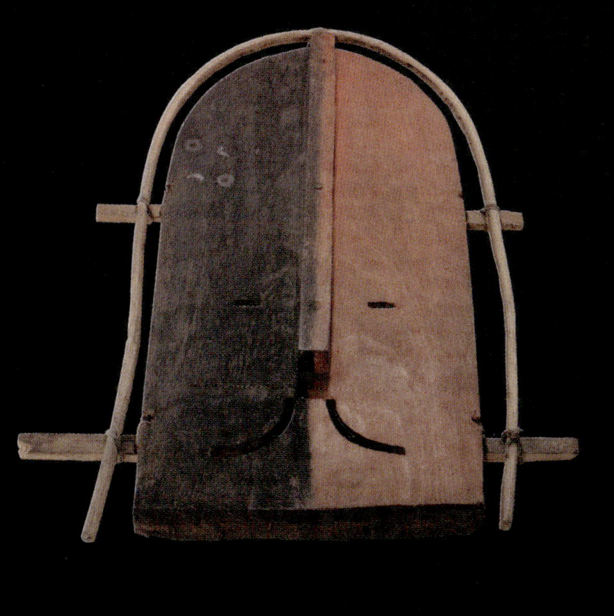

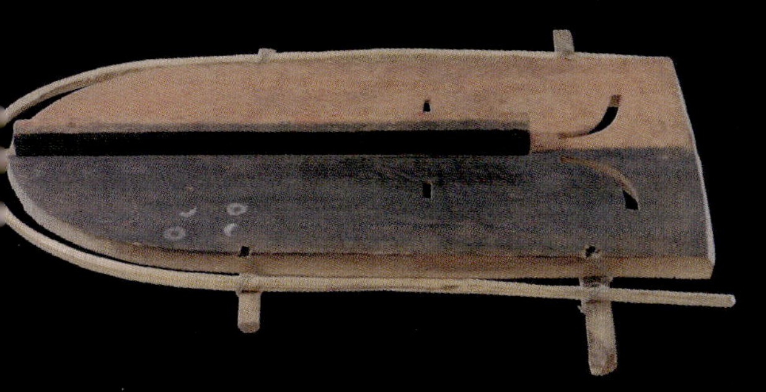

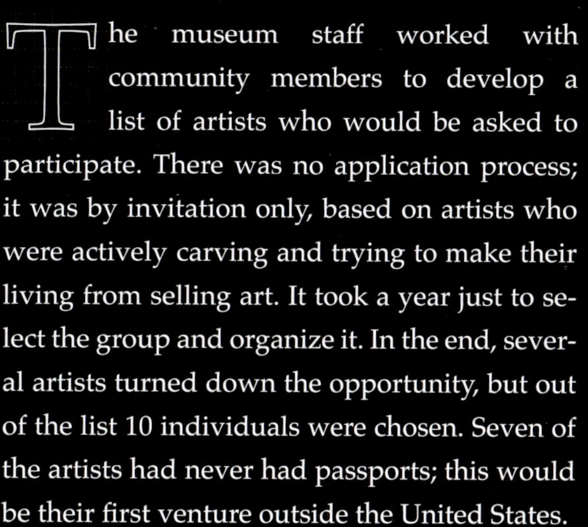

The museum staff worked with community members to develop a list of artists who would be asked to participate. There was no application process; it was by invitation only, based on artists who were actively carving and trying to make their living from selling art. It took a year just to select the group and organize it. In the end, several artists turned down the opportunity, but out of the list 10 individuals were chosen. Seven of the artists had never had passports; this would be their first venture outside the United States.

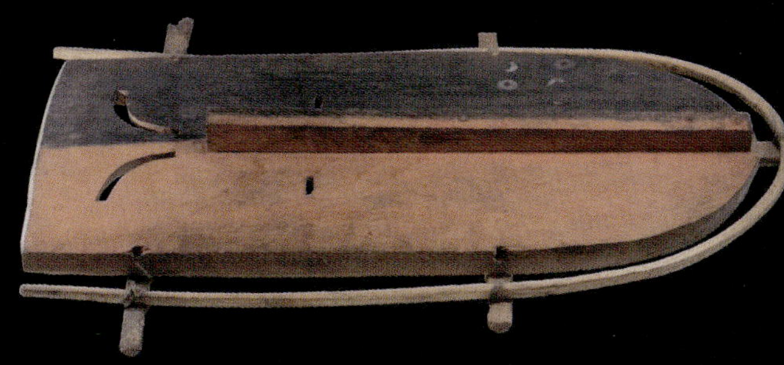

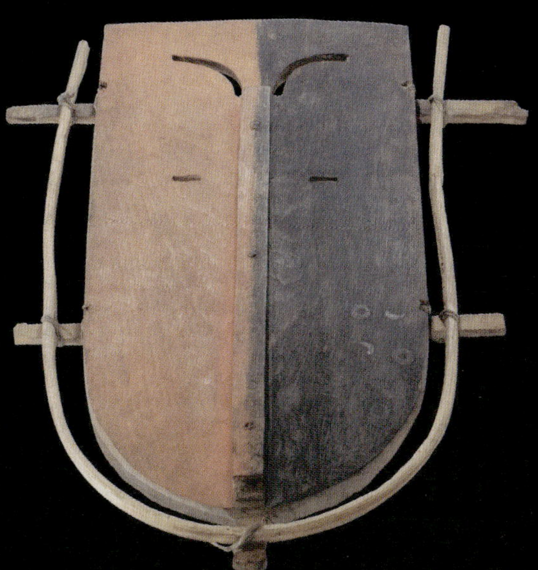

Legend Collected From Afognak In 1872 [8]

Alphonse Pinart recorded many legends and stories from the Alutiiq people during his six months in the Kodiak Archipelago.

The following legend told to Pinart by Nikkepon Celeznoff explains why among the Alutiiq, each kayak of that day had a print on its structure either of a star, a half-moon or another object.

Once near a cape at the entrance to a bay, there lived a marine animal about the size of a cat that would capsize all the angyaat – open boats – that went around the cape. The Alutiiq considered this place with great terror and stayed far away from the cape, not daring to come close. A young Alutiiq man decided one day to try to kill the animal. In order to do so, he built a Kayak with only one hole on top and painted one side of the kayak red and the other one black and on the cover of the kayak the following images.

On the front left, he painted a large crab, on the front right, a human hand, on the back left, a star, and on the other side, a kayak. He repeated the same figures on the float and the palm of his hands. Then he took a spear with which he had killed five men and left without telling his intentions to anyone. In the place where the animal was supposed to be, he heard a sort of whispering, then a lapping, and then he saw the animal moving toward his kayak. "Against me," he said, "you cannot do anything." Then he showed the large crab and said, "You see this figure, the crab? It is the power of the sea, which can seize you." Showing the human hand, he said, "You see this hand, it is the power of man, who can seize you." Now while displaying the star, "You see this star, it shows you the power from higher up, which can also seize you." And finally showing the kayak, "You see this kayak, it shows you how it can contain you."

While he was speaking thus, the animal was forming circles around the kayak. The Alutiiq man grabbed the spear with which he had killed five men, and throwing it, killed the animal. He took it to the shore and spent the night there. When he returned to the village, everybody thought he was dead. He did not say that he had killed the beast, but asked who in the village would go with him in that direction. As everyone refused with terror, he said he had killed the animal.

In commemoration of this event, they now place this figure on their kayak as a safeguard if they meet one of these fantastic animals at sea.

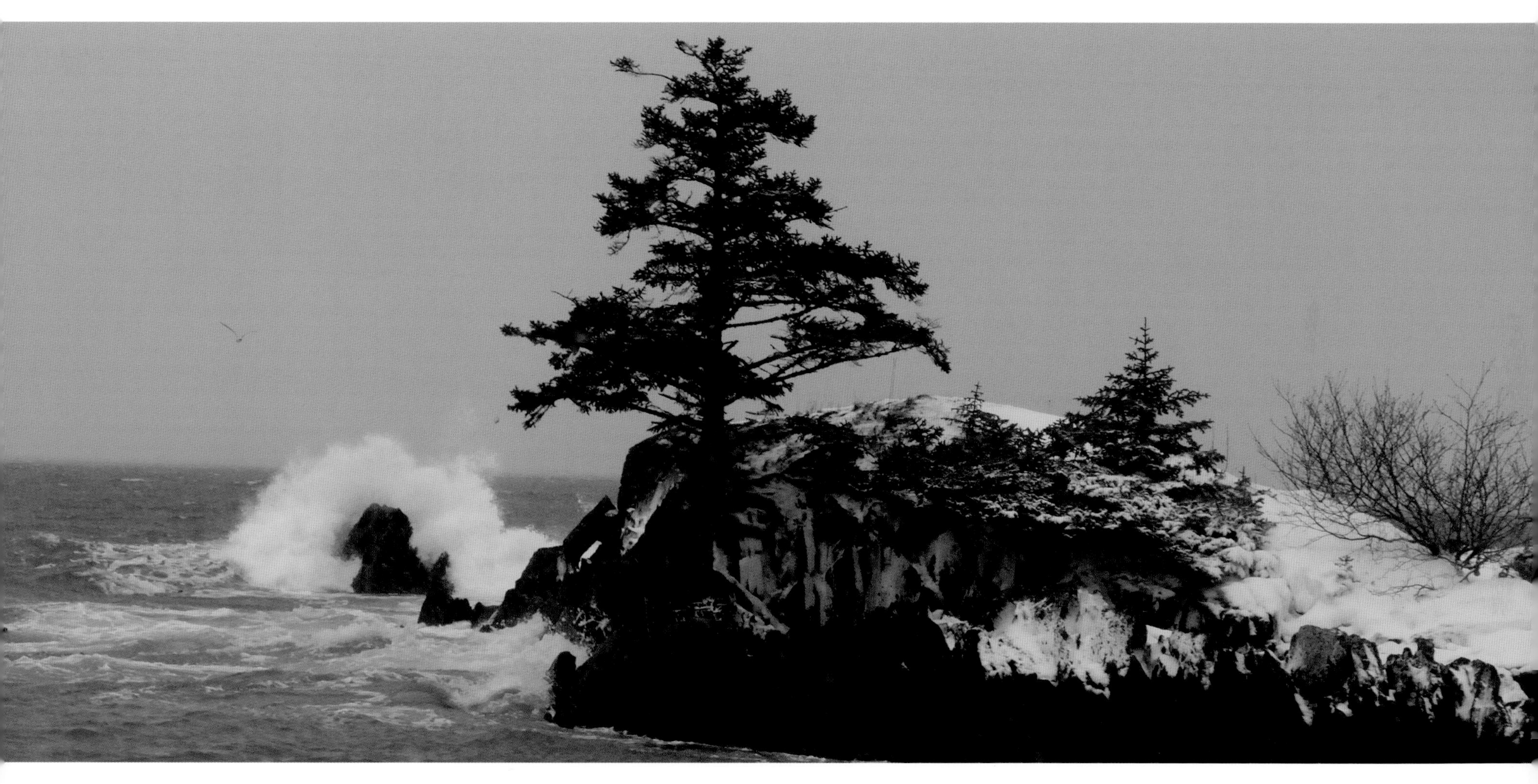

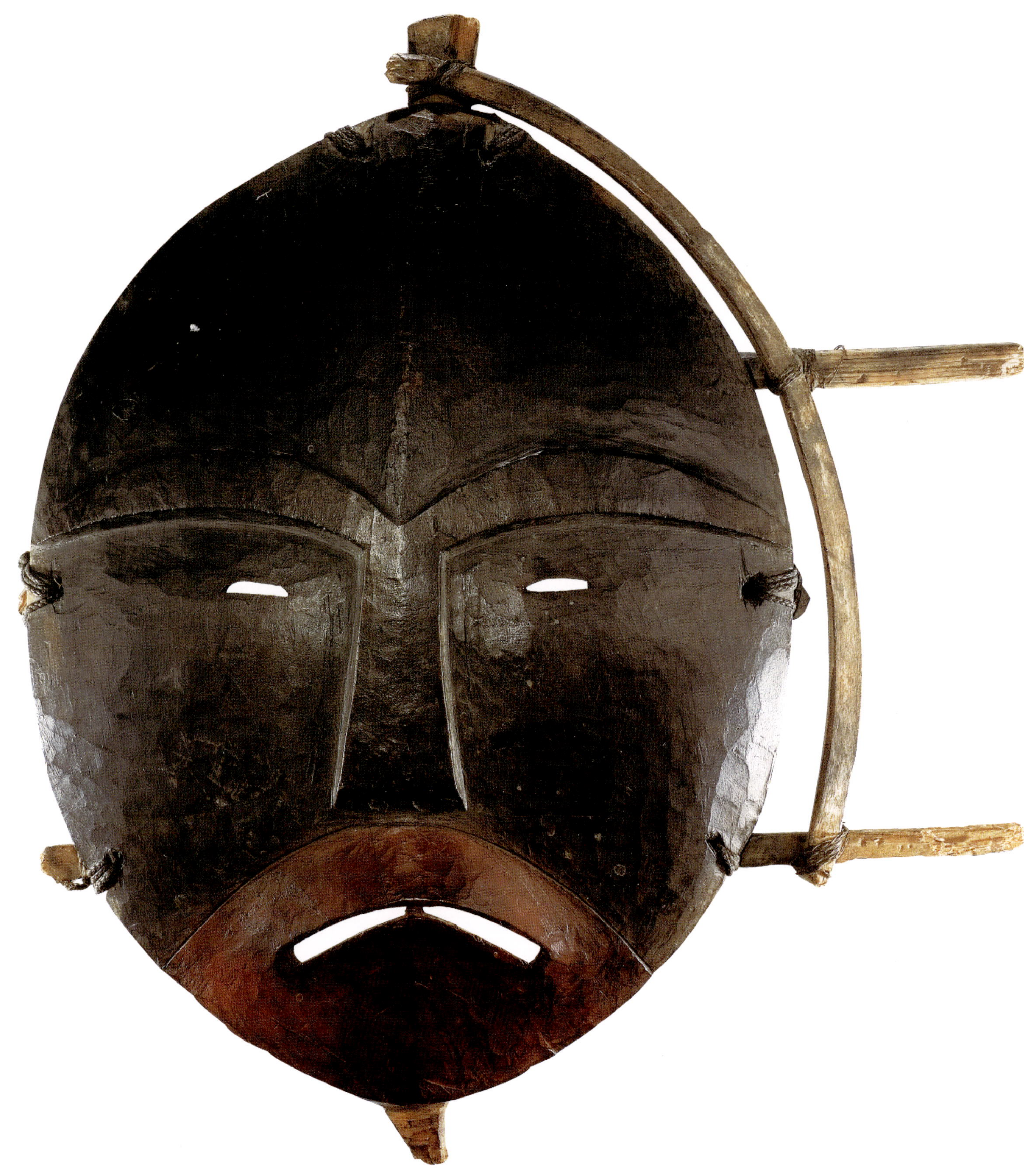

Tamallkuk
"Married Couple"

H. 35 cm;
W. 30.5 cm;
D. 7 cm.

H. 13.78 in;
W. 12.01 in;
D. 2.76 in.

Spruce, paint, tendons

Awe. Joy. Loss.

The Alutiiq contingent arrived in Boulogne on May 30, 2006. The Château Musée staff had laid out the Pinart mask collection on tables in one room, and the artists were given free rein to examine the pieces and even handle them, with gloves. While the artists knew intellectually what they would find, it was still a shock.

It was pretty intense when we first got there. A few of us did cry when we saw them. I had never felt that before – these were the first masks I had seen that were old. Knowing that somebody came and collected them and took care of them for so many years. They are a piece of our history, a connection to our past.
– Speridon Simeonoff

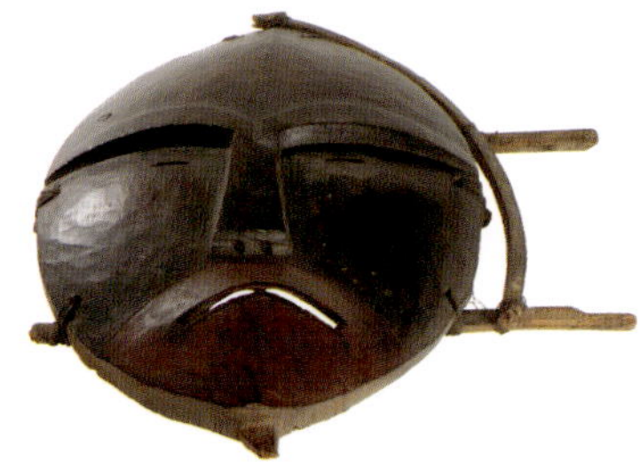

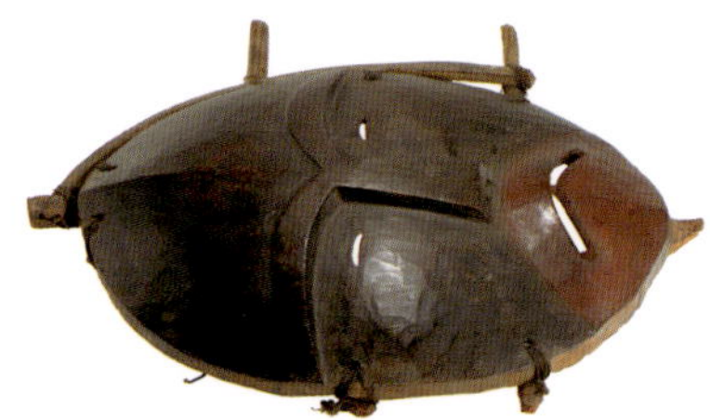

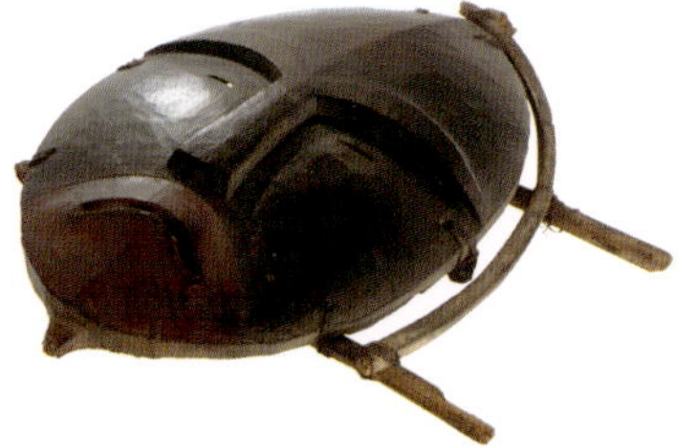

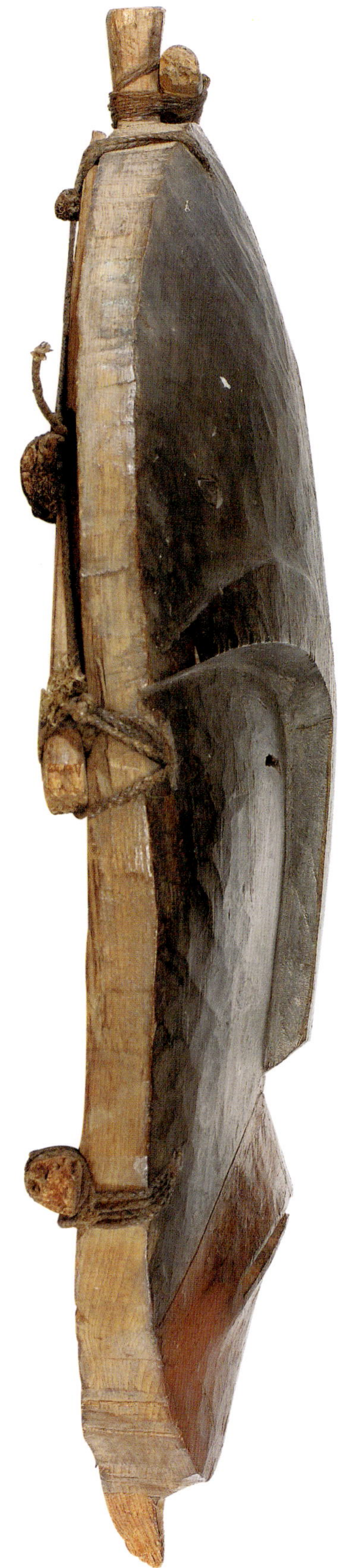

Nakllegnaq
"Pitiful one"

H. 22 cm;
W. 12 cm;
D. 9.5 cm.

H. 8.66 in;
W. 4.72 in;
D. 3.74 in.

White oak, paint

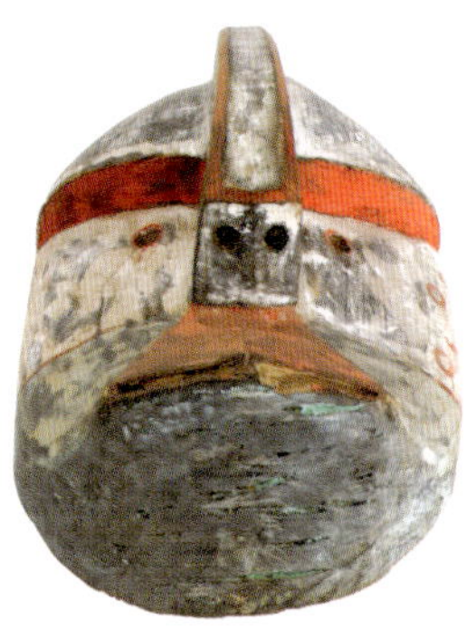

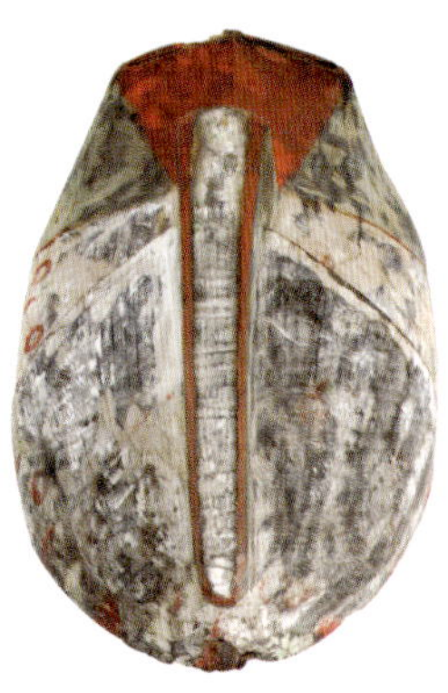

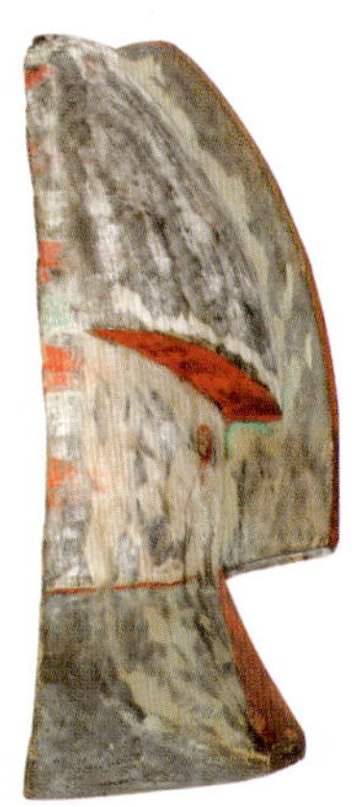

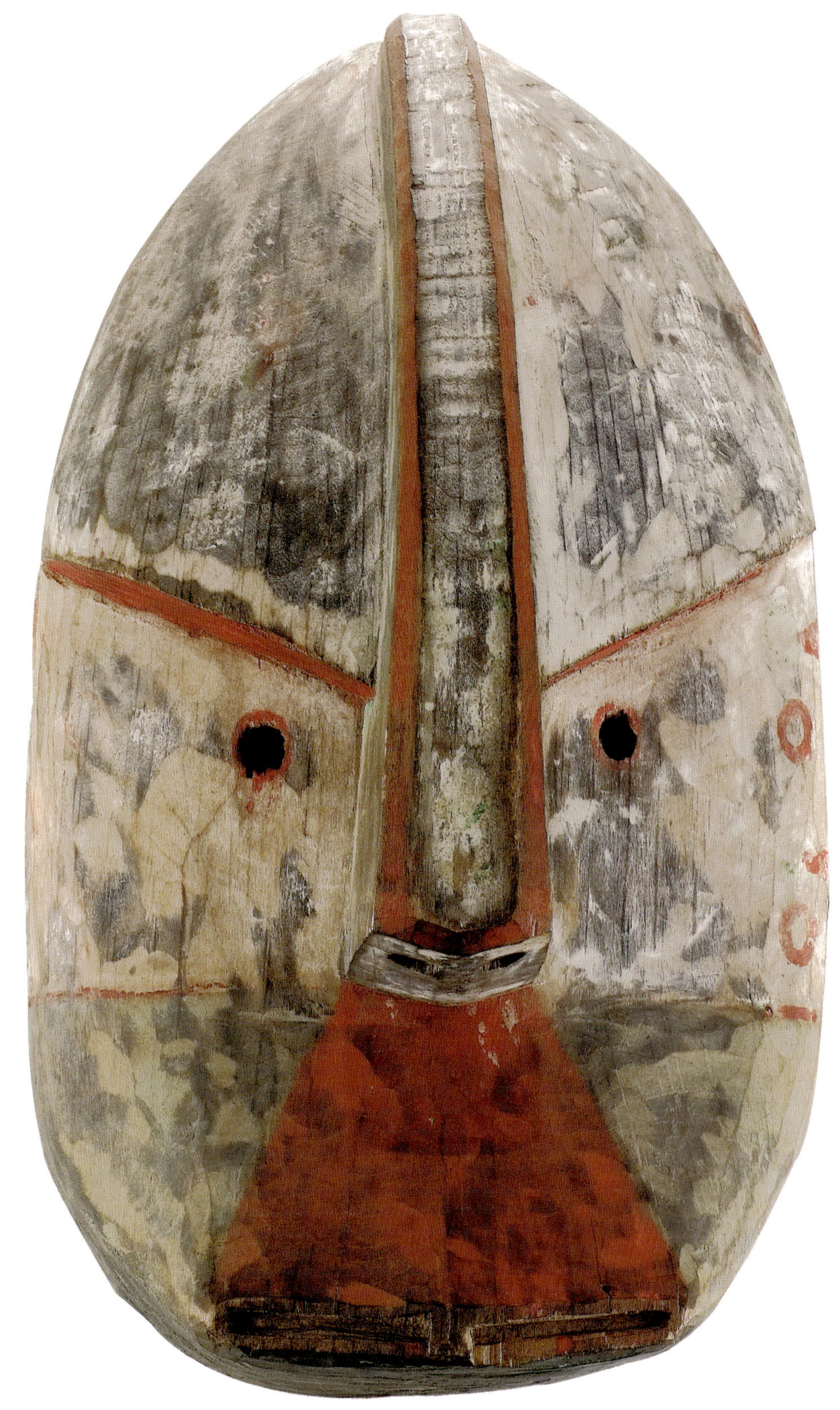

I had to stop at the doorway. It was like walking into a funeral, pretty powerful. I never thought I'd see something like that. It was like being bombarded. I stopped in my tracks. It was an awesome experience but hard to describe. I had to stop and absorb it. I wasn't expecting to feel that way. It was a real spiritual feeling; it was almost painful to see things that had been taken. Yet if they hadn't been taken, they would have been lost. It was a spiritual experience for everyone.
— Alfred Naumoff

I was walking up the stairs to the museum. Everyone was so solemn. I was very excited and just started hollering and yelping with excitement. But I got to the door of the exhibit room, and I couldn't go in. For me to be in the presence . . . it was hard because I knew our people had touched them. . . When I did go in, I was home.
— Doug Inga

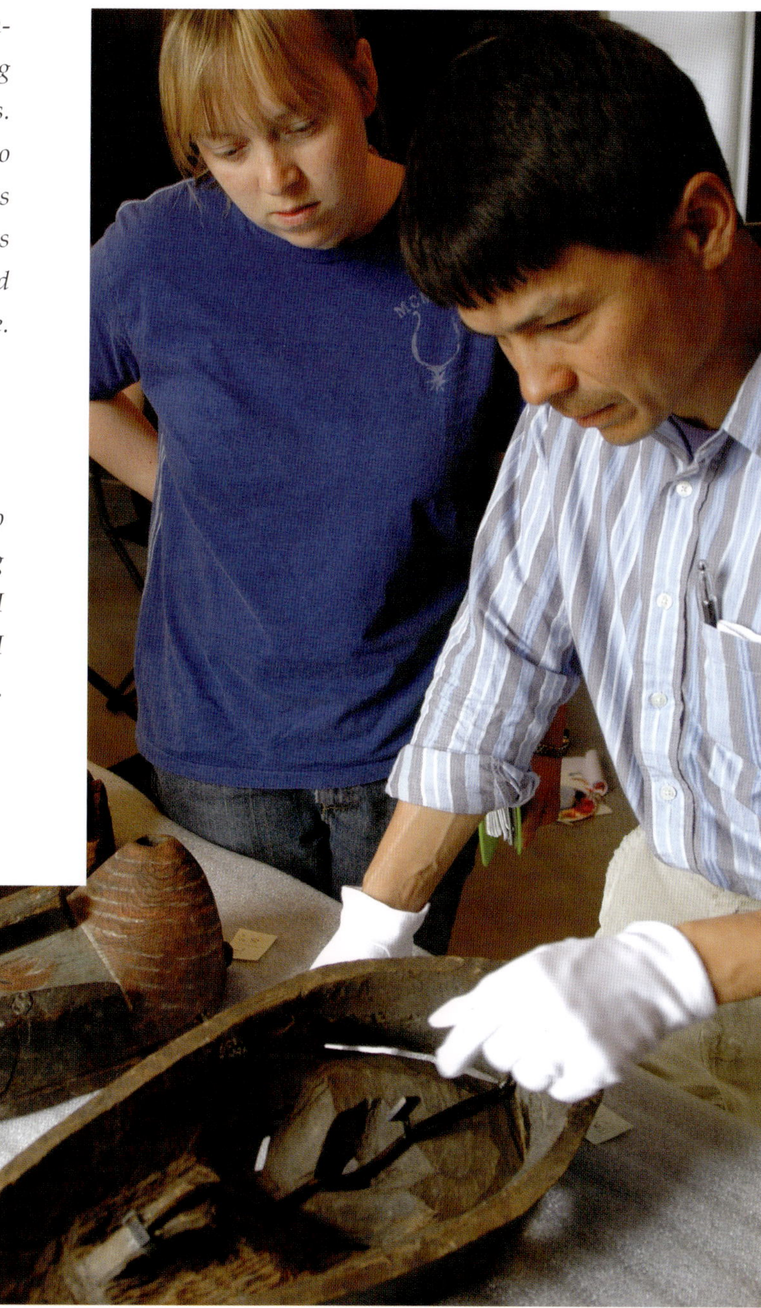

Lena Amason and Sven Haakanson Jr.

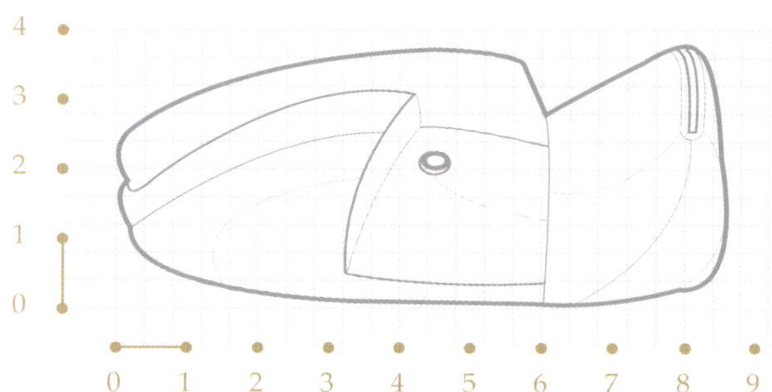

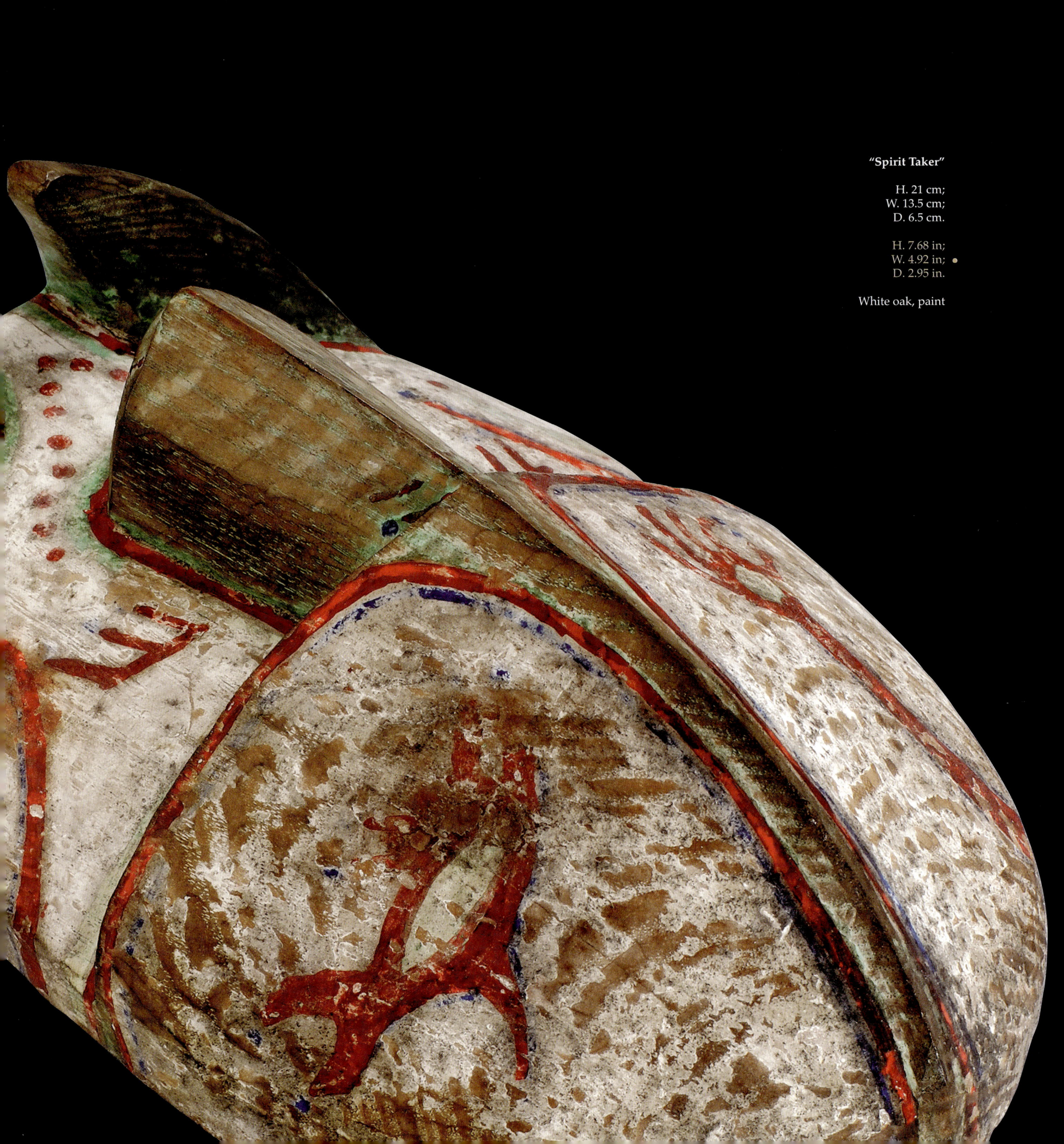

"Spirit Taker"

H. 21 cm;
W. 13.5 cm;
D. 6.5 cm.

H. 7.68 in;
W. 4.92 in;
D. 2.95 in.

White oak, paint

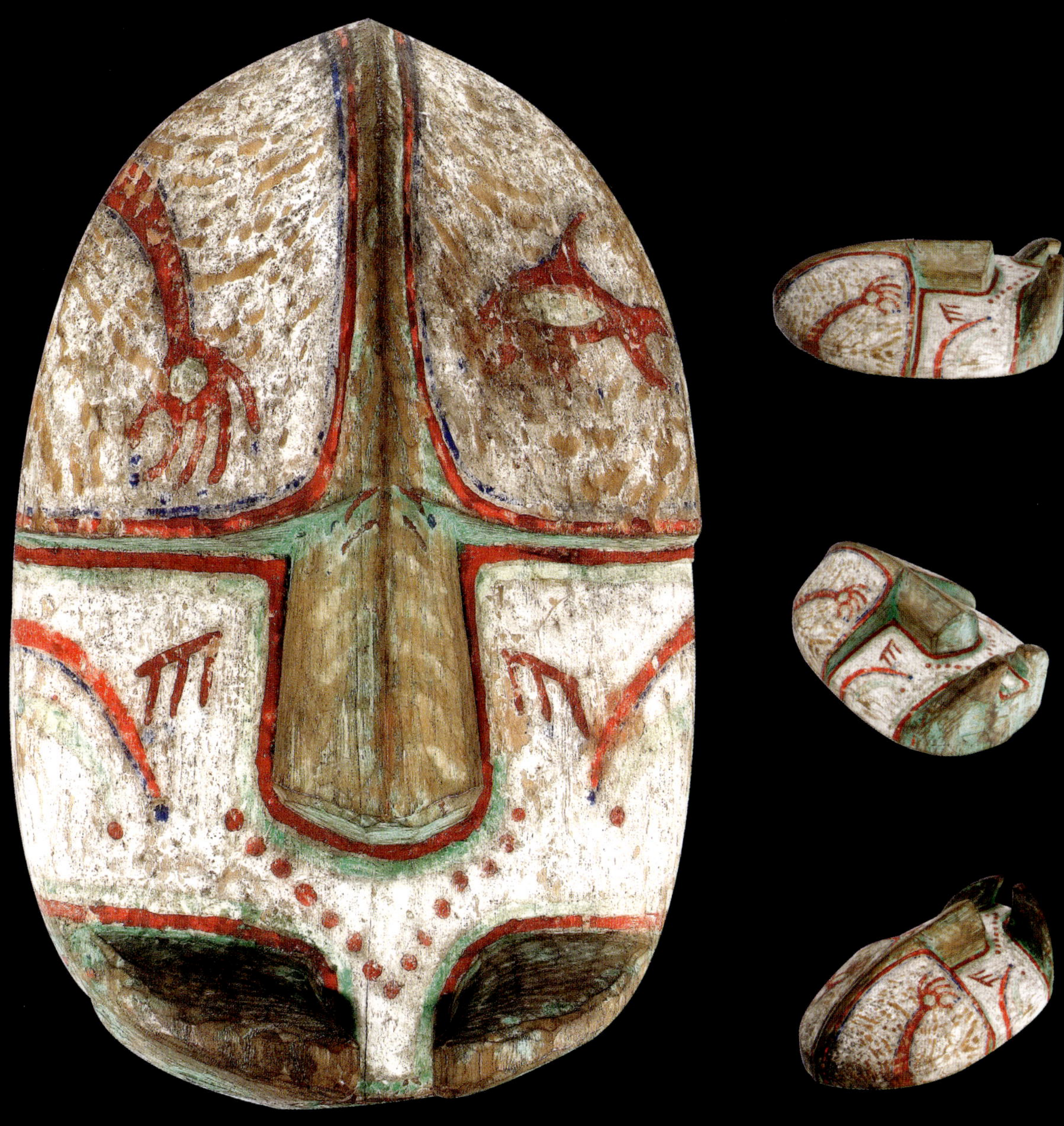

When we all walked into the room where so many Kodiak dance masks were laid out on tables, I think the feelings of awe, of joy, of loss were so overwhelming that we all cried together.

— **Lena Amason**

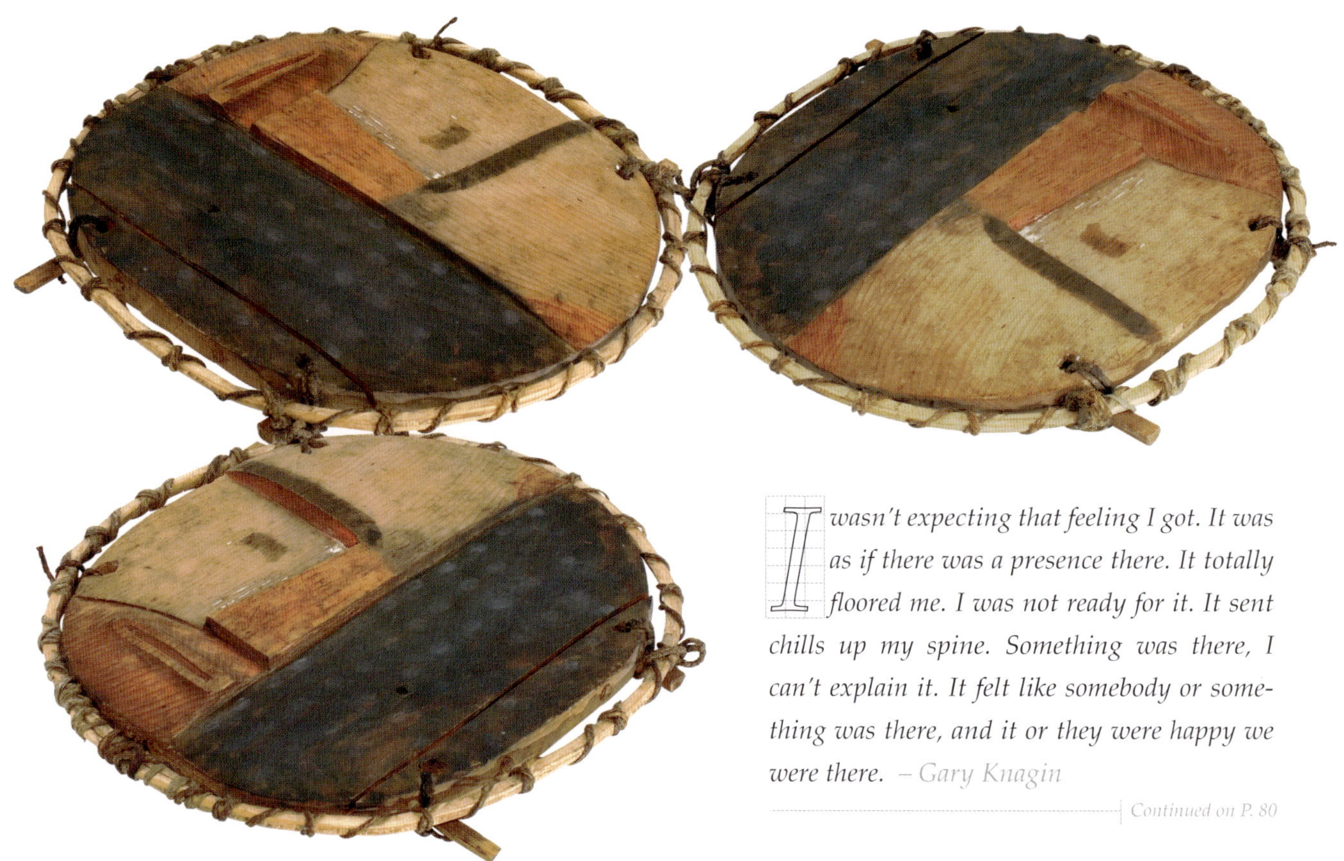

I wasn't expecting that feeling I got. It was as if there was a presence there. It totally floored me. I was not ready for it. It sent chills up my spine. Something was there, I can't explain it. It felt like somebody or something was there, and it or they were happy we were there. – Gary Knagin

Continued on P. 80

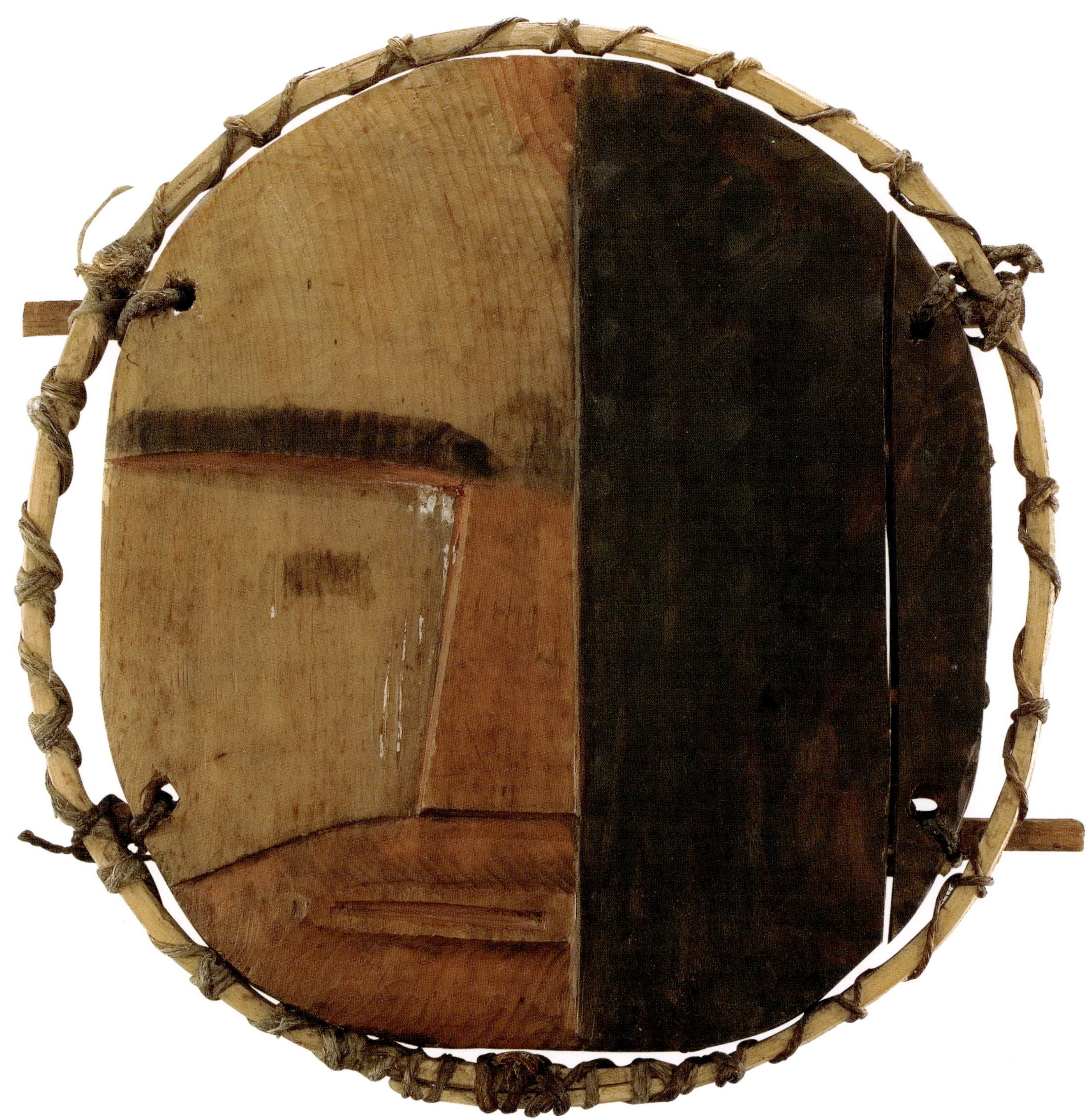

Unnuyayuk
"Night Traveler"

H. 19 cm;
W. 19 cm;
D. 2.5 cm.

H. 7.48 in;
W. 7.48 in;
D. 0.98 in.

Red cedar, paint, tendons, plant fiber

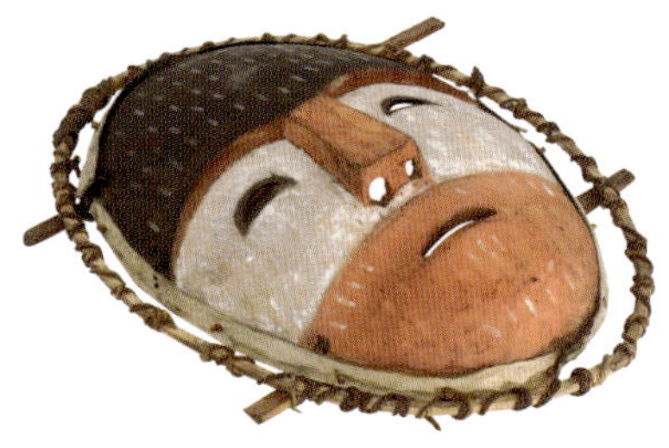

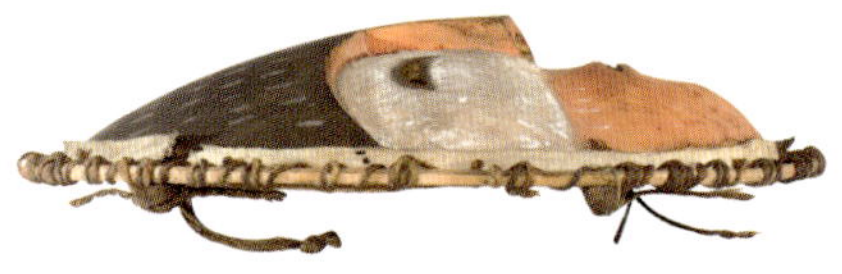

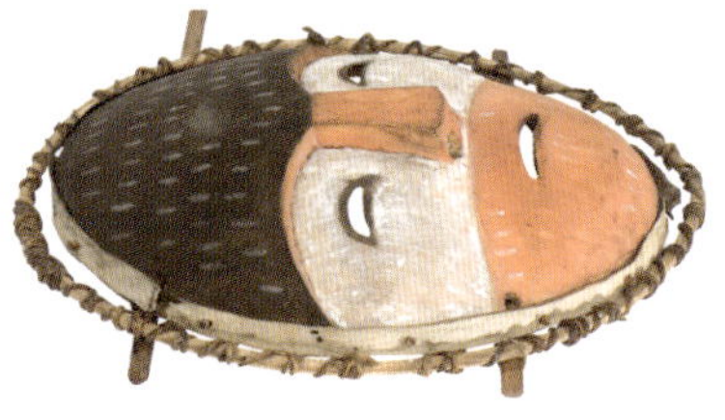

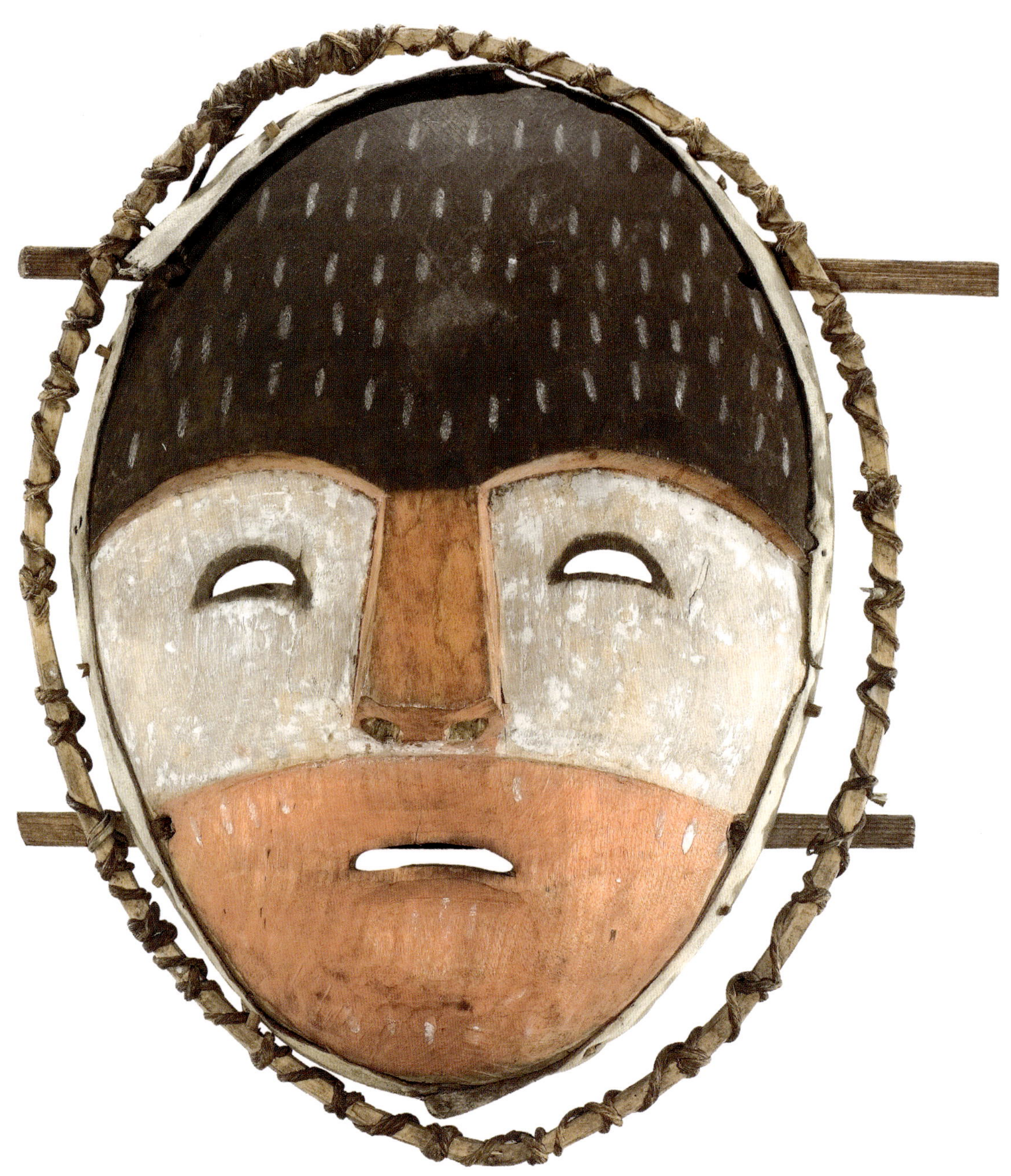

Ingillagayak
"Weatherman"

H. 23.5 cm;
W. 20 cm;
D. 5.5 cm.

H. 9.25 in;
W. 7.87 in;
D. 2.17 in.

White or live oak, paint, tendons, leather, plant fiber

[From the collection] I learned a lot about design and shapes. The cone-shaped pointed head. It took me several months to carve a mask after seeing the collection. Yet when I did carve again, I did the cone-shaped head. Usually, I picture in my head what a piece will look like finished. This one just kind of happened... if you see the carvings with your own eyes. You don't stop until you've finished with your hands. It doesn't leave your mind. It's implanted. Made a lasting change in my carvings. It gets pretty exciting when you learn how they did it. It's mind-blowing. Those guys had stone tools; maybe they used fire, too.
— Alfred Naumoff

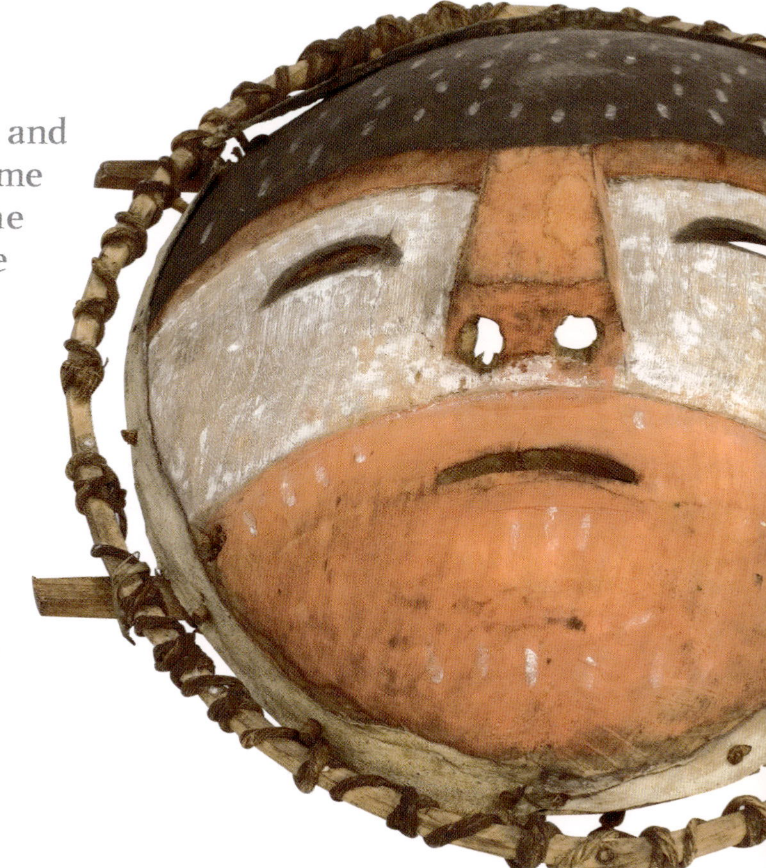

Unartuliq "Talisman"

H. 16 cm;
W. 17 cm;
D. 4.5 cm.

H. 6.3 in;
W. 6.69 in;
D. 1.77 in.

Spruce, paint, tendons, leather

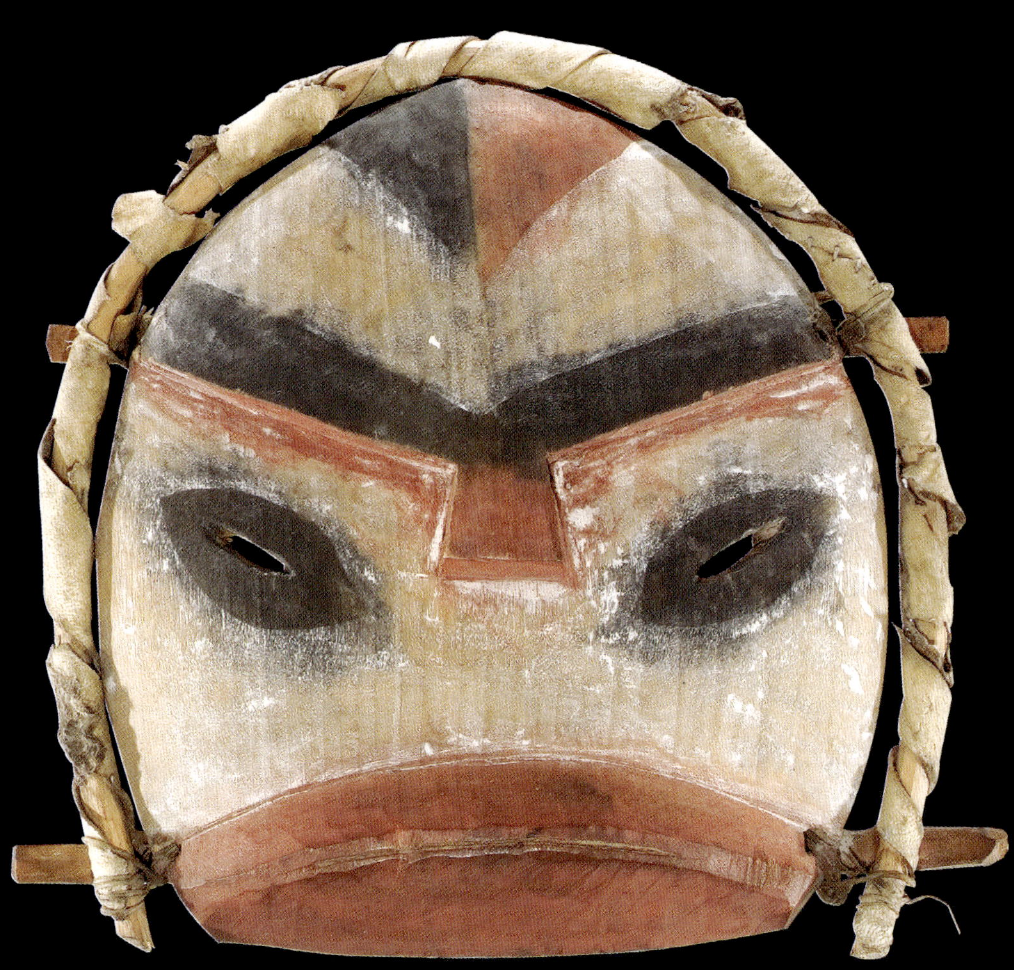

The most surprising thing about the masks, after only seeing them in photographs, was how deeply they were carved, how many angles and lines there are in a single mask, how large some of them were that appeared so small in a photo. Some of them were obviously models of actual dance masks. They could fit in your hand, were solid all the way through and heavy, as if made of hard wood. Seeing them in person, you could tell by the colors and carving style that some masks were made by the same carver. You could tell that certain masks were 'related' to each other.

— **Lena Amason**

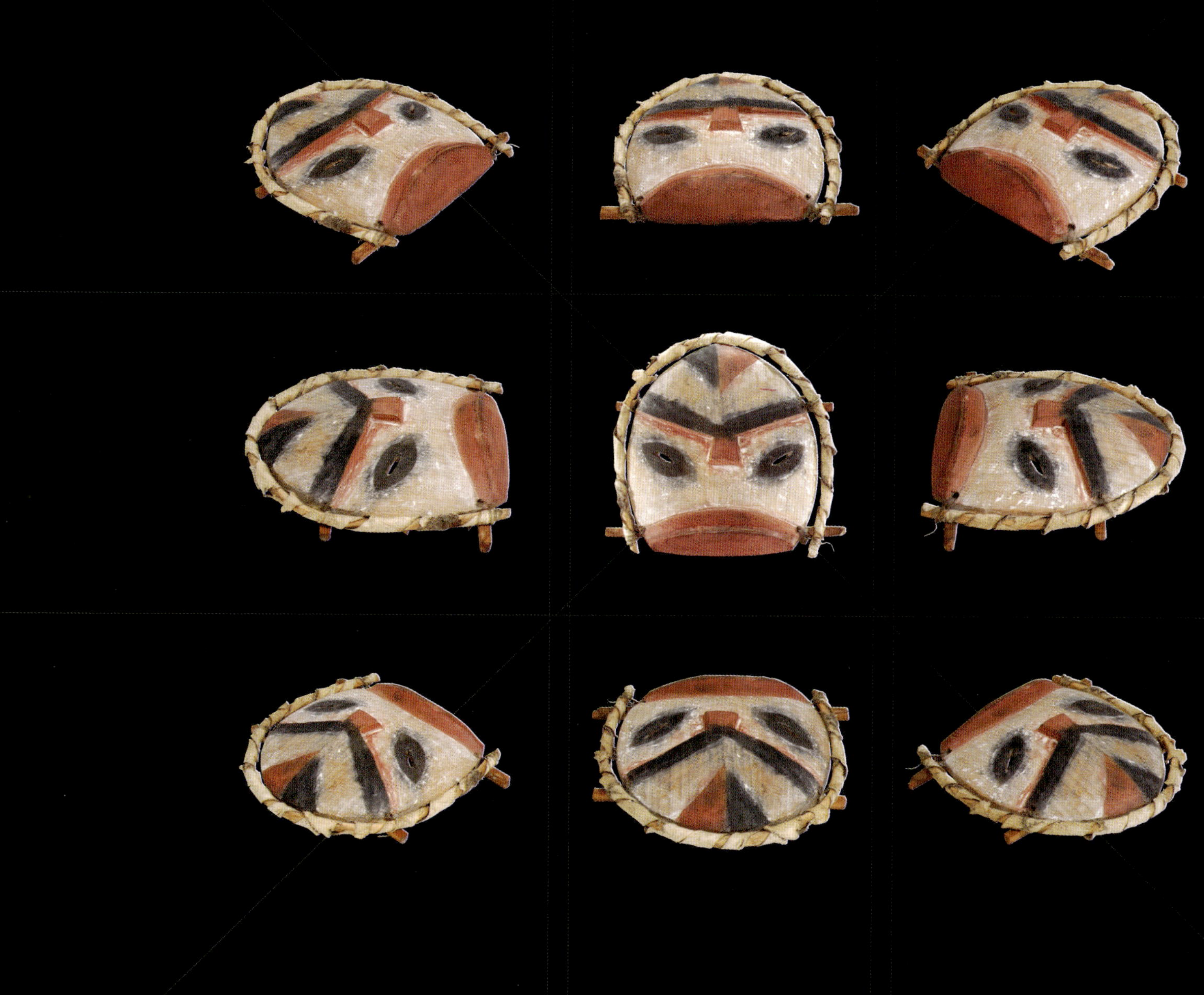

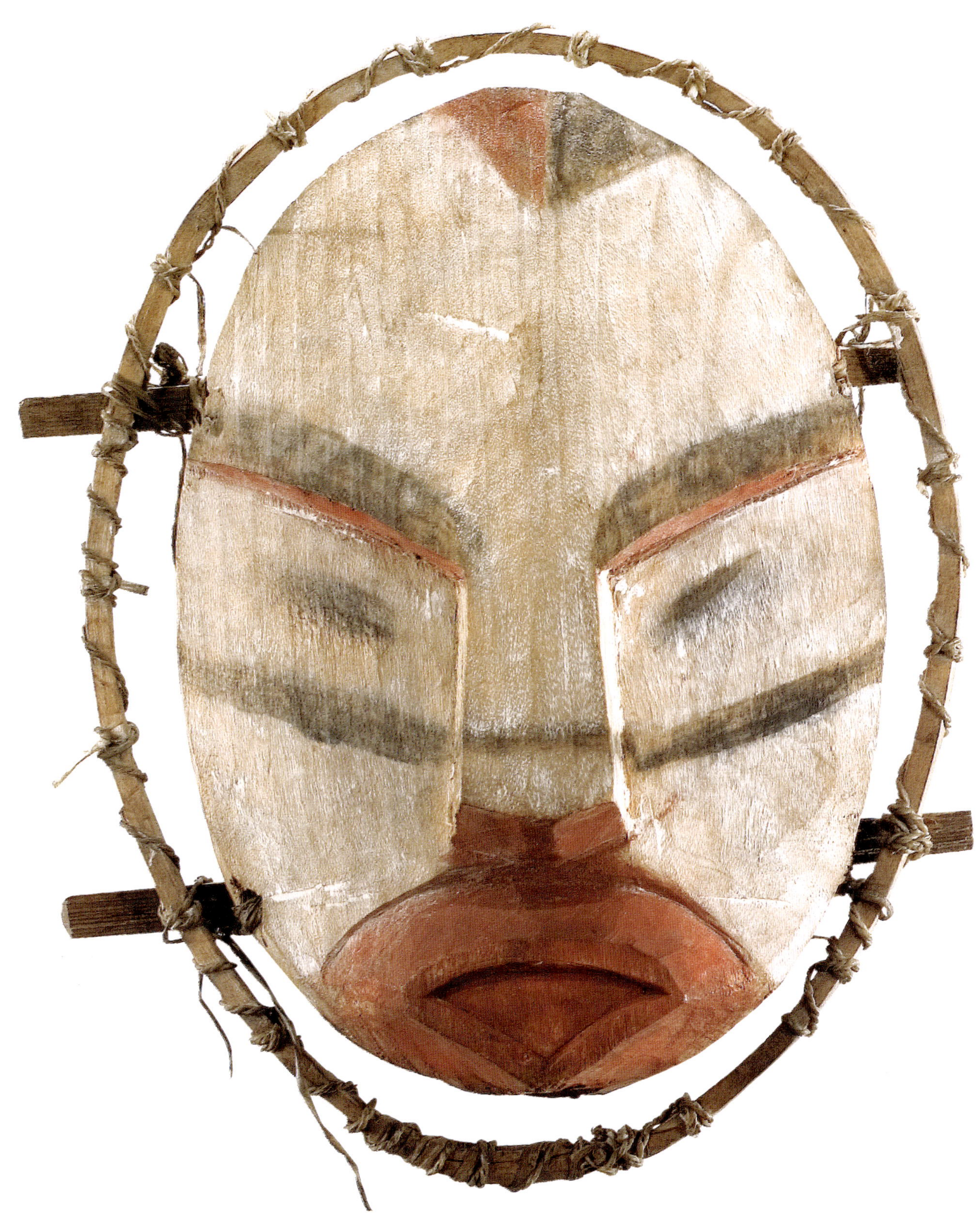

Agayuq
"Mask or Praying"

H. 16.5 cm;
W. 13.5 cm;
D. 3.5 cm.

H. 6.5 in;
W. 5.31 in;
D. 1.38 in.

White oak, paint, tendons, feather stem, remnants

I was hungry to feel reconnected with my 'vanished' culture. It was an overwhelming feeling to see my whole Sugpiaq culture unfold before my eyes, especially when many of the items came out of my mother's village of old Afognak.
— Helen Simeonoff

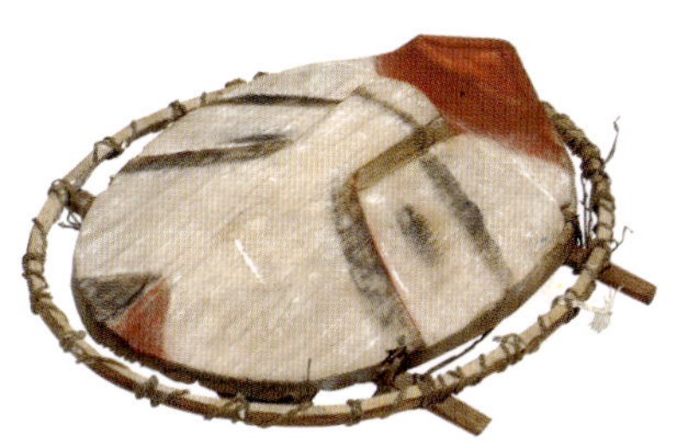

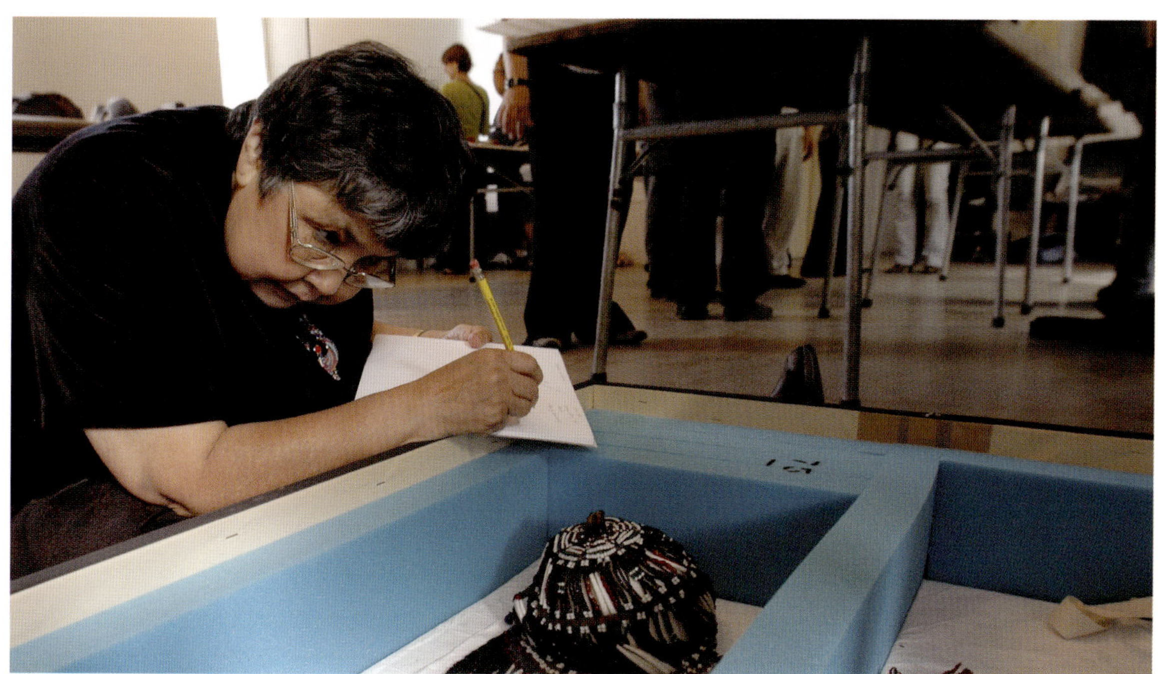

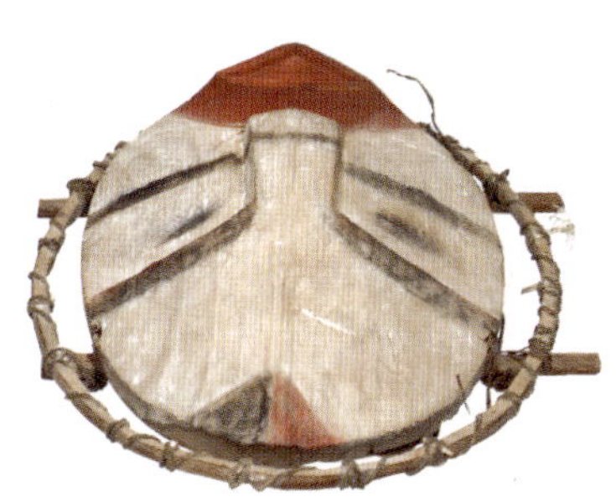

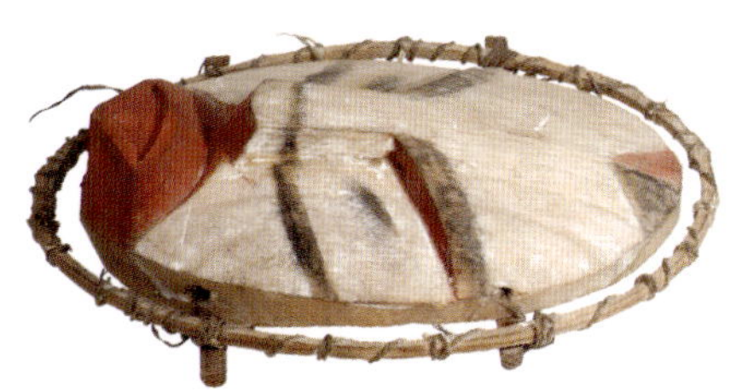

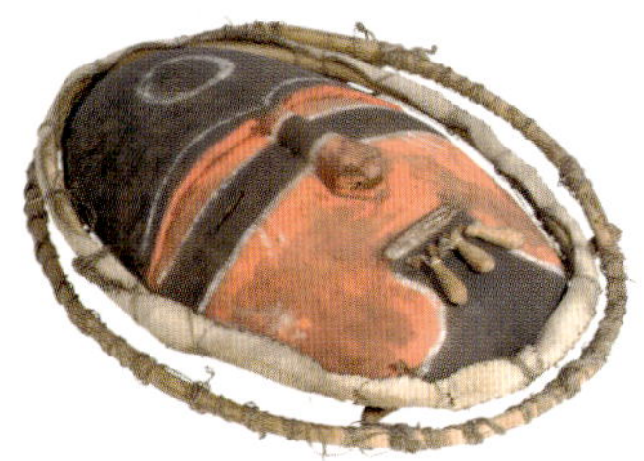

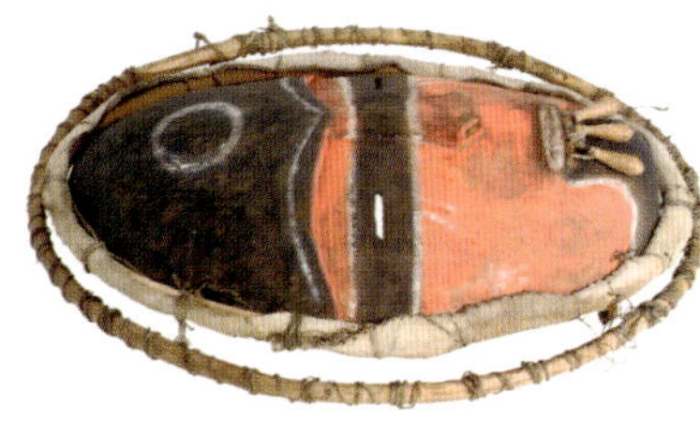

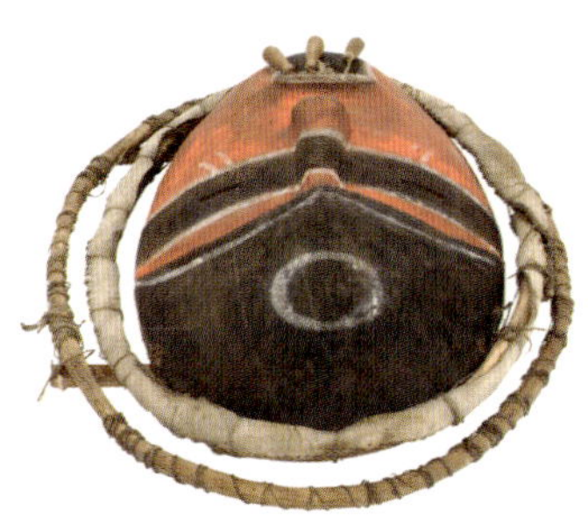

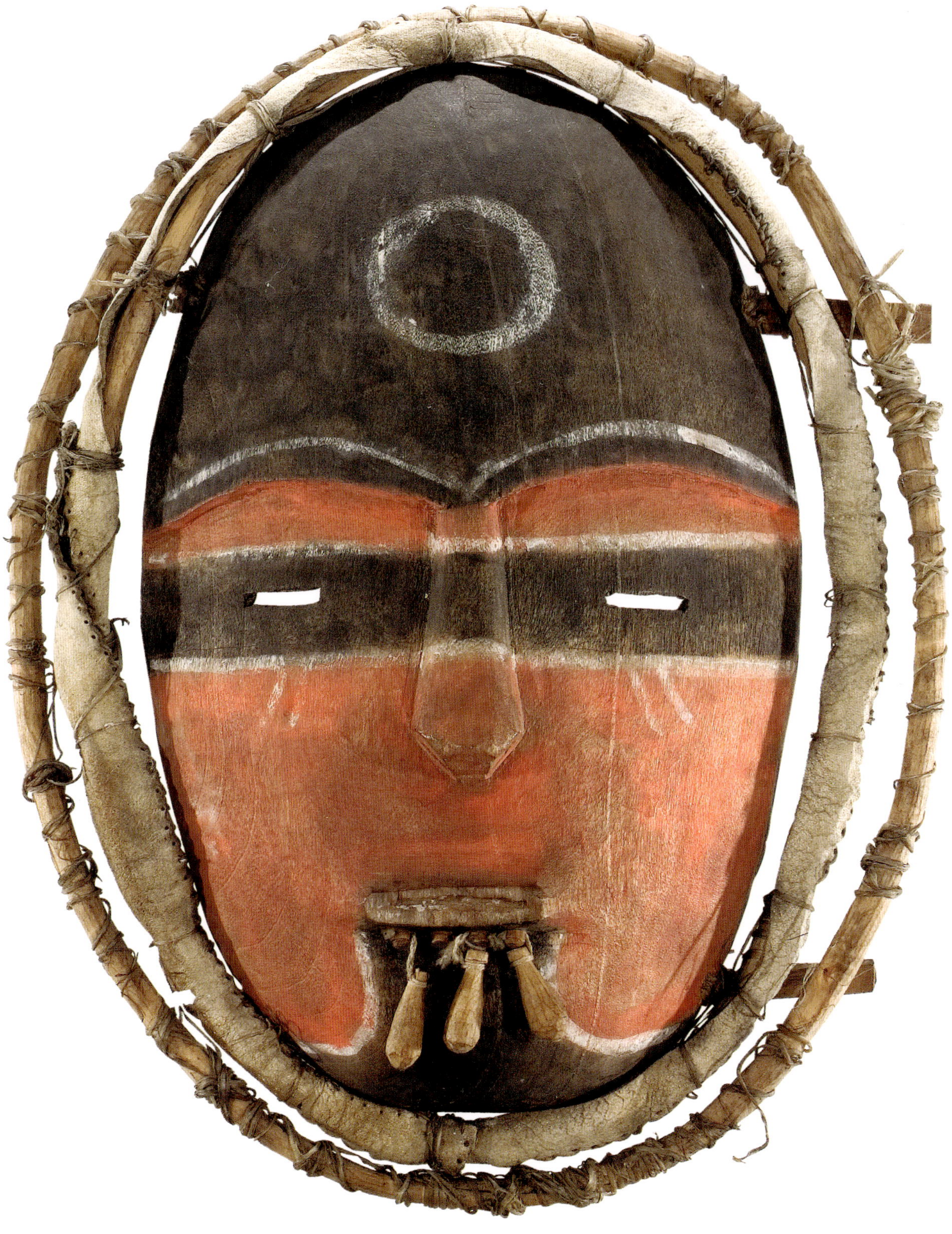

Ashik
"Got Lucky"

H. 22.5 cm;
W. 17.5 cm;
D. 5.5 cm.

H. 8.86 in;
W. 6.89 in;
D. 2.17 in.

Spruce, paint, tendons, cotton, feather remnants

It was an emotional experience that really surprised me. There was a feeling I didn't expect, but I still cannot explain it to people who were not there. The room had a strong presence; it was like there were more people in the room than you could physically see.

– Coral Chernoff

To see and hold these masks for the first time . . . after studying them and wondering about them for so many years in photographs, brought to me the feeling of joy of seeing old friends that you miss and haven't seen for a long time. Only, I had never really 'seen' them. There was also a deep sense of loss for how long it took for us to finally really get to look at and hold them and wonder about them in person. I think the feelings of awe, of joy, of loss were so overwhelming that we all cried together.

– Lena Amason

I went with a very analytical mindset, with a focus on studying the masks' design, proportions and color schemes. I expected to feel a sense of familiarity when I finally had the opportunity to work with the masks first hand. I was surprised to find that when it came time to see the masks for the first time that I was literally overcome with emotion.

– Will Anderson

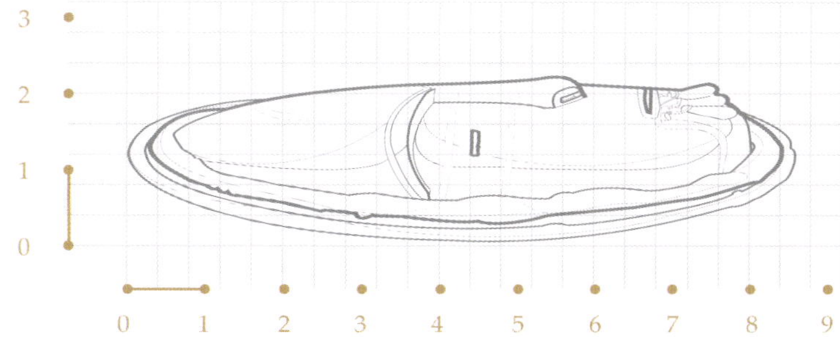

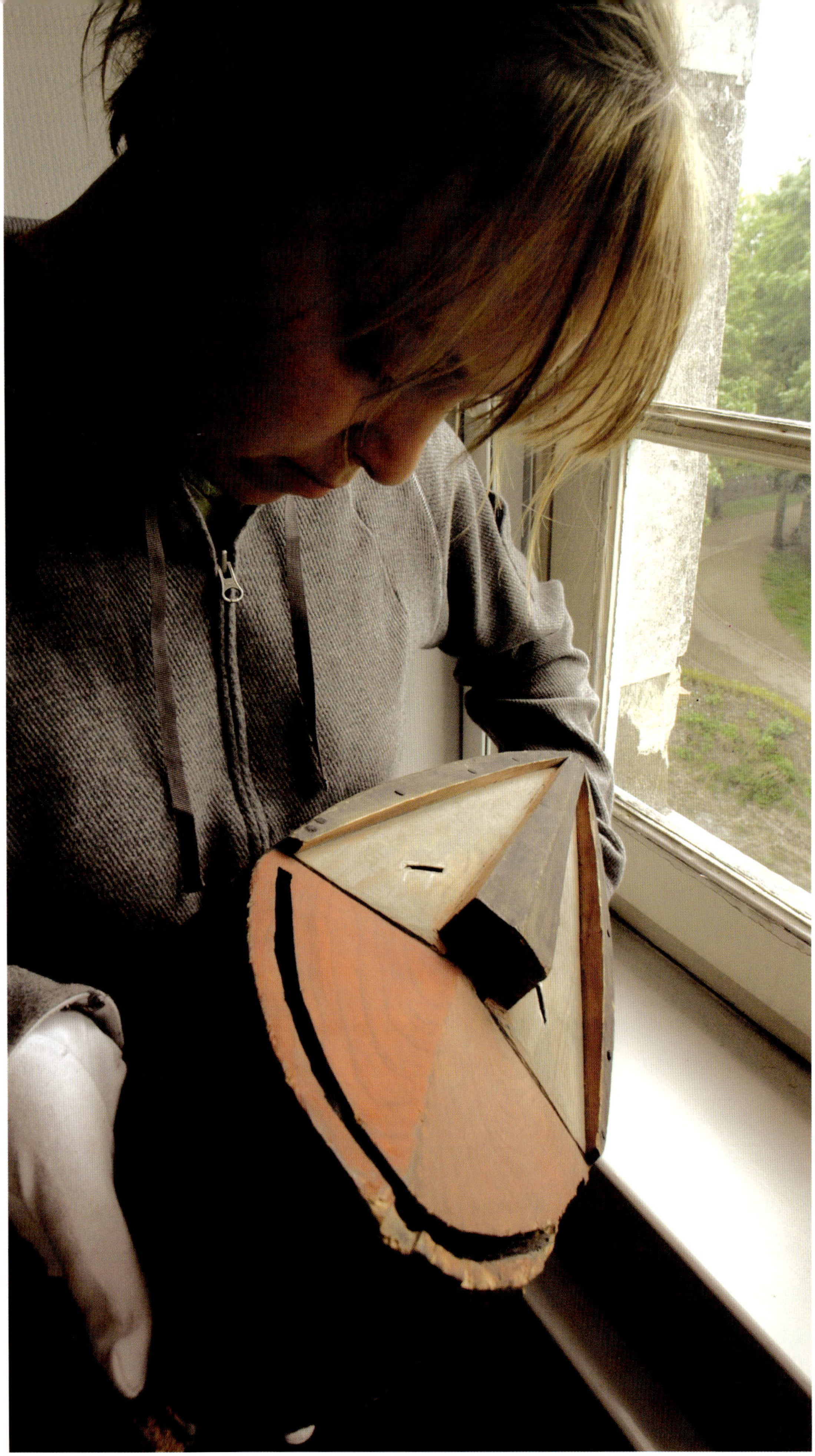

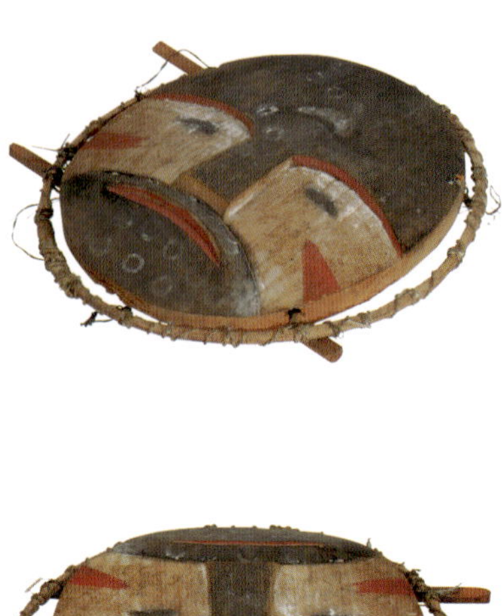

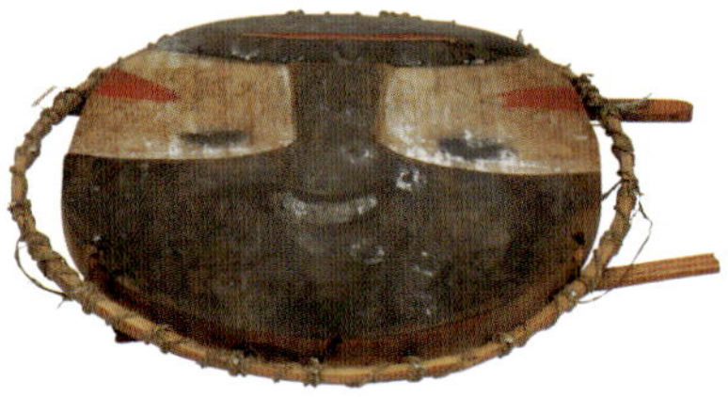

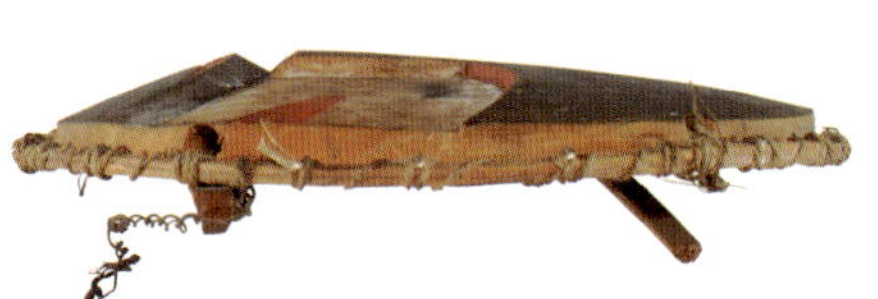

Lena Amason

For three days, the Alutiiq artists studied, sketched and talked. They held pieces to the light, examined colors and carving techniques, marveling at the sophistication and complexity of the work.

The 2006 visit was the linchpin to an agreement for the Alaska exhibition. Until that trip, Haakanson believes, the Château Musée staff didn't truly understand how important the collection is to Alutiiq people.

The French are very proud and protective of their museum collections, which are designated national treasures. They weren't about to loan collections to other countries if there was any suggestion that there would be trouble getting them back. Compounding the problem was misunderstanding about an American law that requires repatriation of Native artifacts. The law applies only to American museums, but the French feared that the Alutiiqs, once they had the Pinart pieces, would not give them back.

Continued on P. 86

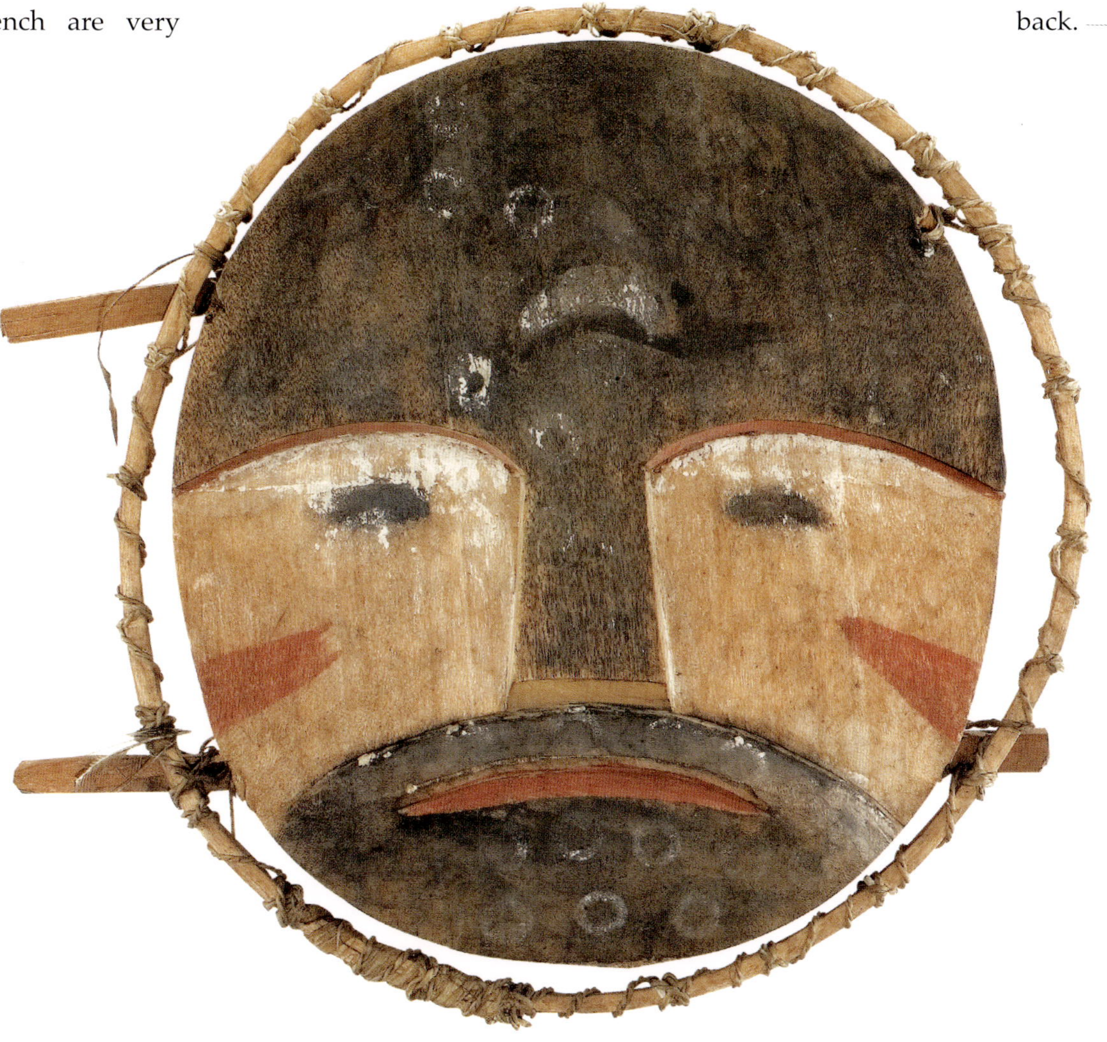

Nalylgalan
"One Who Doesn't Know"

H. 17.5 cm;
W. 18 cm;
D. 3.5 cm.

H. 6.89 in;
W. 7.09 in;
D. 1.38 in.

Spruce, paint, tendons, feather remnants

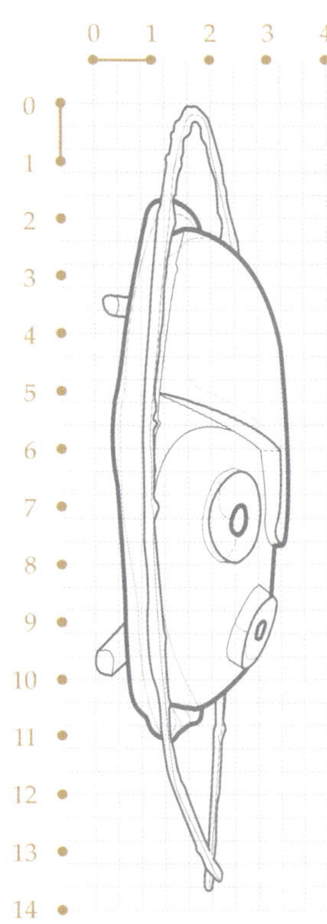

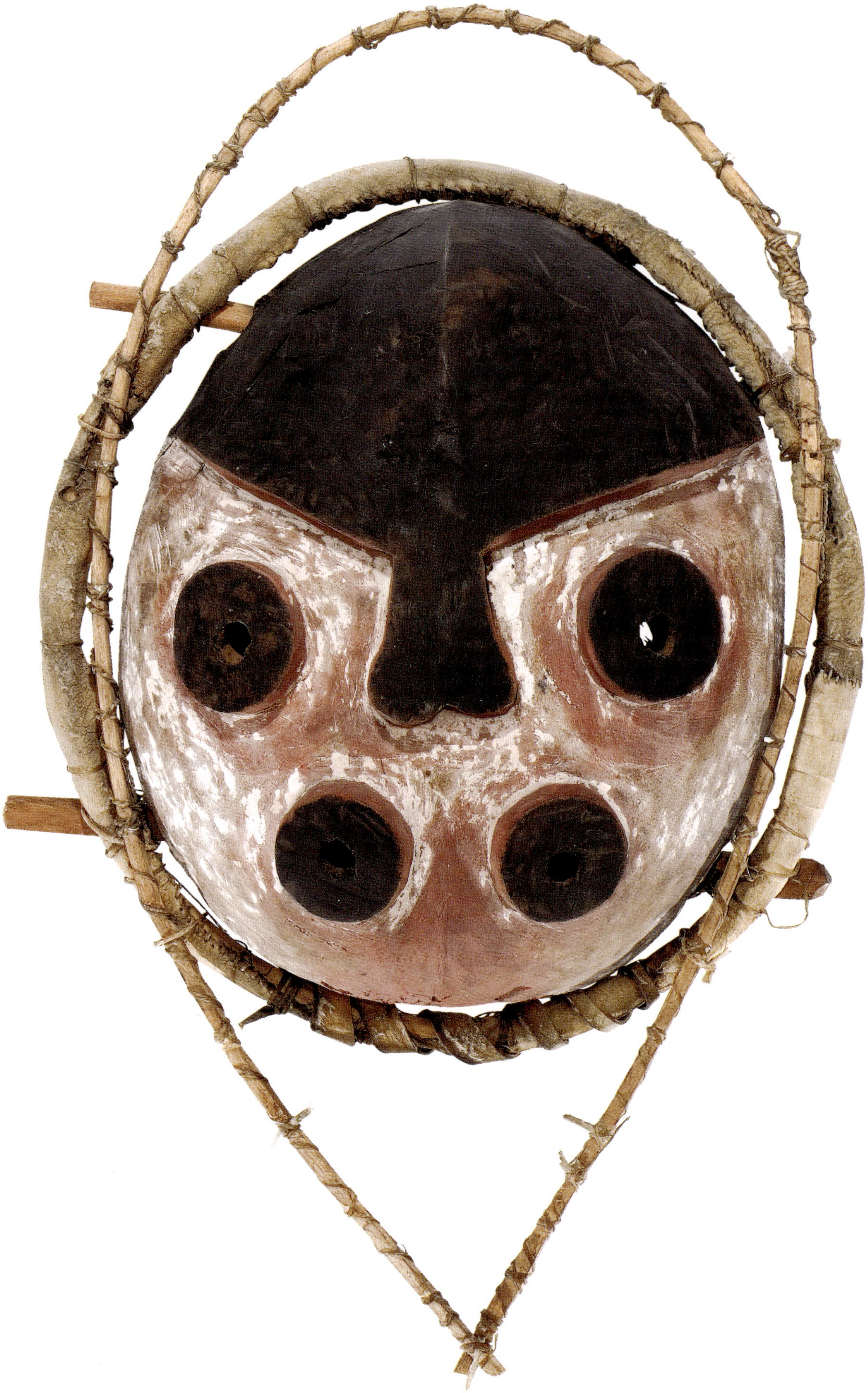

Aningwaat "Boils"

H. 35 cm;
W. 21 cm;
D. 8.5 cm.

H. 13.78 in;
W. 8.27 in;
D. 3.35 in.

Spruce, paint, leather, feathers

Aningwaat "Boils"

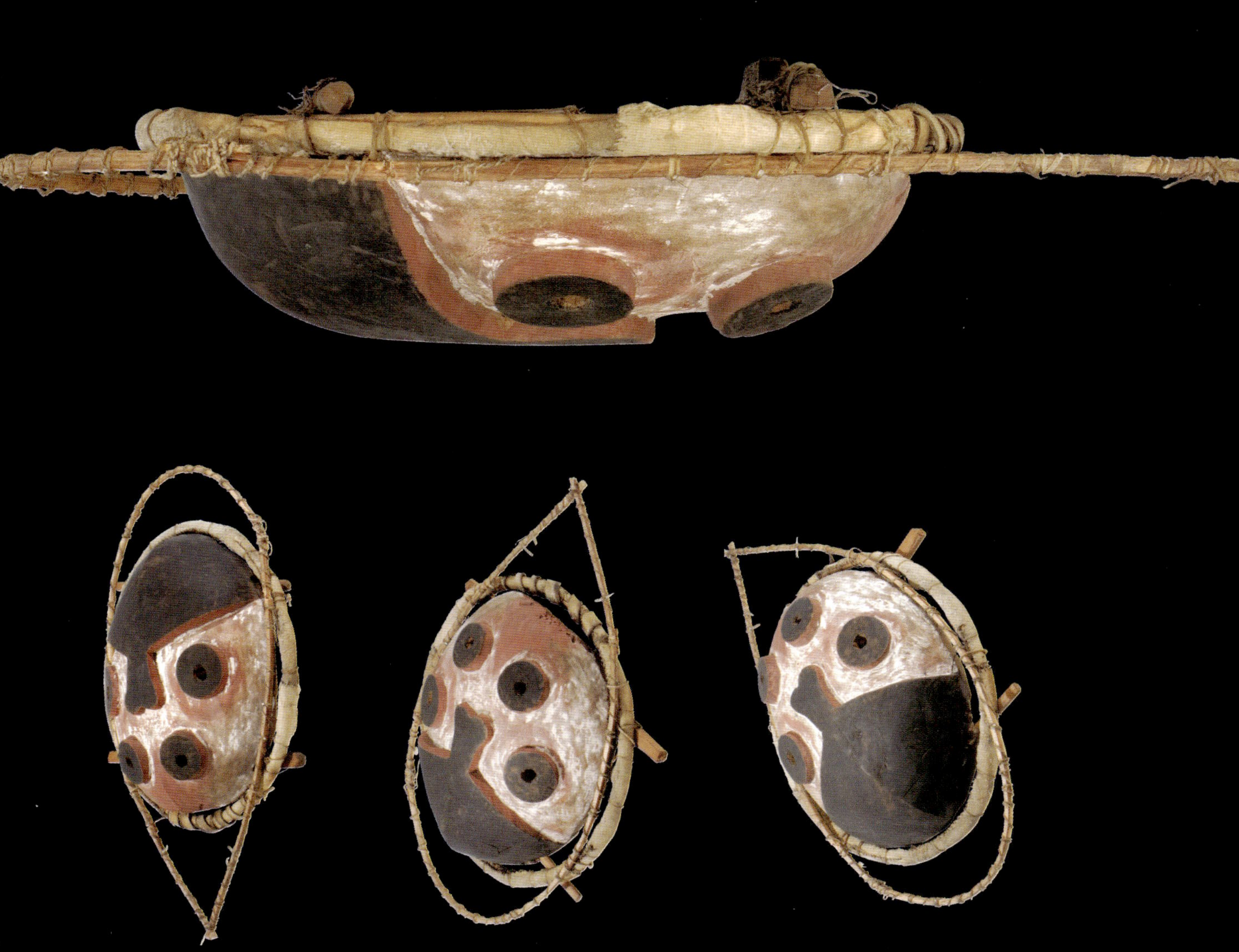

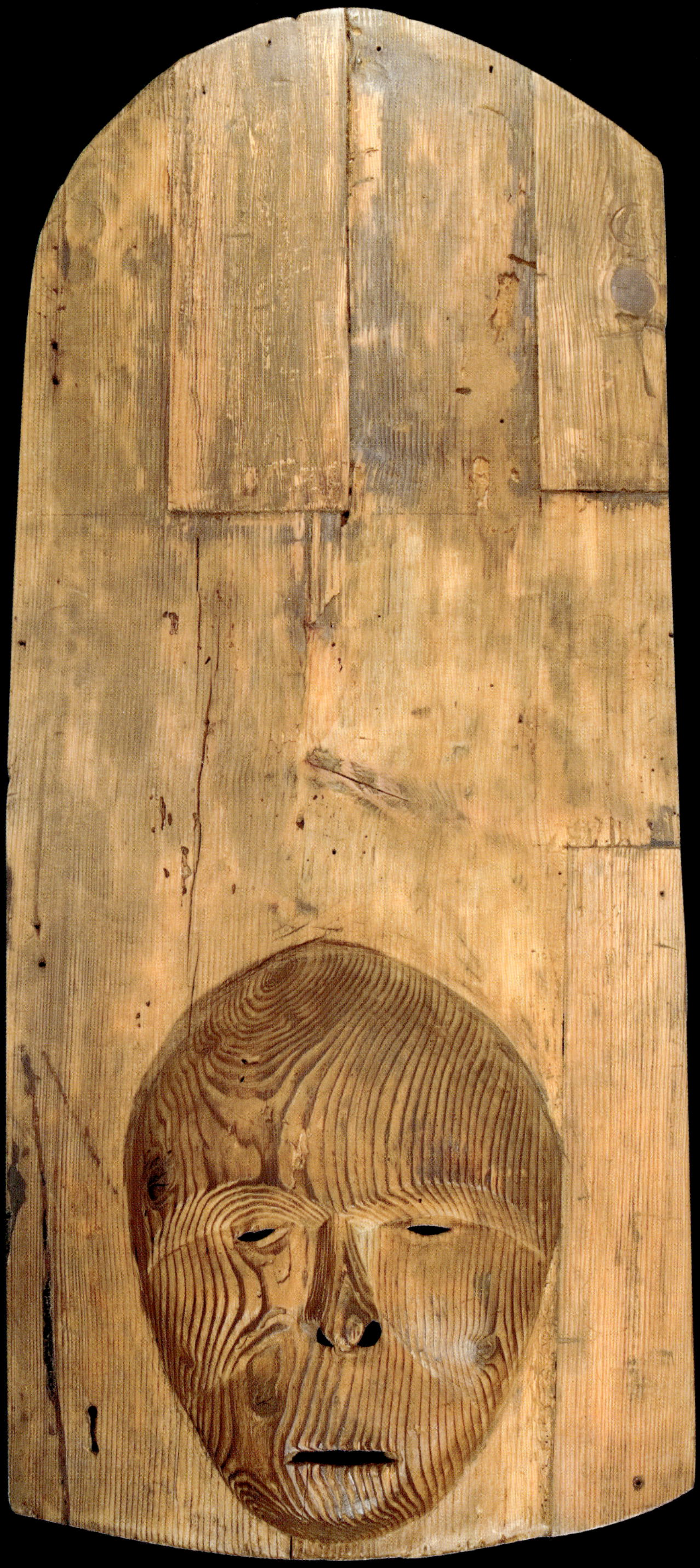

Umyaaqlluku Suumacillra
"Remembering How They Lived"

H. 80 cm;
W. 33 cm;
D. 8 cm.

H. 31.5 in;
W. 12.99 in;
D. 3.15 in.

Douglas fir, remnants of paint

In the early days of June, toward the end of the 2006 pilgrimage, a small group led by Haakanson approached Laronde. She seemed willing. At a lunch with the deputy mayor of Boulogne, they asked if he would work with them to bring an exhibit to the Alutiiq Museum in Kodiak. He said yes.

The deputy mayor's approval was key because the museum, a municipal organization, did not have sole authority to approve a traveling exhibit. Once the city gave its permission, there was little question that the national government would bless it as well. Haakanson credits Laronde, the museum director. She made it happen and pushed it along.

With a grant from Conoco Phillips to the Alutiiq Museum, a group was convened in Kodiak. Artists, elders, educators and museum professionals from the Château Musée and Anchorage Museum at Rasmuson Center came together to start planning the project and select the pieces that would be included in the Alaska exhibit. Thirty-four masks and one bowl were selected.

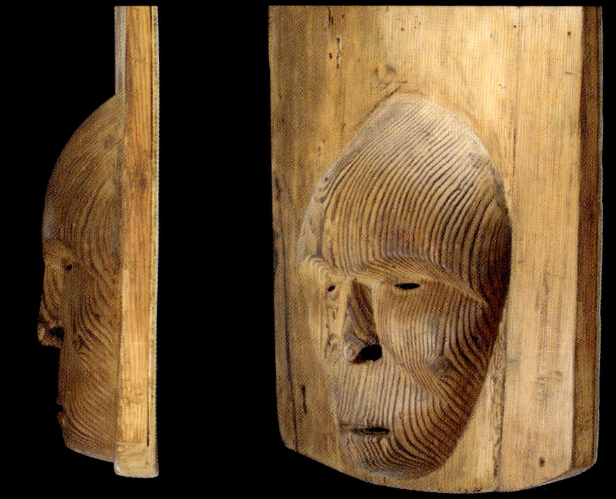

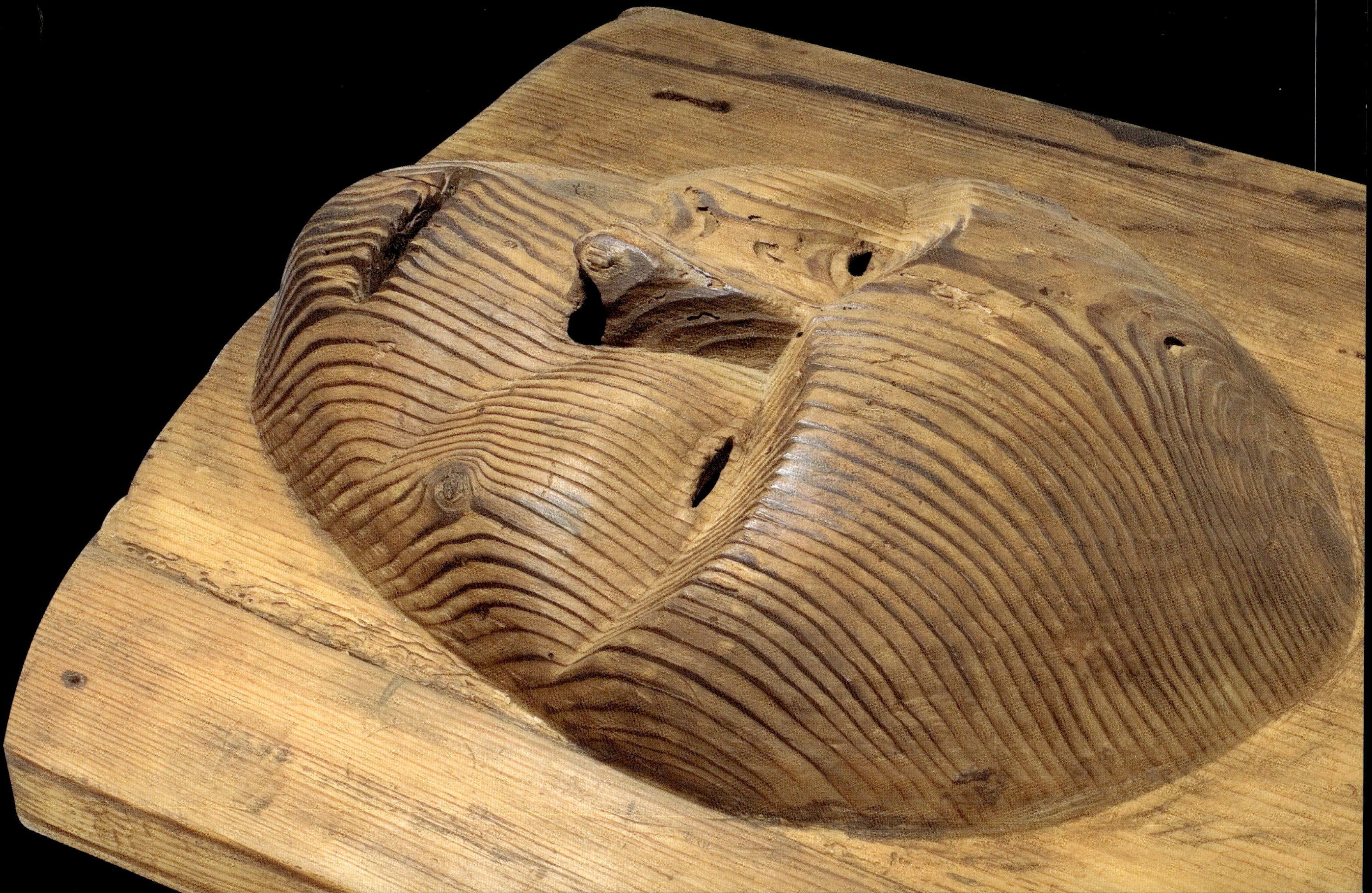

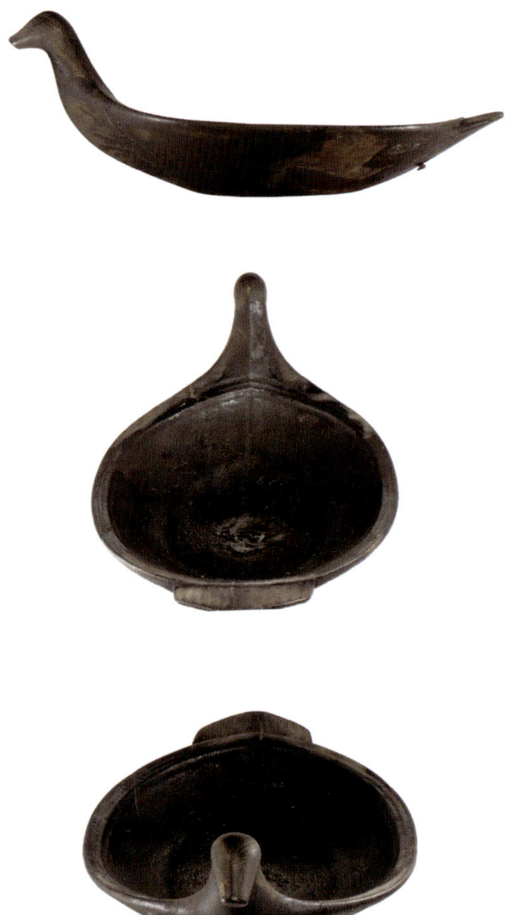

Pinart's Legacy

Alphonse Pinart never returned to Alaska. He spent many years traveling, collecting ethnographic information and artifacts from Arizona, Mexico, Texas, New Mexico, California, Vancouver, British Colombia, and the West Indies, among others. With little financial support from the government, Pinart spent all of his inherited wealth and his first wife's wealth on his travel, his work and an extensive library that he was later forced to sell.

Most of Pinart's writings consisted of magazine articles and essays, papers, speeches, booklets, letters and diaries and copious notes. Yet Pinart never wrote a full-length book. Collections of his papers are at the Bancroft Library, University of California Berkeley, in Paris and Boulogne.

Despite his subsequent work and travels, Pinart is most celebrated for his work in Alaska. By the age of 21, his best work had been completed. In his last years, according to his obituary, Pinart was in poor physical and emotional health.[9] He died in 1911.

Saqullkanam Alutaa
"Bird's Bowl"

H. 16 cm;
L. 40.5 cm;
W. 23 cm.

H. 6.3 in;
L. 15.94 in;
W. 9.06 in.

Spruce

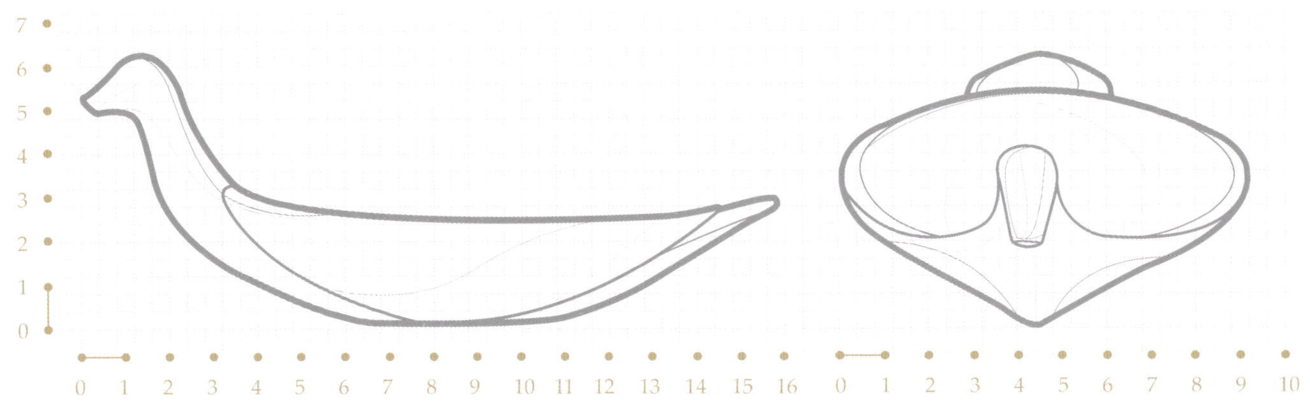

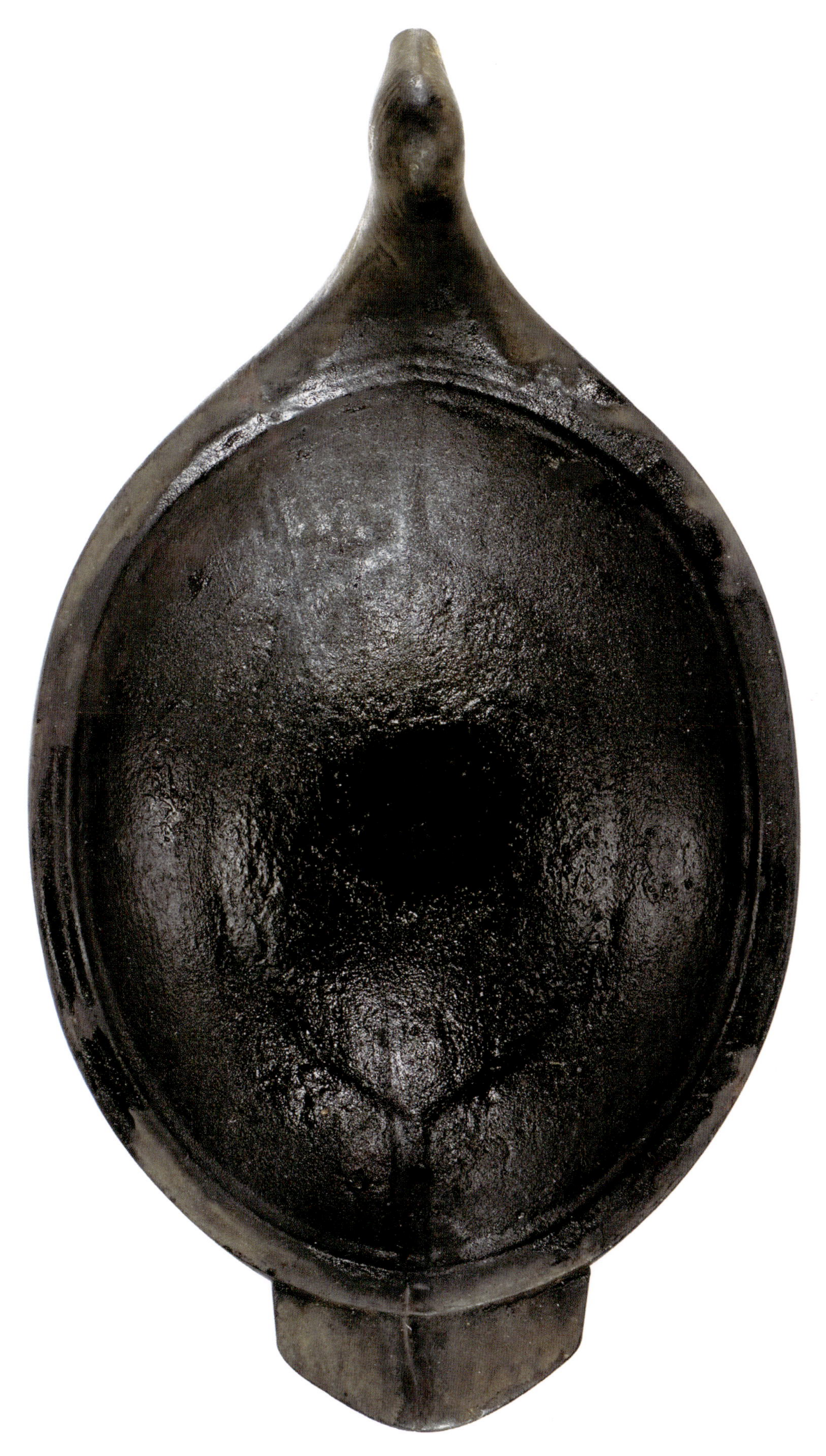

The Alutiiq Artists Group

At the Château Musée: Sven Haakanson Jr., Lena Amason, Helen Simeonoff, Coral Chernoff, Doug Inga, Gary Knagin, Sarah Froning (interpreter), Perry Eaton, Alfred Naumoff, Speridon Simeonoff and Will Anderson.

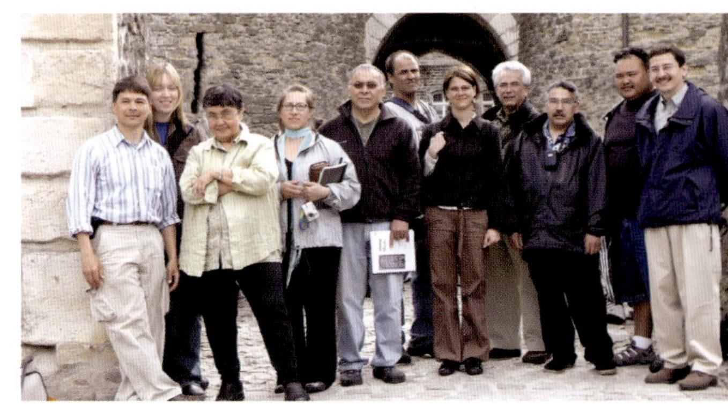

Lena Amason, of Old Harbor, is a mask carver. She is also an Alutiiq language field researcher and co-leads an Alutiiq dance group. She was raised in Port Lions and spent summers commercial salmon fishing with her step-father. Fishing provided Amason with a wealth of imagery for her carving and a strong work ethic.

Will Anderson of Kodiak began carving masks in 2004 after taking a course taught by Perry Eaton. He is also a photographer. On his mother's side, Anderson's family is from Afognak. He is president and CEO of Koniag, Inc.

Coral Chernoff carves ivory and weaves baskets. She is learning to carve wood and is interested in bowls. Her mother is of Northern Cheyenne and Sioux ancestry. Her father was Alutiiq and Russian from Kodiak. Chernoff lives in Kodiak.

Perry Eaton is a mask-maker and photographer. He also teaches mask-making. He was raised in Seattle and Kodiak and lives in Anchorage. Prior to his retirement, Eaton spent nearly 40 years in business and senior management, most recently as an executive with Alyeska Pipeline Service Company.

Sven Haakanson Jr., of Kodiak, is a mask-carver and photographer. An anthropologist with a Ph.D. from Harvard, he is executive director of the Alutiiq Museum and Archaeological Repository. For the past seven years, he has taught carving to students in the Kodiak region. Both of his grandmothers were from Eagle Harbor.

Doug Inga, of Big Lake, carves masks and bowls and makes lamps and jewelry. He has made his living from art for the commercial market for the past 10 years and has traveled throughout Alaska teaching art to children. His family is from Old Harbor.

Gary Knagin, of Kodiak, first carved as a child. His primary art form is painting, but he was introduced to serious carving in 2000 when he managed the Dig Afognak Camp. Knagin enjoys carving masks and paddles. His parents are from Afognak and Karluk.

Alfred Naumoff, of Palmer, has been carving all his life. He primarily makes kayaks — full size and models — and masks. The University of Alaska has purchased several pieces, including a mask based on the Pinart collection. Naumoff was born and raised in Old Harbor, where most of his family is from. He is also a commercial fisherman.

Helen Simeonoff was born in Kodiak and now resides in Anchorage. She specializes in watercolor originals and reproductions, but she also works with oils, acrylics and fused glass. Her ancestors were from Afognak.

Speridon Simeonoff mostly carves masks but also makes paddles and drums. He frequently teaches mask-making through the Alutiiq Museum workshops. A resident of Kodiak, his grandparents are from Akhiok. Simeonoff is employed by the Kodiak Area Native Association (KANA) as a building attendant and security officer.

Sharing Pinart's Collection

The biggest obstacle to bringing the Pinart masks to Alaska was fear among the French that once the masks were in Alaska, the Alutiiqs would not return them. Museum collections in France are considered national treasures and are protected by law. But one country's laws do not apply outside its borders. The Pinart collection has cultural and historic value for the French, as well, since it documents an exploration period in French history.

Once the masks are in Alaska, would the Alutiiqs cite their own federal law on repatriation in order to keep them?

It was an understandable fear, considering the international trend of the past 20 years toward repatriation of cultural items to the descendants of the original owners. Before they would allow the Pinart masks to leave the country, French officials had to be convinced of Alutiiq respect for and commitment to French ownership rights.

The U.S. federal law on repatriation — the Native American Graves Protection and Repatriation Act, or NAGPRA — applies only to public and private museums (other than the Smithsonian Institution, which is governed under a different law) in the U.S. that have received federal funds. Since NAGPRA does not apply outside the U.S., it could not be used as justification to keep the Pinart collection.

Perhaps more important than the legal issues is trust. Alutiiq artists who have seen the collection express only gratitude to Pinart and the French for collecting and preserving these pieces of Alutiiq culture and heritage. Had they not done so, the masks and other artifacts likely would have been lost or destroyed. The Alutiiq people acknowledged the value and importance of the Pinart collection to the French. Statements from the Alutiiq communities affirmed the intent of the Alutiiq Museum to merely borrow the items for the exhibition.

The Alutiiqs' respect for French ownership of the Pinart collection will also make it easier in future negotiations with other countries for traveling exhibits. They will know that the Alutiiq people and their museum are trustworthy and respectful.

Endnotes

1 "Masked Rituals of the Kodiak Archipelago," a Thesis Presented to the Faculty of the University of Alaska Fairbanks in Partial Fulfillment of the Requirements for the Degree of Doctor of Philosophy by Dominique Desson, M.E., M.A. Fairbanks, Alaska May 1995.

2 "Explorer, Linguist and Ethnologist – A Descriptive Bibliography of the Published Works of Alphonse Louis Pinart, With Notes on his Life," Ross Parmenter, Southwest Museum, Los Angeles, California, 1966. Introduction by Carl S. Dentzel.

3 Desson

4 Pinart, A.L., no date, Manuscripts on Ethnography and Folklore, PK-49, Box 1, Bancroft Library, University of California, Berkeley.

5 "Looking Both Ways – Heritage and Identity of the Alutiiq People," Aron L. Crowell, Amy F. Steffian and Gordon L. Pullar, editors, University of Alaska Press Fairbanks, 2001. A project of the Arctic Studies Center, Department of Anthropology, National Museum of Natural History, Smithsonian Institution and The Alutiiq Museum and Archaeological Repository.

6 Desson

7 "Sven Haakanson Sr.'s Memorial Mask," Perry Eaton, Alaska Village Ruralite, October 2004.

8 Pinart, A.L., no date, Manuscripts on Ethnography and Folklore, PK-49, Box 1, Bancroft Library, University of California, Berkeley.

9 Parmenter

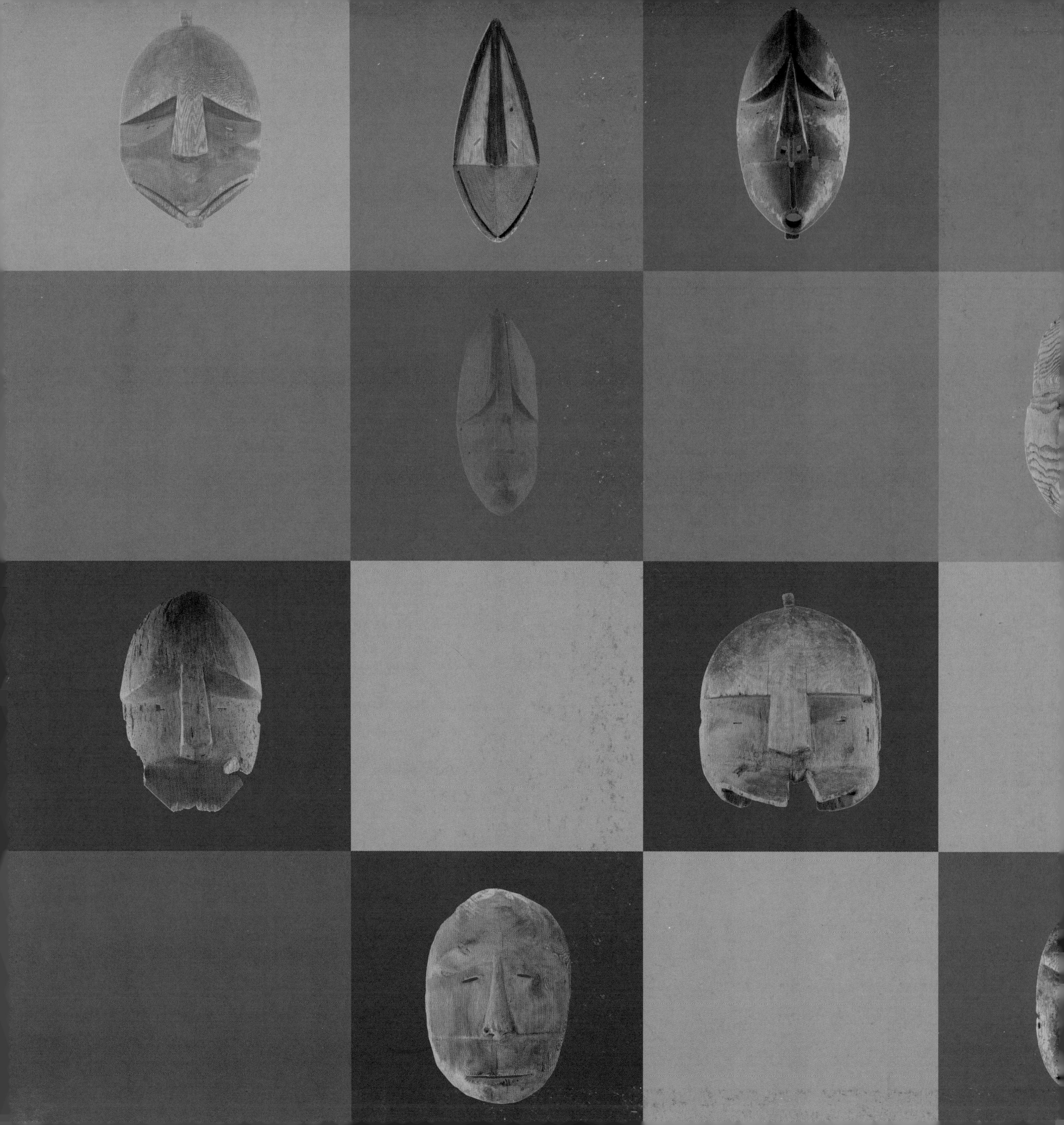